THE FATHERS ACCORDING TO RABBI NATHAN
An Analytical Translation and Explanation

Number 114
THE FATHERS ACCORDING TO RABBI NATHAN
An Analytical Translation and Explanation
by
Jacob Neusner

THE FATHERS ACCORDING TO RABBI NATHAN
An Analytical Translation and Explanation

by
Jacob Neusner

Scholars Press
Atlanta, Georgia

THE FATHERS ACCORDING TO RABBI NATHAN
An Analytical Translation and Explanation

©1986
Brown University

Library of Congress Cataloging in Publication Data

Talmud. Minor tractates. Avot de-Rabbi Nathan. English.
   The Fathers according to Rabbi Nathan.

   (Brown Judaic studies ; no. 114)
   Translation of: Avot de-Rabbi Nathan.
   Includes bibliographical references and index.
   I. Neusner, Jacob, 1932-   . II. Title. III. Series.
BM506.4.A94E5   1986   296.1'2   86-17656
ISBN 1-55540-051-5 (alk. paper)

Printed in the United States of America
on acid-free paper

For

GERSHON SHAKED

Professor of Hebrew Literature
at
The Hebrew University of Jerusalem

Master of the literary approach to the world of
Judaic life and thought
and
generous colleague and co-worker of the intellect.

He exemplifies those virtues of intellect and character
that can make Jerusalem the true spiritual center of the
Judaic renaissance of our times.

A tribute and a token of
appreciation.

CONTENTS

The Fathers According to Rabbi Nathan

Preface

This translation of *The Fathers According to Rabbi Nathan*, in the text of Solomon Schechter, *Aboth de Rabbi Nathan, edited from manuscripts, with an introduction ,notes, and appendices* (Repr. N.Y., 1945: Philipp Feldheim) serves to prepare the way for a number of further inquiries. I plan, for example, to continue my study of the problem of comparing midrash-compilations ("comparative midrash").[1] But *The Fathers According to Rabbi Nathan* has an interest all its own, which is why I present my translation separate from the studies to which the present project will make its contribution. Accordingly, my choice of this particular document requires explanation in its own terms.

I turned to *The Fathers According to Rabbi Nathan (Text A)* for two reasons. First, it seemed a quite different text from any on which I have worked. It is a kind of a Talmud to tractate Avot, and therefore different from the compilations of exegeses of Scriptural books we know as *midrashim*.

But, second, for redactional as well as substantive reasons it is not at all like any other Talmud-tractate we have in hand. Its very odd character therefore attracted my interest. I had in mind examining a document which falls between the midrash-compilations on which I have worked and the two Talmuds, on which, from the present viewpoint, comparative work is hardly pertinent at this time.

I chose this text for yet a third reason, one that turned out to prove false. At the outset, on the basis of my class-room studies at the Jewish Theological Seminary of America, I had the impression that the document was a hodge-podge, a scrapbook, not a composition, such as I had shown Leviticus Rabbah, Genesis Rabbah, Sifra, and Sifré to Numbers, to be. Therefore I wanted to draw a contrast between a scrapbook such as I imagined the text at hand and any of those other cogent documents, each with its own integrity, by comparison to this one. In my further studies of this document in its larger context I shall explain why that original impression was wrong. After I had worked my way through the document, moreover, I realized that my original points of interest

---

[1]*Comparative Midrash. The Program and Plan of Genesis Rabbah and Leviticus Rabbah* (Atlanta, 1986: Scholars Press for Brown Judaic Studies). I am now working on *Comparative Midrash*. Volume II. *The Fathers According to Rabbi Nathan Compared to Genesis Rabbah, Leviticus Rabbah, Sifra, and Sifré to Numbers.*

proved insufficient, and a set of other problems attracted my attention. But I shall work these out in their own setting. For the moment, it suffices to offer this rereading of the text, with a specific set of comments on one principal problem, its principle of agglutination, composition, and redaction. In my analytical explanation, I systematically account for the selection and organization of materials.

My approach to any text is to begin with a complete, fresh translation, helped by earlier translations when such are available, to be sure. But in my view the only way to study a text to begin with is to retranslate it (or translate it for the first time into English, as I have done for the Tosefta, the Yerushalmi, Sifré to Numbers, parts of Sifra, and various other documents). In this way I acquire a thorough knowledge of every aspect of the document as we have it and take a position (perhaps to be modified as further progress requires) on every detail of the text at hand. I know of no better way to proceed. Mine is a different approach, and, as it happens, the difference accounts also for a theory of the purpose and use of a translation different from that which finds sufficient a mere rendition, in one language, of what a text purports to say in another. In line with the larger purposes of this work, I have emphasized in the translation problems of large-scale analysis of the composition, with stress on the components on which the compilers have drawn, and how they have used the materials they have selected.

In the case of *The Fathers According to Rabbi Nathan*, a fresh translation in any event is required for several important reasons. The existing translation, by Judah Goldin, *The Fathers According to Rabbi Nathan* (New Haven, 1955: Yale University Press), despite its literary and philological merits, which are not negligible, lacks any sort of reference system. That means that no analytical work of any kind can proceed, for we have no way of identifying and then signifying the units of thought that comprise paragraphs, the paragraphs that comprise complete expositions or compositions, and so on upward.. I simply do not understand why when Goldin published his translation, he did not think it important to make possible ready reference to the units of thought of which his document was made up. But he is not to be blamed in particular. Before my translations of rabbinic documents, I know of no translator[2] who provided a reference system beyond the received one of the printed texts in the Hebrew. The system in use for centuries for the Bible surely is adequate for the purpose.

Further, in his rather perfunctory introduction, Goldin ignores analytical questions, concentrating, as he chose to do, on a different set altogether. Since

---

[2]Or even editor of a critical text! Theodor-Albeck did not do so for Genesis Rabbah, and I did not find Margulies' system for Leviticus Rabbah adequate. Saul Lieberman's system for the Tosefta demands a double system – chapter and paragraph, on the one side, but also line and page in Lieberman's edition, on the other. In this regard, however, the text-editors did better than any translators known to me, e.g., William G. Braude's translations of Midrash-collections, and the Soncino translations of the Talmud of Babylonia and of the midrash-materials collected under the name Midrash Rabbah. I find all of this rather amateurish.

the one question I wish to answer here through an acute and detailed demonstration of the facts is the redactional principle by which the compilers or authorship of the document made its selections and found their document cogent, I found I had to reread everything from the beginning. My analytical commentary systematically accounts for the work of compilation: what made the framers put things together as they did, how did they know what fit together, and what principle of conglomeration and composition explains what we have in hand: *why this not that*. I found it necessary to retranslate the selection in hand, therefore, because I have had my own set of goals, which required a fresh rendering of the text into English, meant to highlight the matters of special concern here.

Goldin moreover failed in his introduction and footnotes to address to the text, in any way I can discern, a broad range of analytical questions, e.g., concerning redaction, formulation, composition, purpose, and on and on. He gives us long columns of words differentiated only by paragraphs, translated into the idiom he selected as appropriate, but otherwise, essentially allowed to speak for themselves to whom it may concern. His commentary – and every translation is a commentary – extends only to the meanings of words and phrases, and one can only express thanks to him for the important work that he did accomplish: a thorough and reliable exegesis of the document, word for word and phrase for phrase, in the English language. But he asked no important questions beyond the ones concerning philology, so he presents what, in translation, is the counterpart to that scholarship of show and tell, of hunting, gathering, and arranging, that, in general, in his generation and in ours, defined the scholarly program of the ethnic approach to "Jewish studies." In providing a second translation, I in no way suggest that I found material fault with Goldin's,[3] except in his failure to provide a reference system, on the one side, and his failure to make possible an analytical inquiry into the document, on the other.

I certainly did benefit from Goldin's translation, as future commentator-translators of the document will benefit from mine as they render it obsolete. His work on words and phrases is exemplary. I have made constant reference to it, always with thanks for what he accomplished. I used his translation in three ways.

First, where I had difficulty with a word or phrase, I consulted his version, and when I found his rendering suitable, I have copied it. In such cases I have marked the passage in this way: [Goldin:]. What follows then is his phrase.

---

[3]His preference for translating into Elizabethan English is not shared by me, and I found the translation often stilted and jejune. But I would not have undertaken to retranslate a rabbinic document already in English merely because I prefer to translate, so interpret, in the most contemporary and earthy language I can find the sages of ancient Judaism in English. I do not grasp Goldin's reasoning in this regard; it seems to me to have limited merit from a literary viewpoint, none from an academic one. But who is to debate matters of taste?

Second, I treated his translation and notes as a commentary, and from time to time have inserted his reasoning or his explanation of a passage. This too is in square brackets in the translation, indicated as follows: [Goldin, p. 00, n. 0:]. I found some of his notes most illuminating.

Third, I often consulted his (that is, usually the Jewish Publication Society's English version) rendering of verses of Scripture, though, overall, I have tended to a freehand rendition of my own. It goes without saying that, over all, once it was in place, I checked my translation against his.

There are, of course, passages where his translation and mine necessarily are pretty much the same, because I gave what seemed to me the sole possible sense and meaning of the words as they lay before me. There are just so many ways one can say, he said to him. Furthermore, I had no reason to render *king* as *monarch* merely because Goldin rendered king as king. Coincidences of that kind testify not to dependence or borrowing but to the simple requirements of putting Hebrew words into simple and fairly standard English. There are limited numbers of synonyms for a variety of commonplace words. While my translation does not make any material contribution to the basic meaning imputed by Goldin and the prior commentators, particularly Schechter, to the Hebrew text, it is original except where, in the normal course of scholarly study, it relies on the prior work of Schechter in exegesis and of Goldin in translation.

Let me explain my reference system, which aims at allowing immediate reference to any sentence (completed whole unit of thought) or still larger composite. I have marked each whole unit of thought, then each completed and cogent statement ("paragraph" or sizable composition), and upward to each chapter. For the chapters I of course follow Schechter's division of ARNA. I likewise follow his gross paragraphing. Both of these matters are signified with Roman numerals, thus I:I refers to Chapter One, the first indented body of materials, I:II, Chapter One, the second indented body, and so on. Within each such indented body of materials are subdivisions, each of them fully autonomous and a complete thought on its own. These I mark with an Arabic numeral. Then subdivisions of these complete thoughts – those smallest whole units of thought to which I referred – are marked with a letter, thus in all: I:I.1.A and so on.

In presenting my translation on its own, my intent is to prepare the way for a number of further studies. I enjoyed the counsel of my editor at the University of Chicago Press, Mr. Alan Thomas, and my colleague, Professor Calvin Goldscheider, in planning the presentation of this work on its own and in thinking through the several studies to come.

Let me conclude on a personal note. When in my second year at The Jewish Theological Seminary of America, in 1955-1956, the then-chancellor, Louis Finkelstein, taught a course called "theology," I was first introduced to this text. What we did in the course was read and translate *The Fathers According to Rabbi Nathan.* My impression was that Finkelstein maintained Jewish theology finds full expression in *The Fathers According to Rabbi Nathan.* He made that statement on the basis of sheer instinct, since nothing he said for an entire year validated it – or even referred back to his original justification for choosing this text rather than some other. We read words and phrases, and Finkelstein made remarks about them. It was as interesting as any class at JTSA in the half-decade that I spent there. The document remained one of my favorites, partly because Finkelstein did a good job of presenting it, partly because it struck me always as distinctive and in some ways even unique in its setting. Coming back to it after thirty years brought many surprises and much pleasure.

More than ever, I am persuaded that, in the rabbinic canon, we have the notes for great music – but *not* the music. That we, as the musicians of the day, have ourselves not to recreate but to create as if out of nothing but our imagination, disciplined by learning and critical acumen. For no quartet, with its silences and its rhythms and its inner logic, exists on the printed page. It comes to life as music only in the enchanted moment of performance. There alone the music lives.

And the theology of Judaism, which Finkelstein rightly claimed endures in *The Fathers According to Rabbi Nathan,* also demands realization. At stake in this odd component of the rabbinic canon is more than a set of literary-critical problems. We have the printed notes, but we have to train ourselves to hear the music. That defines my next goal.

I call attention to the admirable counterpart to his book, Anthony J. Saldarini, *The Fathers According to Rabbi Nathan (Abot de Rabbi Nathan) Version B. A Translation and Commentary* (Leiden, 1975: E. J. Brill: Studies in Judaism in Late Antiquity Volume Eleven), and Anthony J. Saldarini, *Scholastic Rabbinism. A Literary Study of the Fathers According to Rabbi Nathan* (Chico, 1982: Scholars Press: Brown Judaic Studies Number 14). Saldarini in Text B covers many of the same materials that are contained in Text A, retranslated here. He also provides an introduction to Text B that covers many questions important in analyzing text A as well. His *Scholastic Rabbinism* provides a still more substantial and important approach to *The Fathers* and to both versions of *The Fathers According to Rabbi Nathan* . Since this retranslation pursues a different set of issues, I have not undertaken a systematic dialogue with Saldarini's work, which I greatly admire; points of agreement or disagreement on matters not critical to my analysis and argument do not seem to me to demand discussion here. In my companion study, *Judaism and Story: The Evidence of The Fathers According to Rabbi Nathan*, I shall return to Saldarini's important work where it is pertinent. I do want to make clear my view that he is the most substantial scholar of these documents at work today, and I express my respect and admiration for his achievements.

Jacob Neusner

Program in Judaic Studies
Brown University
Providence, RI 02912-1826 U.S.A.

July 28, 1986
My fifty-fourth birthday: still a learner.

The Fathers According to Rabbi Nathan

Chapter One

The opening chapter covers four matters. First we deal with the figure of Moses and the revelation of the Torah to him. Second, we turn to the chain of tradition beginning with Moses and extending through the men of the Great Assembly and their sayings. Third, we have an amplification of the first of the sayings assigned to that set of authorities, and, finally, we take up the third of those three sayings. The pertinent passage of Avot is as follows:

> Moses received the Torah at Sinai and handed it on to Joshua, Joshua to elders, and elders to prophets. And prophets handed it on to the men of the great assembly. They said three things: Be prudent in judgment. Raise up many disciples. Make a fence for the Torah.

Of the figures on the list, only Moses receives attention. Of the two sayings, we have a brief amplification of the first, and then the introduction to a protracted and ambitious thematic miscellany, triggered to begin with by the amplification of the third, **making a fence around the Torah.** The outline of the chapter follows:

I:I Moses was sanctified in a cloud and received Torah at Sinai.

> I:I.1-2 As above.

> I:I.3 Appendix joined because of a named authority.

I:II By means of Moses the Torah was given at Sinai.

> I:II.1 As above.

> I:II.2 Moses is the one who prepared lambs for the consecration of the priesthood, etc.

I:III-IV The chain of tradition.

> I:III.1-5 Citation of successive names plus proof-text.

> I:IV.1 As above.

I:V Be prudent in judgment.

> **I:V.1** Spelled out ("tarry in giving judgment") plus proof-text.
>
> **I:V.2** Spelled out ("be forebearing in opinions and not too exacting") plus illustration in the case of Moses.
>
> **I:V.3** Continuation of the foregoing.
>
> **I:V.4** Ben Azzai's explanation of the same statement.

I:VI Make a fence for the Torah.

> **I:VI.1** List of eight who made a fence for their words.

I:VII What is the fence that the Holy One Made around his words?

I:VIII What is the fence that the first Man made around his words?

I:IX-XVIII Large Anthology on the first Man.

We see that the basic program of the chapter is lost at **I:VIII**, and the vast anthology on the first Man fills up the bulk of the chapter. That that anthology has been inserted whole and composed without reference to the larger program of the chapter hardly requires argument. The anthology itself follows a fairly careful program from the creation of Man and Woman until the curse of the snake, and the aftermath of the fall from grace. If we ignore the matter of proportion and focus solely on the topical program, however, we see a perfectly simple pattern: saying amplified, then a detail in the amplification itself treated to a systematic anthological amplification of its own. So there is a twin-principle of exposition, first, of the problem at hand, second, of the topic introduced in exemplification of the problem.

I:I

1. A. **Moses** was sanctified in a cloud and **received Torah at Sinai,**
   B. as it is said, *And the glory of the Lord dwelled on Mount Sinai.*
   C. "*[...and the cloud covered* him *for six days]* , (Ex. 24:16), namely, Moses,
   D. "so as to purify him.
   E. "This was an event that took place after the Ten Commandments [were revealed]," the words of R. Yose the Galilean.
   F. And R. Aqiba says, "*And the cloud covered* it *for six days* refers to the mountain, not to Moses.
   G. "[The six days] were counted from the beginning of the new month.
   H. "*And on the seventh day he called to Moses out of the midst of the cloud* (Ex. 24:16) — this was to pay honor to Moses."

2. A. Said R. Nathan, "On what account was Moses held up all those six days, during which time the word did not come to rest on him? It was so that all of the food and drink that was in his belly should be consumed before

the moment at which he was sanctified, so that he might become like one of the ministering angels."

B. Said R. Mattia b. Heresh, "My lord, they said only that it was so as to make him fearful, that he would accept the teachings of the Torah in awe, fear, dread, and trembling, as it is said, *Serve the Lord in fear, rejoice with trembling* (Ps. 2:11)."

3. A. There was a case, in which it happened concerning R. Josiah and R. Mattia b. Heresh that both of them were in session, engaged in the study of words of the Torah. R. Josiah took his leave to do some business [Goldin: "went off to attend to some worldly matters"].

B. Said to him R. Mattia b. Heresh, "My lord, how can you abandon studying the words of the living God to be drawn into common business?"

4. A. They say: So long as they were in session, engaged in the study of the words of the Torah, they acted jealously toward one another. But when they took their leave, it was apparent that they had loved one another from their youth."

At the base is **I:I.1.A-B**, the gloss that prior to receiving the Torah, Moses was sanctified in a cloud. Once the proof-text is introduced, B-C, further exegesis of the verse, distinct from the proposition for which the verse has been adduced, is provided, C-H. The issue, developed further below, has no bearing on the original proposition. Yose, C-E, maintains that the cloud covered Moses on the mountain only after the Ten Commandments had been revealed. Aqiba joins what is a genuine dispute – not a mere juxtaposition of discrete and unrelated opinions – and his statement intersects with Yose's view. His position is that the cloud covered the mountain for six days, from the first through the sixth of Sivan, and then on the seventh day God called Moses. At issue then is the effect of the cloud, its timing and purpose. Yose's position is the same as that of A-B. Aqiba's is that the presence of the cloud had nothing to do with Moses or with the giving of the Torah. On the surface the difference of opinion between Yose and Aqiba has no bearing on A-B; the entire proposition was completed with the statement that, when Moses received the Torah at Sinai, he was sanctified in a cloud. But we see that A-B provides an anonymous version of precisely the opinion attributed to Yose. That accounts for the secondary expansion, Cff., which, superficially, served merely to develop the exegesis of the proof-text, but actually to show that A-B represents the view of Yose, as against that of Aqiba. So we have two versions of the point at issue, C-H, the dispute, and then A-B, the anonymous statement of what is, in fact, only Yose's view.

The composition at **I:I.2**, cogent and unitary, goes over the same issue as the foregoing. Nathan seems to me to repeat the position of Yose. Mattia's view does not find a parallel in Aqiba's. So it is simply an independent statement on the same matter – that is, the exegesis of Ex. 24:16.

The connection between **I:I.3** and **I:I.2** derives from the presence of the name of Mattia.[1] The principle of association derives from the man's name. **I:I.4** seems to me tacked on. It represents a conventional sentiment and contributes nothing to **I:I.3**, which makes the point fully.

I:II

1. A. By means of Moses the Torah was given at Sinai,

   B. as it is said, *And he wrote them down on two stone tablets and handed them over to me* (Deut. 5:19).

   C. And it further says, *These are the ordinances, the laws, and the Torahs which the Lord set forth between himself and the children of Israel at Mount Sinai by means of Moses* (Lev. 26:46).

   D. The Torah which the Holy One, blessed be he, gave to Israel he gave only by means of Moses, as it is said, *...between himself and the children of Israel.*

   E. Moses had the merit of serving as the messenger between the children of Israel and the Omnipresent.

2. A. It was Moses who prepared the lambs for the consecration of the priesthood and the oil for the anointing of the priest, and with it he anointed Aaron and his sons for all the seven days of the rite of consecration.

   B. It was out of that oil that the high priests and kings were anointed.

   C. It was Eleazar who burned the red cow for the preparation of purification-water [Num. 19], from the water of which unclean people were purified for generations to come.

   D. Said R. Eliezer, "The measure of the importance of the former rite is great, for it applies for the generations to come [not only for the original occasion], for Aaron and his sons were sanctified with the anointing oil,

   E. "as it is said, *And Aaron and his sons you will anoint and you will sanctify them to serve as priests for me* (Ex. 30:3)."

I take it that **I:II.1.A** accounts for the inclusion of the entire composition, an anthology on the theme of Moses. The insertion of **I:II.1.A-B** is of course invited as an amplification of Avot 1:1: Moses received Torah at Sinai. A then is simply a paraphrase of that commonplace. The proof-text suffices. C-D then rereads the second proof-text, Lev. 26:46, to make the same point. No. 2 is tacked on as a catalogue of the great deeds of Moses. 2.A-B suffice for that purpose. The intrusion of C shows that No. 2 was originally formed on its own terms and not as part of the Moses-encomium commencing at No. 1. There should then be some sort of debate on the comparative merits of what Moses did and what Eleazar did, and D makes that certain, since it argues a proposition

---

[1]Schechter refers to the story of Yohanan and Ilfa at B. Ta. 21A, which makes the point that it is better to study the Torah than to go off and earn a living. The point is the same, but the story entirely unrelated.

invited by the contrast of A, C.[2] Once more, therefore, we appear to have a composite joined on the principle of associating as a set diverse stories concerning a single name.

I:III

1. A. Joshua received it from Moses,
    B. as it is said, *And you shall set part of your honor on him, so that the entire congregation of the children of Israel will obey* (Num. 27:20).
2. A. And the elders received it from Joshua,
    B. as it is said, *And the people served the Lord all the days of Joshua and all the days of the elders, who outlived Joshua, who had seen all the great deeds of the Lord that he had done for Israel* (Judges 2:7).
3. A. The judges received it from the elders,
    B. as it is said, *And it came to pass during the time that the judges judged* (Ruth 1:25).
4. A. The prophets received it from the judges,
    B. as it is said, *And I sent to you all of my servants, the prophets, sending them every day* (Jer. 7:25).
5. A. Haggai, Zechariah, and Malachi received it from the prophets.

I:IV

1. A. The men of the Great Assembly received it from Haggai, Zechariah, and Malachi.
    B. And they said three things: Be prudent in judgment. Raise up many disciples. Make a fence for the Torah.

Leading up to **I:IV.1**, the composition of **I:III-IV** serves as a prologue to an exposition of traits of the named links in the chain of tradition and follow a simple pattern: citation of a passage of Avot followed by a proof-text. The chain of tradition differs from the version before us by adding some entries. The entire construction serves as a head for what is to follow, which is a systematic amplification of the three sayings. Unlike the interest in Moses expressed at the outset, there is no effort to comment on the names on the list, only on the apophthegms.

I:V

1. A. Be prudent in judgment.
    B. How so? This teaches that a person should take his time in giving a judgment, for whoever takes his time in giving a judgment will give a well-considered judgment,
    C. as it is said, *Also these are the proverbs of Solomon, which the men of Hezekiah, king of Judah, copied* (Proverbs 25:1).

---

[2]Those versions of the same matter that give the name of Moses contradict the rhetoric of the passage before us.

D. It is not that they merely copied them down, but they took their time.

E. Abba Saul says, "It is not that they took their time, but they spelled out the meaning. At first they maintained that Proverbs, the Song of Songs, and Qohelet should be [Goldin:] suppressed, for they maintained that they are mere proverbs and not part of the sacred Writings. They therefore went and suppressed them. Then the men of the Great Assembly came along and spelled out their meaning [and so vindicated their authority]."

F. So it is said, *And I saw among simple youths, there among the boys I noticed a lad, a foolish lad, passing along the street, at the corner, stepping out in the direction of her house at twilight, as the day faded, at dusk, as the night grew dark; suddenly a woman came to meet him, dressed like a prostitute, full of wiles, flighty and inconstant, a woman never content to stay at home, lying in wait at every corner, now in the street, now in the public squares. She caught hold of him and kissed him; brazenly she accosted him and said, "I have had a sacrifice, an offering, to make, and I have paid my vows today; that is why I have come out to meet you, to watch for you and find you. I have spread coverings on my bed of colored linen from Egypt. I have sprinkled my bed with myrrh, my clothes with aloes and cassia. Come, let us drown ourselves in pleasure, let us spend a whole night of love; for the man of the house is away, he has gone on a long journey, he has taken a bag of silver with him; until the moon is full he will not be home"* (Prov. 7:7-20).

G. And it is written in the Song of Songs, *Come, my beloved, let us go out into the fields, to lie among the henna bushes; let us go early to the vineyards and see if the vine has budded or its blossom opened, if the pomegranates are in flower. There will I give you my love* (Song of Songs 7:12-13).

H. And it is written in Qohelet, *Delight in your boyhood, young man, make the most of the days of your youth; let your heart and your eyes show you the way; but remember that for all these things God will call you to account* (Qoh. 11:9).

I. And it is written in the Song of Songs, *I am my beloved's, and his desire is for me* (Song 7:11).

J. One must conclude that it is not that they took their time, but they spelled out [the correct meaning of the books, on which account they were accepted].

2. A. Another meaning of **be prudent in judgment.**

B. How so? This teaches that a person should be forebearing in his opinions and should not be too captious in sticking to his opinions, for whoever is captious in sticking to his opinions forgets his opinions.

C. For so we find in the case of Moses, our master, that when he was captious in sticking to his views, he forgot his learning. [Goldin: This teaches that a man should be patient in his speech and not short tempered in his speech, for whoever is short tempered in his speech forgets what he has to say.]

D. Where do we find with respect to Moses, our master, that when he was captious in sticking to his views, he forgot his learning?

E. As it is said, *And Eleazar the priest said to the men of the army, who had gone out to battle, "This is the law of the Torah which the Lord commanded Moses"* (Num. 31:22). "It was Moses whom he commanded, and not me whom he commanded, Moses, my father's brother, whom he commanded, and not me, whom he commanded."

F. And where do we find with respect to Moses, our master, that he was captious in sticking to his views?

G. Lo, it says in respect to the officers of the army, *And Moses was angry with the officers of the host, and Moses said to them, Have you saved all the women alive? [Remember, it was they who, in Balaam's departure, set about seducing the Israelites into disloyalty to the Lord that day at Peor, so that the plague struck the community of the Lord]* (Num. 31:14).

3. A. *[and Moses said to them, Have you saved all the women alive :]*[3]

B. If so, why does Scripture say, *all the women*?

C. But this is the counsel which the wicked Balaam gave against Israel, as it is said, *And now, lo, I am going to my people. Come, and let me advise you concerning what this people will do to your people in the end of days* (Num. 24:14).

D. He said to him, "This people, whom you hate, is famished for food and parched for drink, and they have nothing to eat or drink except for manna alone. Go and set up stalls for them, and lay out food and drink for them, and station beautiful princesses in them, so that the people will commit whoredom to Baal Peor and fall by the hand of the Omnipresent."

E. Forthwith Balak went and did everything that the wicked Balaam had advised him.

F. Now see how the wicked Balaam made Israel lose twenty-four thousand men, as it is said, *And those who died in the plague were twenty-four thousand* (Num. 25:9).

G. And does that not yield an argument *a fortiori*:

H. Now if Moses, our master, the sage, the greatest of the great, the progenitor of all prophets, when he was too exacting in his opinion, forgot his learning, all the more so is that the rule for us!

I. This teaches that a person should be forebearing in his opinions and should not be captious in sticking to his opinions.

4. A. [The phrase before us means,] Ben Azzai says, "One should be meticulous about his statements, [so preventing it from going] for nothing [Goldin: lest it come to naught]."

The first of the two interpretations of the statement appeals to Abba Saul's interpretation of Prov. 25:1. Without the exposition of E, C-D mean nothing, and therefore the entire passage forms a single statement, C-D+E, standing behind B. The explanations supplied to the cited passages are omitted. J then repeats the opening lines, and the composition as a whole is given the appearance of a cogent and harmonious statement, even without the explicit specification of what the protracted explanation of the cited passages

---

[3]Goldin, p. 176, n. 26: Why should Moses have been angry at the sparing of the women? He had not instructed the Israelites in advance to slay the women along with the men...If so, why should Moses have been angry that they had saved all the women? And the answer given is that these women were indeed guilty of seducing Israel through the counsel of Balaam.

accomplished in making them acceptable to sages. Nos. **2-3** form a single protracted statement. 2.E then points to the result – Moses forgot what he wanted to say. F-G then introduces how Moses lost his temper. The exposition of Num. 31:14/24:14 stands on its own, but, at the same time, it ties in with the foregoing. 3.G makes the connection explicit. That is to say, "*Have you saved the women alive...remember, it was they....*" That statement of Moses stands behind Num. 31:22, which is said by Eleazar and not Moses, as Eleazar makes explicit, E. The exposition is slightly awry, but the point is clear and solidly registered. No. **4** stands entirely by itself, yet another interpretation of the same language.

I:VI

1. A.   **Make a fence for the Torah.**
   B.   And make a fence around your words,
   C.   just as [1] the Holy One, blessed be he, made a fence around his words, and [2] the first man made a fence around his words. [3] The Torah made a fence around its words. [4] Moses made a fence around his words. And so too [5] Job as well as [6] the prophets and [7] writings and [8] sages – all of them made a fence around their words.

This paraphrase and expansion simply introduces what is to follow, as a major and cogent composition, which runs through to the end of ARNA Chapter Two. But what is interesting is the shift in focus, from the Torah to one's rulings or opinions ("words"). For the entire expansion has to do with making a fence around one's words, and, as we shall soon see, there are two understandings of the matter: do it, do not do it.

I:VII

1. A.   What is the fence that [1] the Holy One, blessed be he, made around his words?
   B.   Lo, [Scripture] says, *And all the nations will say, On what account did the Lord do thus to this land* (Deut. 29:24).
   C.   This teaches that it was entirely obvious before Him who by his word brought the world into being that the generations to come were destined to say this.
   D.   Therefore the Holy One, blessed be he, said to Moses, "Moses, write it that way, and leave it for the coming generations to say, *It was because they abandoned the covenant of the Lord* (Deut. 29:24), *And they went and worshipped other gods and bowed down to them, gods which they had not known and which had not been assigned to them* (Deut. 29:25)."
   E.   Lo, in this way you learn that the Holy One, blessed be he, paid out the reward of his creatures [Goldin:] to the letter [lit.: through peace].

The "fence" here refers to the ample explanation of what has happened and why. There can be no misunderstanding or doubt about why God did what he did, because he spelled it out at Deut. 29:24. We must read E as Goldin speculates, or it is irrelevant to what goes before.

I:VIII

1. A. What is the fence that the first man made around his words?

B. Lo, Scripture says, *And the Lord God laid a commandment on Man, saying, Of all the trees of the garden you may certainly eat, but from the tree of knowledge of good and evil you may not eat, for on the day of your eating of it you will surely die* (Gen. 2:17).

C. Man did not want to state the matter to Woman as the Holy One, blessed be he, had stated it to him, but rather he said to her, *Of the fruit of the tree which is in the midst of the garden God has said, You may not eat and* you may not touch it *lest you die* (Gen. 3:3). [He made a fence around his words by extending the matter from eating to merely touching.]

D. At that moment the wicked snake thought to himself, saying, "Since I cannot make Man stumble, I shall go and make Woman stumble." He went and entered discourse with her and had a long conversation with her, saying to her, "If it was as to not touching the tree that you say the Holy One, blessed be he, has laid a commandment on us, lo, I am going to touch it, but I shall not die. You too may touch it and you will not die."

E. What did the wicked snake do at that moment? He went and touched the tree with his hands and feet and shook it until its fruit fell to the ground.

F. But some say he did not touch it at all. But when the tree saw [the snake], it said, "Wicked! wicked! don't touch me!" For it is said, *Let not the foot of pride overtake me and let not the hand of the wicked shake me* (Ps. 36:12).

2. A. Another interpretation of the verse, *Let not the foot of pride overtake me and let not the hand of the wicked shake me* (Ps. 36:12).

B. This refers to the wicked Titus, may his bones be pulverized, for, with wand [penis] in hand he hit the altar saying, "Wolf, wolf! you are a king and I am a king, come and make war against me! How many oxen were slaughtered on you, how many fowl were killed on you, how much wine was poured out on you, how much incense was burned up on you. You are the one who consumes the entire world," as it is said, *Oh Ariel, Ariel, the city where David encamped, add year to year, let the feasts come around* (Is. 29:1).

3. A. [Continuing **I:VIII.1.D**:] And the snake further said to her, "If it was as to not eating of the tree that you say the Holy One, blessed be he, has laid a commandment on us, lo, I am going to eat of it, but I shall not die. You too may eat of it and you will not die."

B. Now what did Woman think to herself? All the things that my lord [Man] has taught me from the very beginning are lies." (For Woman would call the first Man only "my lord.")

C. So she went and took of the fruit and ate it and gave it to Man and he ate, as it is said, *And the woman saw that the tree was good for eating and an appealing sight* (Gen. 3:6).

4. A. At that moment Eve was assigned ten curses [below: three decrees, cf. **I:XIV.3**], as it is said, *To the woman he said, I will greatly multiply* *your pain and your travail; in pain you shall bring forth children; and your desire will be to your husband; and he shall rule over you* (Gen. 3:16).

B. *I will greatly multiply your pain* refers to the two kinds of blood that a woman discharges, one the pain of menstrual blood, the other that of hymeneal blood.

C. *and your travail* refers to the pain of pregnancy.

D. *in pain you shall bring forth children* bears the obvious meaning [and refers to the pain of giving birth].

E. *and your desire will be to your husband* refers to the fact that a woman lusts after her husband when he goes off on a journey.

F. *and he shall rule over you* refers to the fact that a man asks explicitly for what he wants, while a woman just aches in her heart for it, cloaked as in mourning, imprisoned, cut off from all men [other than her husband].

5. A. [Reverting to our opening proposition:] Now what is it that led to the woman's touching the tree? It was the fence that the first Man erected around his words.

B. On this basis they have said: If someone puts too much of a fence around what he says, he will not be able to [Goldin:] stand by his words.

C. On this basis they have said: A person should not embellish [a report, when repeating] what he hears.

D. R. Yose says, "Better a fence ten handbreadths high that stands than one a hundred handbreadths high that falls down."

Now fence bears a different meaning from that imputed in **I:VII**. Specifically, it is an embellishment or an addition to what one says, aimed at adding to effect. That is something one should not do – rather than something one should do. So when at **I:VI.1.B** we were told that the first man made a fence around his words, we expected that that is something we should emulate. But as we see, the point is just the opposite. The first Man embellished the instructions that God had given to him, with the result that is spelled out. It seems to me this composition is singularly inappropriate to the present context. At least part of it, a systematic collection conglomerated around Ps. 36:12, surely took shape before insertion here. Then there is an independent exegesis of Gen. 3:16. **I:VIII.5** pretends to carry us all the way back to our opening proposition. But, of course, as we already realize, that is an error, since the opening proposition was that one should set up a hedge around one's statements, but the closing one – quite appropriate to the large and complex composition before us – is that one should not do so too much, a separate and essentially contradictory position. We now go on to a further exposition of the topic that has made possible this treatment of the proposition, that is, the fall of Man and Woman. This accumulation of thematic appendices is by no means random; it is a trait of the document over all, as we shall see.

I:IX

1. A. At that time, the wicked snake reflected, "I shall go and kill Man and marry his wife and be king over the whole world and walk upright and eat all the gourmet foods of the world."

B. Said to him the Holy One, blessed be he, "You have said, I shall kill Man and marry Woman." Therefore: *I shall put hatred between you and woman* (Gen. 3:15).

C. "You have said, be king over the whole world. Therefore: *You are most cursed of all cattle* (Gen. 3:14).

D. "You have said, I shall walk upright. Therefore: *On your belly you shall walk* (Gen. 3:15).

E. You have said, I shall eat all the gourmet foods of the world. Ttherefore: *You will eat dirt all the time you live.*"

The systematic exegesis of Gen. 3:14-15, reasoning backward from God's curse to the original motivation of the snake, simply serves as a thematic supplement to the foregoing. In no way does it advance the argument concerning setting up (or not setting up too high) a fence around one's words. This same thematic miscellany continues.

I:X

1. A. R. Simeon b. Menassia says, "What a loss of a great servant, for if the snake had not been cursed, every Israelite would have had two snakes in his house, one to send westward, the other eastward, to bring back good sardonix, jewels, pearls, every sort of desirable thing in the world, and no one could do them any harm.

B. "Not only so, but they would have served as beasts of burden in place of camels, asses, mules, bringing manure out to the fields and orchards."

The principle of aggregation is simple: more on the same theme as the foregoing.

I:XI

1. A. R. Judah b. Bathera says, "The first Man was reclining in the Garden of Eden, with the ministering angels serving as his retinue, roasting meat for him, cooling wine for him.

B. "The snake came and saw all this glory and was filled with envy."

The principle of aggregation is as before.

I:XII

1. A. What was the order of the creation of the first Man? [The entire sequence of events of the creation and fall of Man and Woman took place on a single day, illustrating a series of verses of Psalms that are liturgically utilized on the several days of the week.]

B. In the first hour [of the sixth day, on which Man was made] the dirt for making him was gathered, in the second, his form was shaped, in the third, he was turned into a mass of dough, in the fourth, his limbs were made, in the fifth, his various apertures were opened up, in the sixth, breath was put into him, in the seventh, he stood on his feet, in the eighth, Eve was made as his match, in the ninth, he was put into the Garden of Eden, in the tenth, he was given the commandment, in the eleventh, he turned rotten, in the twelfth, he was driven out and went his way.

C. This carries out the verse: *But Man does not lodge overnight in honor* (Ps. 49:13).

D. On the first day of the week [with reference to the acts of creation done on that day], what Psalm is to be recited? *The earth is the Lord's and the fullness thereof, the world and they who dwell in it* (Ps. 24:1). For [God] is the one who owns it and transfers ownership of it, and he is the one who will judge the world.

E. On the second day? *Great is the Lord and greatly to be praised in the city of our God* (Ps. 48:2). He divided everything he had made [between sea and dry land] and was made king over his world.

F. On the third day? *God is standing in the congregation of the mighty, in the midst of the mighty he will judge* (Ps. 82:1). He created the sea and the dry land and folded up the land to its place, leaving a place for his congregation.

G. On the fourth day? *God of vengeance, O Lord, God of vengeance, appear* (Ps. 94:1). He created the sun, moon, stars, and planets, which give light to the world but He is going to exact vengeance from those [who serve them.]

H. On the fifth? *Sing aloud to God our strength, shout to the God of Jacob* (Ps. 81:2). He created the fowl, fish, mammals of the sea, who sing aloud in the world [praises of God].

I. On the sixth? *The Lord reigns, clothed in majesty, the Lord is clothed, girded in strength, yes, the world is established and cannot be moved* (Ps. 93:1). On that day he completed all his work and arose and took his seat on the heights of the world.

J. On the seventh? *A Psalm, a song for the Sabbath day* (Ps. 92:1). It is a day that is wholly a Sabbath, on which there is no eating, drinking, or conducting of business, but the righteous are seated in retinue with their crowns on their heads and derive sustenance from the splendor of God's presence, as it is said, *And they beheld God and ate and drank* (Ex. 24:11), like the ministering angels.

K. And [reverting back to B] why [was man created last]?

L. So that [immediately upon creation on the sixth day] he might forthwith take up his Sabbath meal.

The order of creation is worked out at A, B. The sizable insertion, D-J, then goes over the order of creation as it is celebrated in Psalms recited in the cult. Only K-L take up where B has left off. That D-J has been composed in its own terms we need not doubt, and the entire complex has been tacked on for essentially the same reason as the foregoing: an enormous thematic supplement to what was, to begin with, irrelevant to the exposition of the matter at hand.

I:XIII

1. **A.** R. Simeon b. Eleazar says, "I shall draw a parable for you. To what may the first Man be compared? He was like a man who married a proselyte, who sat and gave her instructions, saying to her, 'My daughter, do not eat a piece of bread when your hands are cultically unclean, and do not eat produce that has not been tithed, and do not profane the Sabbath, and do not go around making vows, and do not walk about with any other man. Now if you should violate any of these orders, lo, you will be subject to the death penalty.'

   B. "What did the man himself do? He went and in her presence ate a piece of bread when his hands were cultically unclean, ate produce that had not been tithed, violated the Sabbath, went around taking vows, and with his own hands placed before her [an example of what he had himself prohibited].

   C. "What did that proselyte say to herself? 'All of these orders that my husband gave me to begin with were lies.' So she went and violated all of them."

2. **A.** R. Simeon b. Yohai says, "I shall draw a parable for you. To what may the first Man be compared? He was like a man who had a wife at home. What did that man do? He went and brought a jug and put in it a certain number of dates and nuts. He caught a scorpion and put it at the mouth of the jug and sealed it tightly. He left it in the corner of his house.

   B. "He said to her, 'My daughter, whatever I have in the house is entrusted to you, except for this jar, which under no circumstances should you touch.' What did the woman do? When her husband went off to market, she went and opened the jug and put her hand in it, and the scorpion bit her, and she went and fell into bed. When her husband came home from the market, he said to her, 'What's going on?'

   C. "She said to him, 'I put my hand into the jug, and a scorpion bit me, and now I'm dying.'

   D. "He said to her, 'Didn't I tell you to begin with, "Whatever I have in the house is entrusted to you, except for this jar, which under no circumstances should you touch."' He got mad at her and divorced her.

   E. "So it was with the first man.

   F. "When the Holy One, blessed be he, said to him, *Of all the trees of the garden you certainly may eat, but from the tree of knowledge of good and evil you may not eat, for on the day on which you eat of it, you will surely die* (Gen. 2:17),

   G. "on that day he was driven out, thereby illustrating the verse, *Man does not lodge overnight in honor* (Ps. 49:24)."

I am puzzled by the point of Simeon's statement at **I:XIII:1.** I do not see how the parable is relevant to Adam as the story has been expounded here. For it was Eve who violated Adam's instructions, and the one error Adam made was stated above, "Man did not want to state the matter to Woman as the Holy One, blessed be he, had stated it to him, but rather he said to her, *Of the fruit of the tree which is in the midst of the garden God has said, You may not eat and you may not touch it lest you die* ." That has no bearing on Adam's violating his *own* instructions, which is the point of the story before us. Clearly, the point of pertinence comes at C, which intersects explicitly with the following: "Now what did Woman think to herself? All the things that my lord [Man] has taught me from the very beginning are lies." But that is on account of the exaggeration of Man's statement of God's instruction, that is to say, Man had built too high a fence around God's words. But that point has no bearing here. The upshot is that the parable intersects with, but does not illustrate, the materials before us. That forms a still stronger argument for the proposition that the person who has collected these materials as a thematic appendix has had very little role in making the materials up, and also had no strong theory of what he wished to say through the compilation of the document, beyond the mere development of a scrapbook on certain themes.

The pertinence of the second parable, **I:XIII.2**, is clear. Simeon's point is somewhat odd, however, since what he wishes to say is that by giving Man the commandment, God aroused his interest in that tree and led man to do what he did. So God bears a measure of guilt for the fall of man. F-G clearly is tacked on and out of place, since it does not revert to the parable at all and makes its own point, Ps. 49:24.

I:XIV

1. A. On the very same day Man was formed, on the very same day Man was made, on the very same day his form was shaped, on the very same day he was turned into a mass of dough, on the very same day his limbs were made and his various apertures were opened up, on the very same day breath was put into him, on the very same day he stood on his feet, on the very same day Eve was matched for him, on the very same day he was put into the Garden of Eden, on the very same day he was given the commandment, on the very same day he went bad, on the very same day he was driven out and went his way,

   B. thereby illustrating the verse, *Man does not lodge overnight in honor* (Ps. 49:24).

2. A. On the very same day two got into bed and four got out.

   B. R. Judah b. Beterah says, "On the very same day two got into bed and seven got out."

3. A. On that very same day three decrees were issued against Man,

   B. as it is said, *And to Man he said, Because you have obeyed your wife, cursed is the ground on your account; in labor you shall eat its produce...Thorns also and thistles it will produce for you, and you shall eat the herb of the field* (Gen. 3:17-18).

   C. When the first man heard what the Holy One, blessed be he, said to him, namely, *You shall eat the herb of the field,* his limbs trembled, and he said before him, "Lord of the world, shall I and my cattle eat in a single crib?"

   D. Said to him the Holy One, blessed be he, "Since your limbs have trembled, *in the sweat of your face you shall eat bread* (Gen. 3:19)."

   E. And just as three decrees were issued against the first Man, so three decrees were issued against Woman.

   F. For it is said, *To the woman he said, I will greatly multiply your pain and your travail; in pain you shall bring forth children; and your desire will be to your husband; and he shall rule over you* (Gen. 3:16).

G. *I will greatly [multiply] your pain* refers to the fact that, when a woman produces menstrual blood at the beginning of her period, it is painful for her.

H. *I will [greatly] multiply your pain* refers to the fact that when a woman has sexual relations for the first time, it is painful for her.

I. *in pain you shall conceive* refers to the fact that, when a woman first gets pregnant, for the first three months her face is distorted and pale.

No. 1 goes over familiar materials. It is tacked on because it goes over the same proof-text as is given earlier. No. 2 carries forward the formulaic pattern of No. 1, and so does No. 3.

I:XV

1. A. When evening fell, the first Man saw the world growing dark as the sun set. He thought to himself, "Woe is me! Because I turned rotten, the Holy One, blessed be he, on my account brings darkness to the entire world." But he did not know that that is how things are.

   B. At dawn when he saw the world grow light with sunrise, he rejoiced. He went and built altars and brought an ox whose horns extended beyond it hooves and offered it up as a whole offering [retaining no parts for his own food],

   C. as it is said, *And it shall please the Lord better than an ox whose horns extend beyond its hooves* (Ps. 69:32).

2. A. As to the ox that the first Man offered, the bull that Noah offered, and the ram that Abraham, our father, offered in place of his son on the altar, all of them were *beasts in which the horns extended beyond the hooves.*

   B. For it is said, *And Abraham looked up, and he saw, lo, another ram, caught by its horns in the bush* (Gen. 22:13).

The anthology on the first man runs its course. We have at No. 1 a set piece item, which, so far as I can see, does not continue any prior discussion. It is simply inserted whole. No. 2 is attached to No. 1 because of its pertinence to the theme of the particularly desirable animal for sacrifice.

I:XVI

1. A. At that moment three groups of ministering angels descended, with lutes, lyres, and diverse other musical instruments in their hands, and with [the first Man] they recited a song.

   B. For it is said, *A Psalm, a song, for the sabbath day. It is good to give thanks to the Lord...to declare your loving-kindness in the morning and your faithfulness at night* (Ps. 92:1-3).

   C. *To declare your loving-kindness in the morning* refers to the world to come, as it is said, *They are new every morning, great is your faithfulness* (Lam. 3:23).

   D. *And your faithfulness at night* refers to this world, which is compared to night, as it is said, *The burden of Dumah. One calls to me out of Seir, watchman, what of the night? watchman, what of the night?* (Is. 21:11).

The long narrative about the first Man on the day of the fall from grace proceeds on its own lines. The rhetorical-formulaic that links one piece to the next, on that very same day or, at that time, provides the outline of a reasonably cogent narrative program.

I:XVII

1. A. At that time said the Holy One, blessed be he, "If I do not judge the snake, I shall turn out to destroy the entire world."
   B. And he thought to himself, "This one that I crowned and made king over the entire world has gone wrong and eaten of the fruit of the tree."
   C. He forthwith turned on him and cursed him,
   D. as it is said, *And the Lord God said to the snake* (Gen. 3:14).
   E. R. Yose says, "If the curse concerning the snake had not been stated in Scripture [following Goldin, p. 15:] after theirs [the curse of Man and Woman], [the snake] would have destroyed the entire world."

The narrative proceeds apace. The reason for including it – the reference to the first Man and the fence that he (wrongly) erected around his words – has long since fallen from sight.

I:XVIII

1. A. When the Holy One, blessed be he, created the first Man, he formed a face on him both in front and in back,
   B. for it is said, *You have fashioned me in back and in front and laid your hand upon me* (Ps. 139:5).
   C. Then the ministering angels came down to destroy him, so the Holy One, blessed be he, took him and placed him under his wings, as it is said, *and laid your hand upon me.*
2. A. Another interpretation of the clause, *And laid your hand upon me* :
   B. Once [the first Man] went rotten, the Holy One, blessed be he, took away one of [the two faces he had originally given to Man].
3. A. On this basis [we derive the fact that] the first Man and the Temple, when they were created, were created with both of God's hands.
   B. How do we know that [when man was created,] he was created with both hands?
   C. As it is said, *Your hands have made me and formed me* (Ps. 119:73).
   D. How do we know that the Temple was created with two hands?
   E. As it is said, *The sanctuary, O Lord, which your hands have established* (Ex. 15:17), *And he brought them to his holy border, the mountain, which his right hand had gotten* (Ps. 78:543), *The Lord shall reign for ever and ever* (Ex. 15:18).

The long narrative on the creation of the first Man reaches its conclusion with a final miscellany. Pertinent verses are adduced to provide a further fact, Nos. 1-2. No. 3 follows as an appropriate appendix.

The Fathers According to Rabbi Nathan

Chapter Two

We revert in this chapter to the introductory statement at **I:VI.1.B** of the exposition of the sentence, **Make a fence for the Torah**, *"And make a fence around your words, just as [1] the Holy One, blessed be he, made a fence around his words, and [2] the first man made a fence around his words. [3] The Torah made a fence around its words. [4] Moses made a fence around his words. And so too [5] Job as well as [6] the prophets and [7] the writings and [8] sages – all of them made a fence around their words."* Now that ARNA Chapter One has completed the exposition of clauses one and two, we proceed to the remainder, 3-8, in order. The chapter follows the following outline:

II:I

II:I.1 What sort of fence did the Torah make around its words? It was a stricter requirement than the law really demands in connection with separation from a woman during her menstrual period.

II:I.2 As above.

II:I.3 As above.

II:I.4 As above.

II.I.5 The same theme, namely, sexual taboos, is focused on a different conception, namely, there are minor religious duties that produce a great reward.

II:II

II:II.1 What sort of fence did Moses make around his words? Moses on his own volition added to the instructions God gave him.

II:III

II:III.1-4 Other instances in which Moses on his own volition did something with which, after the fact, God concurred.

II:IV

II:IV.1 Instances in which Hezekiah on his own volition did something with which, after the fact, God [elsewhere: sages] concurred.

II:V

II:V.1 What sort of fence did Job make around his words? He avoided not only transgression but even something that might appear to lead to transgression.

II:V.2 Because the foregoing refers to Job 1:8, which says that Job was unblemished, and which sages understand to mean, Job was born circumcised, we have a catalogue of others born circumcised.

II:V.3 Specific instance of Job's making a fence around the divine law, by avoiding something that might appear to lead to transgression, specifically, gazing even upon an unmarried woman.

II:VI What sort of fence did prophets make for their words? This question is not given a clear answer. They understated God's attributes, rather than exaggerating the law's requirements.

II:VII What sort of fence did the Writings make around their words? The basic point is that one should not only avoid wicked people but also not go anywhere near them.

II:VII.1 Avoid heretics and do not feel overconfident of being able to resist them.

II:VII.2 Avoid whores as above.

II:VIII What sort of fence did sages make around their words?

II:VIII.1 Recite the *Shema* before taking a nap in the evening.

II:VIII.2 The same basic point about hedges around proper recitation of the *Shema*.

The chapter follows its own program, though sizable units have been inserted whole, and not all of these units advance the exegesis of the statement that is under study.

II:I

1. A. What sort of fence did [3] the Torah make around its words?
   B. Lo, Scripture says, *To a woman during the unclean time of her menstrual period you shall not draw near* (Lev. 18:17).
   C. Is it possible to suppose that one may nonetheless hug and kiss her and exchange billets-doux with her?
   D. Scripture says, *you shall not draw near.*
   E. Is it nonetheless possible to suppose that if she is fully clothed, one may sleep with her in the same bed?
   F. Scripture says, *you shall not draw near.*
   G. Is it possible to suppose that a woman may pretty her face and put on eye-makeup?

H. Scripture says, *And of her that is sick with her impurity* (Lev. 15:33), meaning, all the days of her menstrual period she shall be put away.

I. On this basis they have said: whoever neglects herself during her menstrual period enjoys the approbation of sages, and whoever pretties herself during her menstrual period does not enjoy the approbation of sages.

2. A. There is the precedent of a man who studied much Scripture, repeated much Mishnah, extensively served as a disciple of sages, but died when his years were only half done, and his wife took his *tefillin* and made the circuit of synagogues and school-houses, crying and weeping, saying to them, "My lords, it is written in the Torah, *For it is your life and the length of your days* (Deut. 30:20).

B. "On what account did my husband, who studied much Scripture, repeated much Mishnah, extensively served as a disciple of sages, die when his years were only half done?"

C. No one knew what to answer her. But one time Elijah, of blessed memory, was appointed to deal with her, saying to her, "My daughter, on what account are you crying and weeping?"

D. She said to him, "My lord, my husband studied much Scripture, repeated much Mishnah, extensively served as a disciple of sages, but died when his years were only half done."

E. He said to her, "When you were in your period, on the first three days of your period, what was your practice?"

F. She said to him, "My lord, God forbid, he never touched me, even with his little finger. But this is what he said to me, 'Do not touch a thing, perhaps you may come into doubt about something.'"

G. "As to the last days of your period, what was your practice?"

H. She said to him, "My lord, I ate with him, drank with him, and in my clothing slept with him in the same bed, and, while his flesh touched mine, he never had the intention of any inappropriate action [such as sexual relations before the period had fully ended]."

I. He said to her, "Blessed be the Omnipresent, who killed him. For so is it written in the Torah: *To a woman during the unclean time of her menstrual period you shall not draw near* (Lev. 18:17)."

3. A. Lo, Scripture says, *None of you shall approach any one that is near of kin to him* (Lev. 18:6).

B. On the basis of this verse sages have ruled:

C. One should not spend time in an inn alone with any woman, and that applies even to his sister, his daughter, his mother in law,

D. on account of what people will think.

E. Someone should not engage in conversation with a woman in the market place,

F. and that applies even to his wife, and, it goes without saying, any other woman,

G. because of what people might say.

H. And a man should not walk behind a woman in the market place, even behind his own wife, and, it is hardly necessary to say, any other woman,

I. because of what people might say.

4. A. Here it is said, *You shall not draw near* (Lev. 18:6) and elsewhere, *You shall not draw near* (Lev. 18:19).

B. The point is that one should not come anywhere close to something which will lead him to a transgression.

C. One should keep his distance not only from something that is despicable, but also from something that seems despicable.

D. Therefore sages have ruled: Keep your distance from a minor sin, lest it bring you to a major one.

E. Run to do a minor religious duty, which will bring you to carry out a major religious duty.

5. A. Lo, Scripture states, *Your belly is like a heap of wheat hedged in by lilies* (Song 7:3).

B. *Your belly is like a heap of wheat refers to the congregation of Israel.*

C. *...hedged in by lilies* refers to the seventy elders.

D. Another interpretation of *Your belly is like a heap of wheat hedged in by lilies* :

E. *Your belly is like a heap of wheat* refers to the minor religious duties, which are easy.

F. *...hedged in by lilies* means this: when the Israelites carry them out, lo, they bring them into the life of the world to come.

G. How [does the hedge of lilies serve to bring someone into the life of the world to come]? When one's wife, in her menstrual period, is with him in the house, if he wants to have sexual relations, he does so, and if not, he does not do so.

H. For is there anyone who sees him or knows about it so as to say anything at all to him?

I. Lo, he fears only him who gave the commandment to them concerning not having sexual relations with a menstruating woman.

J. [Along these same lines,] if one has produced a seminal emission, if he wants, he immerses, and if not, he does not do so.

K. For is there anyone who sees him or knows about it so as to say anything at all to him?

L. Lo, he fears only him who gave the commandment to them concerning immersion.

M. And one may make the same statement concerning the separation of the dough offering, and so too concerning setting aside the first fleece [that go to the priest].

N. These all fall into the category of minor religious duties, which are easy.

O. They are like lilies. When the Israelites carry them out, lo, they bring them into the life of the world to come.

No. 1 is apropos up to H-I, which goes on to a secondary question. But the whole surely pertains to placing secondary restrictions on rules of the Torah, to make sure that the primary prohibition is observed. This clear meaning imputed to the base-saying about putting a fence around one's words surely contradicts the view that Adam made a mistake by doing so. No. 2 continues No. 1 with a story that illustrates the exegesis of No. 1 but not the proposition that, for its part, No. 1 is meant to spell out. No. 3 carries forward the work of illustrating the same point, about raising a high fence around one's rule. No. 4 makes the same point in more general terms. No. 5 provides a sustained exposition of **II:I.4.E**, which refers to a minor religious duty, and No. 5 should be regarded as essentially continuous with No. 4. We cannot identify the hedge of lilies as relevant to the exposition of Song 7:3, since at issue is solely the definition of minor religious duties that make a major difference. So the concluding materials have their own interest.

II:II

1. A. What sort of fence did [4] Moses make around his words?

   B. Lo, Scripture says, *And the Lord said to Moses, "Go to the people and sanctify them today and tomorrow"* (Ex. 19:10).

   C. But that righteous man, Moses, did not wish to speak to Israel in the way in which the Holy One, blessed be he, had spoken to him. Rather, this is how he spoke with them: *Be ready against the third day; do not come near a woman* (Ex. 19:15).

   D. [And as to the fence that Moses made around his words,] it was on his own that he added a third day.

   E. For this is how Moses reasoned matters: "If a man goes near his wife and produces a drop of semen on the third day, they will be unclean, and the Israelites will turn out to receive from Mount Sinai the words of the Torah in a state of uncleanness. Therefore I shall add a third day so that a man may not go near his wife, and hence will not produce a drop of semen on the third day, so the people will be in a state of cultic cleanness, and the Israelites will turn out to receive from Mount Sinai the words of the Torah in a state of cleanness."

How Moses made a hedge around his words is not stated, since the hedge serves the commandment that God gave, not Moses' *own* opinion. But the point is clear as given: one should take precautions by adding to the requirement of a religious duty, so that there is no possibility of not carrying out the critical action that is required. And that point is completely coherent with the foregoing, which stresses that one should make a hedge around the words of the Torah by adding to the restrictions imposed by the Torah itself. The allusion to Moses' doing so at his own volition leads the compiler to insert a sizable exposition on that theme.

II:III

1. A. This is one of the matters which Moses carried out on his own volition, and his plan coincided with the plan of the Omnipresent.

   B. He kept away from his wife, and his plan coincided with the plan of the Omnipresent.

   C. He kept away from the tent of meeting, and his plan coincided with the plan of the Omnipresent.

   D. He broke the tablets, and his plan coincided with the plan of the Omnipresent.

2. A. He kept away from his wife, and his plan coincided with the plan of the Omnipresent.

   B. How so? He reasoned in this way: "If concerning the Israelites, who are sanctified only for a brief moment, and who have been designated only so as to accept upon themselves the Ten Commandments from Mount Sinai, the Holy One, blessed be he, has instructed me, *Go to the people and sanctify them today and tomorrow* (Ex. 19:10), I, who am designated for that task every single day and every single hour, and do not know when [God] will speak with me, whether by day or by night, all the more so that I should separate from having sexual relations.

C.   And his plan coincided with the plan of the Omnipresent.

D.   [Rejecting this view,] R. Judah b. Batera says, "Moses separated from having sexual relations with his wife only when he was explicitly instructed to do so by the Almighty, for it is said, *With him do I speak mouth to mouth* (Num. 12:8).

E.   "Mouth to mouth I made it explicit to him, 'Separate from having sexual relations with a woman,' and he did so."

F.   And some say that Moses separated from having sexual relations with his wife only when he was explicitly instructed to do so by the Almighty, as it is said, *Go, say to them, Return you to your tents* (Deut. 5:27), and it is written, *But as for you, stay here by me* (Deut. 5:28).

G.   He went back [following Goldin, p. 19] but he separated [from having sexual relations with his wife].

H.   And his plan coincided with the plan of the Omnipresent.

3. A.   He kept away from the tent of meeting, and his plan coincided with the plan of the Omnipresent.

B.   How so? He reasoned in this way: "If my brother Aaron, who has been anointed with anointing oil and with a profusion of priestly vestments and who serves at the altar in those vestments in a state of sanctification, has been told by the Holy One, blessed be he, *Speak to your brother Aaron, that he not come at any unspecified time to the sanctuary* [but only at strictly regulated intervals] (Lev. 16:2), I, who have not been designated for that purpose, all the more so that I should take my leave of the tent of meeting."

C.   He therefore kept away from the tent of meeting, and his plan coincided with the plan of the Omnipresent.

4. A.   He broke the tablets, and his plan coincided with the plan of the Omnipresent.

B.   How so? They tell: When Moses went up to the height to receive the tablets,

C.   (which were inscribed and kept in readiness from the six days of creation, for it is said, *The tablets were the work of God, and the writing the writing of God, incised on the tablets* (Ex. 32:16) – do not read inscribed but rather freedom [from *harut* to *herut*] for whoever is occupied in the Torah, ₁o, in his own context he is a free man –)

D.   at that moment the ministering angels were forming a conspiracy against Moses, saying, "Lord of the ages, *What is man, that you are mindful of him? and the son of man, that you think of him? Yet you have made him but little lower than the angels and have crowned him with glory and honor. You have made him to have dominion over the works of your hands, you have put all things under his feet, sheep and oxen, all of them, yes, and the beasts of the fields, the fowl of the air, and the fish of the sea* (Ps. 8:5-9),"

E.   and so they kept up the talk against Moses, saying, "What sort of creature is this one, born of woman, who has come up to the height?"

F.   So it is said, *You have ascended on high, you have led captivity captive, you have taken gifts* (Ps. 68:19).

G.   He took the [tablets] and went down, greatly rejoicing. When, however, he saw that offense that the people committed through the making of the calf, he thought, "How shall I give them the tablets? [If I do so,] I shall impose on them the duty of carrying out most weighty religious duties, on which account I shall also impose on them the liability to the death penalty inflicted at the hand of Heaven, for so it is written in them, *You shall not have any god other than me* (Ex. 20:3)."

H.   He went back, and the seventy elders saw him and ran after him. He took hold of one end of the tablets, and they took hold of one end of the tablets. The strength of Moses was greater than that of all the rest of them, as it is written, *And in all the mighty hand and in all the great terror which Moses wrought in the sight of all Israel* (Deut. 34:12).

I.   He looked at the tablets and realized that the writing had floated up from them. He said, "How shall I gave the Israelites tablets on which there is nothing of substance? Rather, I shall take and break them." For it is said, *So I took hold of the two tablets and I threw them out of my two hands and broke them* (Deut. 9:17).

J.   R. Yose the Galilean says, "I shall make a parable for you. To what may the matter be likened? To the case of a mortal king, who said to his messenger, 'Go and betroth a pretty girl for me, one who is pious, whose deeds are graceful.' The messenger went and betrothed such a woman. After he betrothed her, he went and found out that she committed an act of whoredom with another man. Forthwith he constructed an argument *a fortiori* on his own authority, saying, 'If now I give her a marriage-contract, it will turn out that I shall impose on her liability to the death penalty, and she will be removed from the possibility of marrying my lord for all time.'

K.   "So Moses, that righteous man, constructed an argument *a fortiori* on his own authority, saying, 'How shall I give the Israelites these tablets? [If I do so,] I shall impose on them the duty of carrying out most weighty religious duties, on which account I shall also impose on them the liability to the death penalty inflicted at the hand of Heaven, for so it is written in them, *One who sacrifices to other gods, instead of the Lord alone, will be utterly wiped out* (Ex. 22:19). Rather, I shall take hold of these and shatter them, and [later on] the Israelites will revert to good conduct.'"

L.   [Following Goldin:] *And I broke them before your eyes* (Deut. 9:17):

M.   "[I did so in your sight] lest the Israelites say, 'Where are those first tablets, which you brought down? The whole matter is nothing but a joke.'"

N.   [Rejecting the entire line of argument from A onward,] R. Judah b. Betera says, "Moses broke the tablets only because he was explicitly instructed to do so from the mouth of the Almighty, as it is said, for it is said, *With him do I speak mouth to mouth* (Num. 12:8).

E.   "Mouth to mouth I made it explicit to him, 'Break the tablets,' [and he did so]."

F.   And some say that Moses broke the tablets only when he was explicitly instructed to do so by the Almighty, as it is said, *And I saw, and behold, you have sinned against the Lord your God* (Deut. 9:17). It says, *And I saw,* only because he saw that the writing had floated up from the tablets.

G. And others say that Moses broke the tablets only when he was explicitly instructed to do so by the Almighty, as it is said, *And there they are as he commanded me* (Deut. 10:5). It says, *He commanded me* only because since he had been commanded to do so, he broke them.

H. R. Eleazar b. Azariah says, "Moses broke the tablets only when he was explicitly instructed to do so by the Almighty, as it is said, *which Moses did before the eyes of all Israel* (Deut. 34:12). Just as in that latter case Moses had been commanded and so did what he did, likewise here, it was because he had been commanded that he did what he did."

I. R. Aqiba says, "Moses broke the tablets only when he was explicitly instructed to do so by the Almighty, as it is said, *And I took hold of the two tablets* (Deut. 9:17). What someone takes hold of is what he can [following Goldin, citing Ginzberg, p. 180, n. 37:] hold on to. This teaches that Moses was so told by the mouth of the Almighty and Moses held on, as it were, to his creator."

J. R. Meir says, "Moses broke the tablets only when he was explicitly instructed to do so by the Almighty, as it is said, *which you broke* (Deut. 10:2). 'Good for you that you broke them!'"

After **II:II**, we proceed to amplify the theme introduced there, namely, Moses' reasoning on his own. But this has nothing to do with making a hedge around one's words. It is another thematic anthology, nothing more. Nos. 2., 3.,. and 4 then provide the information to which **II:III.1** refers. No. 4 presents an autonomous discussion of its issue, with A-M representing the position that Moses did what he did on his own volition, a view associated with the name of Yose the Galilean, and then a sequence of named authorities taking the opposite position. This pattern of presenting anonymously, then in Yose's name, one view, and presenting in the names of dissidents the contrary view, is of course familiar from the opening of Chapter One.

II:IV

1. A. Hezekiah, king of Judah, carried out four actions, and his plan coincided with the plan of the Omnipresent.

    B. He suppressed the book of remedies, and his plan coincided with the plan of the Omnipresent.

    C. He pulverized the copper snake, and his plan coincided with the plan of the Omnipresent.

    D. For it is said, *And he broke in pieces the copper snake...for up to that time the children of Israel made an offering to it and it was called Nehushtan* (2 Kgs. 18:4).

    E. He removed the high places and altars, and his plan coincided with the plan of the Omnipresent.

    F. For it is said, *Hezekiah removed the high places and altars and said to Judah and Jerusalem, saying, You shall worship before one altar and on it you shall offer* (2 Chr. 32:12).

    G. He stopped up the stream of Gihon, and his plan coincided with the plan of the Omnipresent.

H.   For it is said, *Hezekiah stopped up the upper spring of the waters of Gihon and brought them straight down on the west side of the city of David* (2 Chr. 32:30).

I.   *And Hezekiah prospered in all his works* (2 Chr. 32:30).

The information on Hezekiah is spelled out as required by this context. The parallels list other things Hezekiah did, with which the Omnipresent did not concur, but they are not relevant to the present composition. Clearly we are in the middle of an appendix of a thematic character. We now revert to the main topic subject to exposition.

II:V

1. A.   What sort of fence did [5] Job make around his words?

     B.   Lo, it is written, *An unblemished and upright man, who fears God and avoids evil* (Job 1:8).

     C.   This verse teaches that Job kept himself far not only from a matter that leads to transgression and anything offensive but even something that appears to be offensive.

2. A.   If so, why [Goldin: And why...] does Scripture say, *An unblemished and upright man?*

     B.   This is to teach that Job came forth circumcised.

     C.   So too the first Man came forth circumcised, for it is said, *And God created Man in his image* (Gen. 1:24).

     D.   So too Seth came forth circumcised, for it is said, *And he begot a son in his own likeness, after his image* (Gen. 5:3).

     E.   So too Noah came forth circumcised, for it is said, *He was righteous, flawless in his generation* (Gen. 6:9).

     F.   So too Shem came forth circumcised, for it is said, *And Melchizedek, king of Salem* (Gen. 14:18).

     G.   So too Jacob came forth circumcised, for it is said, *And Jacob, a flawless man, who dwelled in tents* (Gen. 25:27).

     H.   So too Joseph came forth circumcised, for it is said, *These are the generations of Jacob, Joseph* (Gen. 37:2).

     I.   Now what it should say is, *These are the generations of Jacob: Reuben.* Why then does Scripture say, *Joseph?* It is to indicate that just as Jacob came forth circumcised, so too Joseph came forth circumcised.

     J.   So too Moses came forth circumcised, for it is said, *And she saw him that he was good* (Ex. 2:2).

     K.   Now what was it that his mother saw in him? Was he prettier or more beautiful than anyone else? It was that he came forth circumcised.

     L.   So too the wicked Balaam came forth circumcised, for it is said, *The saying of him who hears the words of God* (Num. 24:4).

     M.   So too Samuel came forth circumcised, for it is said, *And the youth, Samuel, grew bigger and increased in goodness* (1 Sam. 2:26).

     N.   So too David came forth circumcised, for it is said, *Michtam, of David. Keep me, O God, for I have taken refuge in you* (Ps. 16:1).

     O.   So too Jeremiah came forth circumcised, for it is said, *Before I formed you in the belly I knew you, and before you come forth from the womb I had sanctified you* (Jer. 1:5).

P. So too Zerubbabel came forth circumcised, for it is said, *In that day I shall take you, O Zerubbabel, my servant, son of Shealtiel, says the Lord, and I will make you as a signet* (Hag. 2:23).

3. A. Lo, Scripture says, *I made a covenant with my eyes, how then should I look at a woman* (Job 31:1).

B. This teaches that Job applied to himself a very strict rule and never looked even at an unmarried woman.

C. And that fact produces an argument *a fortiori*:

D. Now if in the case of an unmarried woman, whom, if he wishes, he might take as a wife for himself, his son or brother or other relative, he imposed on himself a very strict rule, not looking at her, as to a married woman, how much the more so!

E. On what account did Job impose on himself so strict a rule as not to gaze even upon an unmarried woman?

F. It was because Job reasoned, "If I do so, perhaps today I shall gaze upon her and tomorrow someone else will come and marry her, and I shall turn out to have gazed upon a married woman."

No. 1 goes over the basic proposition, now with respect to Job, and No. 3 reverts to it, giving a concrete example. This is a good instance of imposing a hedge around one's own words, which coincide of course with the rule of the Torah. No. 2 forms a vast intrusion, attached for obviously thematic reasons, but with no bearing on matters at all.

II:VI

1. A. What sort of fence did [6] the prophets make for their words?

B. Lo, Scripture says, *The Lord will go forth as a mighty man, he will stir up jealousy like a man of war, he will cry, yes, he will shout aloud* (Is. 42:13).

C. He is not like only a single mighty man, but equivalent to all the mighty men in the world.

D. Along these same lines: *The lion has roared, who will not fear? The Lord God has spoken, who can but prophesy?* (Amos 3:8).

E. He is not like only a single lion, but equivalent to all the lions in the world.

F. Along these same lines: *And behold the glory of the Lord God of Israel came from the east, and his voice was like the sound of many waters, and the earth did shine with his glory* (Ez. 43:2):

G. ...*the sound of many waters* alludes to the angel Gabriel, *and the earth did shine with his glory* speaks of the Presence of God in the world.

H Now does the matter not yield an argument *a fortiori*:

I. if the voice of Gabriel, who is merely one among thousands of thousands and hosts of hosts of the retinue that stands before him, goes from one end of the world to the other, the King of kings of kings, the Holy One, blessed be he, who has created the entire world, who has created the upper creatures, who has created the lower creatures, all the more so.

J. But to the eye is shown what the eye can see, and to the ear is conveyed what the ear can hear.

The point is hardly self-evident, since the hedge around the prophets' words is not made explicit. Goldin, p. 180, n. 55, explains: "The hedge of the prophets is this, that they employed some metaphor in the description of God who, strictly speaking, is beyond description and comparison." While plausible, that explanation ignores the context, because it makes the hedge at hand different from the ones attributed to the first five heroes on the list, all of whom went beyond the limits of the statement they wished to make, to make certain that the rule they set forth would not be violated. So a hedge earlier required overstatement, while here, following Goldin, we find a hedge that requires understatement. It seems to me more plausible, therefore, that we have no picture of the sort of fence the prophets set up, but rather a set-piece exposition of prophetic understatement, which has no bearing on the proposition it is supposed to amplify. What follows is far more appropriate to the context.

II:VII

1. A. What sort of fence did [7] the Writings make around their words?
   B. Lo, Scripture says, *Remove your way far from her and come not near the door of her house* (Prov. 5:8).
   C. *Remove your way far from her* refers to heresy.
   D. For people say to someone, "Do not associate with heretics and do not go to such a place, lest you stumble among them."
   E. If one replies, "I am confident of myself that, even though I go there, I shall not stumble among them,"
   F. or if you might suppose, "I shall listen to what they say and then go my way,"
   G. the verse of Scripture states, *None that go to her return, nor do they gain the paths of life* (Prov. 2:19).
   H. It is written, *She has prepared her meat, she has mixed her wine, she has also set her table* (Prov. 9:2).
   I. This refers to wicked people. When someone associates with them, they give him food and drink and clothe him and give him a lodging place and plenty of money. Once he becomes as one of them, each one recognizes his own and grabs it away from him. Of them it is said, *Till an arrow strike through the liver; as a bird that runs to the trap and does not know that it is at the cost of his life* (Prov. 7:23).

2. A. Another matter concerning the verse: *Remove your way far from her and come not near the door of her house* (Prov. 5:8):
   B. This refers to a whore, concerning whom people say to someone, "Do not go into that marketplace, and do not walk through that alley, for there is a whore there, really built."
   C. Then he says, "I am quite sure of myself that, even if I go to such a place, I am not going to stumble on her account."
   D. They say to him, "Even though you have confidence in yourself, do not go there, lest you stumble on her account."
   E. For lo, sages have said, "Do not routinely go by the door of a whore, for it is said, *For she has cast down many wounded, yes, a mighty host are all those whom she has slain* (Prov. 7:26)."

No. 1.A-B provides a good example of a fence, that is, one should not only not have dealings with such a disreputable person, one should not even pass near by. That is a fine instance of going beyond the limits of the law, so as to avoid violating the law. C-G go on to their own interests. They are hardly essential for the purpose at hand. But they do fit the larger context in a way in which II:VI's materials do not. H-I seem to me attached to C-G because of a general congruence, not because they make the same point at all. No. 2 follows along the lines introduced already, in that it makes the point that one should not rely on his own strength but should avoid temptation, which, in a general way, forms a good illustration of the rule to establish a fence around one's principles.

II:VIII

1. A. What sort of fence did [8] sages make around their words?
    B. Sages rule: The recitation of the *Shema* in the evening may be done up to midnight. Rabban Gamaliel says, "Up to the cock's crow [in the morning]."
    C. How so [did sages make around their words]?
    D. If someone comes home tired after work, he should not say, "I shall eat a bite and drink a bit and go to sleep for forty winks, and then I shall recite the *Shema*." He may turn out to sleep all night and not recite the *Shema*.
    E. But when someone comes home, tired from work, he should go to the synagogue or the school house. If he is accustomed to study Scripture, let him recite Scripture, and if he is accustomed to repeat Mishnah-sayings, let him repeat Mishnah-sayings, but if not, let him merely recite the *Shema,* then say the Prayer.
    F. And whoever violates the teachings of sages is liable to the death penalty.
    G. Rabban Simeon b. Gamaliel says, "There are times that a person recites the *Shema* two times in the same night, once before the morning star rises, once afterward. He then turns out to fulfill his obligation to say the *Shema* both by day and by night.
    H. Sages went and imposed a substantial requirement, so making a fence around their words. [Goldin, p. 181, n. 64: Sages...declared that one is not to recite the evening *Shema* after midnight nor the morning *Shema* before sunrise.]

The exposition of the sages' fence is somewhat confused. D-E seem to me an adequate answer to the question. Prior to reciting the *Shema*, one should not take a nap in the evening, lest he sleep all night. So a hedge is to require immediate recitation, E. G-H present a separate matter, and why the requirement specified by G may represent a violation of the law is not clear, though Goldin attempts to explain the matter and to show the link between H and G.

The Fathers According to Rabbi Nathan

Chapter Three

ARNA Chapter Three is devoted to the exposition of the middle saying of the Men of the Great Assembly:

> **They said three things: Be prudent in judgment. Raise up many disciples. Make a fence for the Torah.**

As to that matter, discourse is brief and rather tangential. Goldin, p. 182, n. 28, states, "The whole of the preceding chapter, except for the opening paragraph, is out of place and properly should form part of the discussion in the next chapter on 'acts of loving-kindness.'" But the discourse on acts of loving-kindness in ARNA Chapter Four at no point approaches the theme of charity. In fact the entire treatment of that topic focuses upon the destruction of the Temple, because in a proof-text in a story on that matter Hos. 6:6, which refers to acts of loving-kindness, happens to occur. So Goldin's suggestion is not plausible. The outline shows the rest.

III:I

III:I.1 Raise up many disciples + the Houses on whether one should teach only appropriate candidates or whoever comes.

III:II

III:II.1-4 Aqiba-sayings: If one lies about a condition from which he does not suffer, he will end up suffering from that condition.

III:III

III:III.1 Aqiba's ruling in a case. Not related to foregoing.

III:IV A set of sayings illustrative in diverse ways of Qoh. 11:6.

III:IV.1 R. Dosa b. R. Yannai: Persist in what you do, because you do not know the result of your earlier effort, so keep it up.

III:IV.2 Ishmael: Study Torah when young and old.

III:IV.3 Aqiba: Study Torah when young and old, [Goldin adds:] teach disciples when young and old].

III:IV.4 Meir: Study with different masters.

III:IV.5 Study with four masters, such as Eliezer, Joshua, Aqiba, Tarfon.

III:IV.6 Joshua: Marry and have children when young and when old.

III:IV.7 Give charity to a beggar in the morning and do the same at night.

III:V

III:V.1 Story about a man who gave to charity.

III:VI

III:VI.1 Story about a man who gave to charity.

III:VII

III:VII.1 Story about a man who gave to charity.

The principle of compilation is therefore essentially associative. If the compilers found an available composition that at some point, in some detail, intersected with the theme of a saying in Avot, they took the entire composition and inserted it whole. As we shall see, the only reason for making use of this rather sizable composite, itself made up of prior compositions, is the supposition that Aqiba's statement at **III:IV:3.B** refers to raising disciples both in one's youth and in one's old age. And in the text as we have it, that element is not present at all!

III:I

1. A. **Raise up many disciples.**
   B. For the House of Shammai say, "A person should teach only one who is wise, modest, well-born, and rich."
   C. And the House of Hillel say, "A person should teach everybody, for there were many sinners in Israel who drew near to the study of the Torah, and from such as they came forth righteous, pious, and wholly acceptable persons.

The opening entry places the philosophy at hand into the framework of the House of Hillel. The House of Shammai directly contradicts the saying, and the House of Hillel implicitly affirms its philosophy. But the two Houses do not respond directly to the saying at all. For its issue – raising up many disciples – is not the focus of either saying, since the dispute concerns not the numbers but assessing the character of prospective disciples.

III:II

1. A. R. Aqiba says, "Whoever takes a penny from the poor-fund when he does not need it will not leave this world before he falls into need of help from other people."

2. A. He also would say, "One who covers his eyes or his loins with bandages and cries, 'Give to a blind man' or '...a suffering man' will end up telling the truth [about his afflictions]."

3. A. He also would say, "He who [in anger] bangs his bread on the ground or in temper throws his money around will not leave this world before he falls into need of help from other people."

    B. He also would say, "He who in anger tears his clothes or in anger breaks his property in the end will serve idolatry.

    C. "For that is the skill of the evil impulse. Today it says to someone, 'Tear your clothes,' and the next day it will say to him, 'Serve an idol,' and the man goes and serves an idol."

4. A. He also would say, "He who gazes upon his wife and wishes that she would die so that he might inherit her estate, or so that she would die and he might marry his sister,

    B. "and whoever wishes that his brother would die so that he might marry his wife in the end will be buried while they are alive.

    C. "In this regard Scripture says, *He who digs a hole will fall into it, and whoever breaks through a fence will be bitten by a snake lurking in it* (Qoh. 10:8)."

This collection of sayings, joined by both the name of the authority and also the philosophy, in no way proves relevant to the basic statement of Avot that is supposedly amplified. Aqiba's point throughout is that if one lies about his condition, saying that it is worse than it is, he will end up telling the truth. That point is made three times. Then **III:II.3.B** shifts the ground of discourse, making a separate point. No. 4 goes on to yet a fresh proposition, which is that if one wants something he should not want, he will be punished by getting the opposite. That is congruent in a general way to the opening proposition, 1-3. Why the redactor found this entire composition useful I cannot say. What follows is no more pertinent.

III:III

1. A. There was a man who violated the instructions of R. Aqiba by pulling off a woman's hair-covering in the market place.

    B. She brought complaint before R. Aqiba and he imposed on the man a fine of four hundred *zuz*.

    C. The man said to him, "My lord, give me time [to pay up this substantial sum]."

    D. He gave him time.

    E. When the man left court, his friend said to him, "I'll tell you how you won't have to pay her even something worth a penny."

    F. He said to him, "Tell me."

    G. He said to him, "Go and get yourself some oil worth an *issar* and break the flask at the woman's door."

    H. [He did so.] What did that woman do? She came out of her house and let her hair down in the marketplace and mopped up the oil with her hands and wiped it on her hair.

I. Now the man had set up witnesses and came back to R. Aqiba's court and said to him, "Should I pay off four hundred *zuz* to this contemptible woman? Now because of a mere issar's worth of oil, this woman could not forego the dignity owing to herself, but rather came out of her house and let her hair down in the marketplace and mopped up the oil with her hands and wiped it on her hair."

J. He said to him, "You have no legitimate claim at all. For if a person inflicts injury on herself, even though one is not permitted to do so, she is exempt from penalty, others who do injury to that person are liable. She who does injury to herself is exempt from penalty, while you, who have done injury to her [are liable]. Go and pay her the four hundred *zuz*."

The relevance of this story to the basic saying is nil, and there also is no connection, other than Aqiba's name, to what has gone before. If Aqiba's name appeared in the original statement of Avot, we might imagine that Aqiba's collection has been inserted whole because of an interest in assembling stories about authorities named on the base-list. But of course Aqiba is nowhere to be seen, and why the present materials, assembled because all are told about Aqiba, have been inserted remains a mystery.

But in **III:IV.3** the mystery will be solved. There we have a sustained disquisition on the importance of continuing at a project in a persistent manner, e.g., study of the Torah, and, in context, it is stated that one should raise up disciples both in one's youth and also in old age, an illustration of the larger principle. That saying is assigned to Aqiba. On that account, it would appear, the enormous complex made up of the present and following compositions has been pasted in to this pastiche of materials that, in some ways and at some points only, intersect with the themes of sayings in Avot.

III:IV

1. A. R. Dosa b. R. Yannai says, "If you went ahead and sowed seed during the early rains, again go and sow in the later rains, for it is entirely possible that a hail may come down and destroy the earlier crop, while the later crop [still in the ground and not yet sprouted] will survive.

   B. "*For you do not know which will prosper, the one or the other*, or perhaps both of them will survive, *and they shall both turn out well* (Qoh. 11:6) [following Goldin], as it is said, *In the morning sow your seed and in the evening keep it up* (Qoh. 11:6).

   C. "If you went ahead and sowed seed during the early rains and again during the later rains, again go and sow in the final rains, for a blight may descend and ruin the first crops, while the later ones may survive.

   D. "*For you do not know which will prosper, the one or the other*, or perhaps both of them will survive, *and they shall both turn out well* (Qoh. 11:6) [following Goldin], as it is said, *In the morning sow your seed and in the evening keep it up* (Qoh. 11:6)."

2. A. R. Ishmael says, "If you have studied the Torah in your youth, do not conclude, 'I shall not study the Torah in my old age.' Study the Torah, *For you do not know which will prosper, the one or the other*.

B. "If you have studied the Torah in a time of prosperity, do not let up in a time of need, if you have studied the Torah in a time of satisfaction, do not let up in a time of famine, if you have studied the Torah in a time of plenty, do not let up in a time of penury,

C. "for better for a person is one thing in distress than a hundred in ease.

D. "For it is said, *In the morning sow your seed and in the evening keep it up* (Qoh. 11:6)."

3. A. R. Aqiba says, "If you have studied the Torah in your youth, do not conclude, 'I shall not study the Torah in my old age.' Study the Torah, *For you do not know which will prosper, the one or the other,* or perhaps both of them will survive, *and they shall both turn out well* (Qoh. 11:6).

B. "And [add, following Goldin, p. 28], [If you have raised disciples in your youth, raise disciples in your old age also,] as it is said, *In the morning sow your seed and in the evening keep it up* (Qoh. 11:6).

4. A. R. Meir says, "If you have studied the Torah with one master, do not say, 'That is enough,' but go to another sage and study the Torah.

B. "But do not go to just anyone, but rather, go to someone to whom to begin with you have an affinity.

C. "So it is said, *Drink waters out of your own cistern and running water out of your own well* (Prov. 5:15)."

5. A. One is obligated to serve as disciple four disciples of sages, for example, R Eliezer, R. Joshua, R. Aqiba, and R. Tarfon.

B. For it is said, *Happy is the one who listens to me, watching daily at my gates, waiting at the posts of my doors* (Prov. 8:34).

C. Instead of *my doors*, read the letters as if they spelled out the words, *my four gates.*

D. *For you do not know which will prosper, the one or the other,* or perhaps both of them will survive, *and they shall both turn out well . In the morning sow your seed and in the evening keep it up* (Qoh. 11:6)."

6. A. R. Joshua says, "Marry a wife when you are young, and marry a wife when you are old, beget children when you are young, and beget children when you are old.

B. "Do not say, 'I shall not get married,' but get married and produce sons and daughters and so increase procreation in the world.

C. "*For you do not know which will prosper, the one or the other,* or perhaps both of them will survive, *and they shall both turn out well . In the morning sow your seed and in the evening keep it up* (Qoh. 11:6)."

7. A. He would say, "If you have given a penny to a beggar in the morning and another beggar comes and stands at your door in the evening, give him too,

B. "*For you do not know which will prosper, the one or the other,* or perhaps both of them will survive, *and they shall both turn out well. In the morning sow your seed and in the evening keep it up* (Qoh. 11:6)."

The theory I offered on why **III:III-IV** has been inserted rests entirely on Goldin's interpolation at **III:IV.3.B.** Otherwise the composition is parachuted down without any target at all. But Goldin's interpolation rests on solid ground, and so does the redactional reason that derives from it. What we have is a rather cogent set of expositions of examples of the basic notion of Qoh. 11:6: "*For* *you do not know which will prosper, the one or the other*, or perhaps both of them will survive, *and they shall both turn out well. In the morning sow your seed and in the evening keep it up.* Each sage's entry gives its own example of the same matter. Not all are equally relevant, and Meir is irrelevant. The rule of studying with four masters is pertinent only if we know that one does not know which one's teachings will work out well, but that is not made explicit. The ultimate compiler of ARNA then has taken the entire composition, the basic point of which is in no way germane to the sayings he is purporting to amplify, and simply given it its place here.

III:V

1. A. There was the case of a pious man who gave a *denar* to a poor man during the time of famine. His wife criticized him [for giving away what little they had in need], so he went and spent the night in the graveyard. He heard two spirits gossiping with one another, saying to one another, "My friend, come on and let's fly around the world and see what sort of disaster is coming into the world."

B. The other said to her, "I can't go forth, because I am buried in a wrapping made of a reed mat, but you go, and whatever you hear come and report to me."

C. The other went and came back, and the former said to her, "My friend, have you heard anything from [following Goldin:] beyond the veil about what sort of disaster is coming upon the world?"

D. She said, "I heard that whoever sows in the time of the earlier rains [will lose out, because] hail will hit his crops."

E. The man went and sowed in the second, not in the first rain. The crops of everybody were hit by hail, but his crop was not smitten.

F. The next year the man went and spent the night in the graveyard.

G. He heard two spirits gossiping with one another, saying to one another, "My friend, come on and let's fly around the world and see what sort of disaster is coming into the world."

H. The other said to her, "Didn't I tell you, I can't go forth, because I am buried in a wrapping made of a reed mat, but you go, and whatever you hear come and report to me."

I. The other went and came back, and the former said to her, "My friend, have you heard anything from [following Goldin:] beyond the veil about what sort of disaster is coming upon the world."

J. She said, "I heard that whoever sows in the time of the later rains [will lose out, because] blast will hit his crops."

K. The man went and sowed in the first rain. The crops of everybody were hit by blast, but his crop was not smitten.

L. His wife said to him, "How come when the disasters came upon everyone in the world, the crops of everybody were hit by hail and smitten by blast, but yours were not hit by hail or smitten by blast." He told her the whole story.

M. Some time later the pious man's wife had a fight with the mother of the girl [who had been buried in a cheap matting of reed as her shroud]. She said to her, "Go and I shall show you how your daughter is buried in a cheap matting of reed as a shroud."

N. The next year the man went and spent the night in the graveyard.

O. He heard two spirits gossiping with one another, saying to one another, "My friend, come on and let's fly around the world and see what sort of disaster is coming into the world."

P. The other said to her, "My friend, leave me alone. The words that have passed between you and me have now been heard among the living."

The only reason I can imagine the redactor has inserted this complete story is that it is joined to the theme of Joshua's second statement, **III:IV.7**, which, by the way, has introduced the theme of philanthropy. Once that theme comes to the fore, philanthropy-stories will find their way to center stage.

III:VI

1. A. There was the case of a pious man who regularly gave charity. Once he took his place on a ship, a strong wind came and his ship sank in the sea. R. Aqiba saw [that this had happened to] him [and wished to make certain that testimony of the man's death was provided in court, so that the man's widow would be free to remarry].

B. He came to court to give testimony in behalf of the man's widow, so that she might wed. But before the sage had taken the stand, the man himself came and stood before him.

C. [Aqiba] said to him, "Are you the man who sank into the sea?"

D. He said to him, "Yes."

E. "And he dredged you up from the sea?"

F. He said to him, "It is the charity that I carried out that brought me up from the sea."

G. He said to him, "How do you know?"

H. He said to him, "When I had descended to the depths of the ocean, I heard the great thunder coming from the waves of the ocean, with this one saying to that, and that one to the other, 'Run and let us raise up this man from the sea, who has carried out acts of charity for his entire life.'"

I. At that moment R. Aqiba commenced discourse, "Blessed is God, the God of Israel, who has chosen the words of the Torah and the words of sages.

J. "For the words of the Torah and the words of sages endure for ages and ages to come.

K. "For it is said, *Cast your bread upon the waters, for you shall find it after many days* (Qoh. 11:1), and, *Charity delivers from death* (Prov. 109:2)."

The established theme finds yet another exemplification.

III:VII

1. A. There was the case of Benjamin, the righteous man, who was appointed in charge of the charity fund. A woman came before him and said to him, "My lord, feed me."

B. He said to her, "By the Temple service! There is nothing in the charity-fund to give you."

C. She said to him, "My lord, if you do not feed me, you will turn out to have killed a widow and her seven children."

D. He went and provided for her from his own funds.

E. After a while Benjamin the righteous man fell sick and lay in bed in distress.

F. The ministering angels said before the Holy One, blessed be he, "Lord of the world, you have said that whoever saves a single life in Israel is as if he had saved the entire world. Benjamin the righteous, who kept alive a widow and her seven children, how much the more so, and now he is suffering in bed on account of this illness."

G. Forthwith they sought mercy for him, and the decree against him was torn up, and he was given twenty-two more years in addition to the years that had been allotted to him.

The established theme finds yet another exemplification.

The Fathers According to Rabbi Nathan

Chapter Four

ARNA Chapter Four moves us on to the saying of Simeon the Righteous:

> Simeon the Righteous was one of the last survivors of the
> men of the great assembly. He would say: On three things
> does the world stand, [1] on the Torah, and [2] on the
> Temple service, and [3] on deeds of loving-kindness.

The chapter unfolds in line with the three clauses, as the following outline shows. But the chapter also contains diverse materials tacked on on the principle of thematic association.

IV:I

IV:I.1 Citation of Simeon's statement.

IV:II

IV:II.1 On the Torah: how so? Burnt-offering is most desirable. But study of the Torah is superior.

IV:III

IV:III.1 Sages should interrupt their study to carry out deeds of loving-kindness, if there is no one else available to do so.

IV:III.2 Judah b. Ilai interrupted his teaching to celebrate a bride. [Omitted: if there is no one else available to do so.]

IV:III.3 Same.

IV:IV

IV:IV.1 On the Temple service: how so? When the Temple service is carried on, nature gives its blessings.

IV:IV.2 Same point, different proof-text. Nothing is more beloved than the Temple service.

IV:V

> **IV:V.1** Deeds of loving-kindness: how so? World was created only for loving-kindness.
>
> **IV:V.2** Yohanan ben Zakkai: Deeds of loving-kindness are a means of atonement as effective as cult.
>
> **IV:V.3** Daniel did such deeds, and not sacrifices. They were acts of celebration of the bride, burial of the dead, charity, and prayer.

IV:VI

> **IV:VI.1** Destruction of the Temple.
>
> **IV:VI.2** Same.
>
> **IV:VI.3-4** Same.

IV:VII

> **IV:VII.1** God diversified human beings in three aspects.

The movement from Simeon's statement about the world standing on the service of the Temple to Yohanan's discourse on the destruction of the Temple shows wit and subtlety. We shall see some flaws in the exposition, to be sure, since materials illustrative of the first of Simeon's statements – the Temple service – in fact serve the third, deeds of loving-kindness. That is only one example of the imperfection of the redactional work. As usual, once the redactor has decided to compose a set of materials on Simeon's sayings, he has selected rather large composites and not cut them down for his own purposes, but reproduced them whole. The inclusion of **IV:VII.1** is incomprehensible to me, except as it may repeat a key-word of **IV:VI.4**.

IV:I

1. A. Simeon the Righteous was one of the last survivors of the great assembly. He would say: On three things does the world stand, [1] on the Torah, and [2] on the Temple service, and [3] on deeds of loving-kindness.

IV:II

1. A. ...on the Torah: how so?

    B. *For I desire mercy and not sacrifice, and the knowledge of God rather than burnt-offerings* (Hos. 6:6):

    C. On the basis of this statement we learn that the burnt-offering is the most desired offering of all, because the burnt-offering is entirely consumed on the altar fires [and yields nothing for either the priest or the farmer who brought the beast, hence it is a mark of total generosity to the altar].

    D. As it is said, *And the priest shall make the whole smoke on the altar* (Lev. 1:9).

E.   And further: *And Samuel took a sucking lamb and offering it for a whole burnt-offering to the Lord* (1 Sam. 7:9).

F.   Nonetheless, study of the Torah is more beloved still for the Omnipresent than burnt-offerings.

G.   For if someone studies the Torah, he knows the mind [Goldin: will] of God,

H.   for it is said,*Then you will understand the fear of the Lord and find the mind of God* (Prov. 2:5).

I.   On the basis of this statement we learn of a sage who sits and expounds [the Torah] in the community that Scripture credits it to him as though he had offered fat and blood on the altar.

A-E set the stage for F, with its reference to the whole-offering as less desirable than the study of the Torah. G-I are congruent to the foregoing. I does not make reference to the whole-offering in particular.

IV:III

1.   A.   When two disciples of sages are in session and occupied with the Torah, if before them came a bride [to whom they owe the honor of bringing rejoicing] or the bier of a corpse [to whom they are obligated to attend], if the one or the other has adequate provision for the need of the occasion, let the disciples not interrupt their repetition of their traditions.

B.   But if not, then let them go and [Goldin:] cheer and praise the bride or accompany the corpse.

2.   A.   There was the case of R. Judah b. Ilai who was in session and repeating Mishnah-traditions to his disciples, and a bride came by.

B.   He took in his hand myrtle twigs and cheered her until the bride had gone by him.

3.   A.   There was the further case of R. Judah b. Ilai who was in session and repeating Mishnah-traditions to his disciples, and a bride came by.

B.   He said to them, "What's going on?"

C.   They said to him, "It's a bride going by."

D.   He said to them, "My sons, get up and get busy with the bride.

E.   "For so we find with the Holy One, blessed be he, that he occupied himself with the needs of the bride.

F.   "For it is said, *And the Lord God built the rib* (Gen. 2:22).

G.   "Since [God] occupied himself with the needs of the bride, how much the more so should we."

H.   And where do we find that the Holy One occupied himself with the needs of the bride?

I.   It is said, *And the Lord God built the rib* (Gen. 2:22).

J.   Now in the coastal towns they call [Goldin:] plaiting the hair by the same word that in this verse means *built*.

K.   On the basis of the cited verse we learn that the Holy One, blessed be he, attended to Eve and adorned her as a bride and brought her to Adam, as it is said, *And he brought her to man* (Gen. 2:22).

L. On that one occasion the Holy One, blessed be he, served as Adam's best man. From that point onward, a man acquires a best man for himself, as it is said, *Bone of my bone and flesh of my flesh* (Gen. 2:23).

M. On that one occasion he took Eve from Adam. From that time onward a man betrothes the daughter of his fellow.

The materials of **IV:II.1-3** have no bearing on the exposition of the clause of Simeon's saying. Indeed, they contradict what has gone before, because we have just been told that the study of the Torah takes precedence even over a whole-offering. But at **IV:II.1** the proposition is that certain acts of supererogatory grace, caring for the bride and burying the dead, take precedence even over the study of the Torah. These materials would seem to me to serve Simeon's third clause, that the world stands on deeds of loving-kindness still more than on either study of the Torah or the Temple service. But the redactor has not indicated that that is his meaning, and since at **IV:III.1** he will move on to the Temple service, it is certain that it is not. The secondary expansion of No. 1 and Nos. 2, 3 pursues a line of thought entirely remote from the point at which we began, and clearly has been worked out without interest in the context in which the entire composition finally located itself.

IV:IV

1. A. ...on the Temple service: how so?

    B. So long as the Temple service of the house of the sanctuary went on, the world was blessed for its inhabitants and rain came down in the proper time.

    C. For it is said, *To love the Lord your God and to serve him with all your heart and with all your soul that I will provide the rain of your land in its season, the former rain and the latter rain...and I will provide grass in your fields for your cattle* (Deut. 11:13-14).

    D. But when the Temple service of the house of the sanctuary ceased to go on, the world was not blessed for its inhabitants, and rain did not come down in the proper time,

    E. as it is said, *Take heed to yourselves lest your heart be deceived...and he shut up the heaven so that there shall be no rain* (Deut. 11:16-17).

2. A. And so Scripture says, *I pray you, consider from this day onward, before a stone was laid upon a stone in the Temple of the Lord, through all that time, when one came to a heap of twenty measures, there were but ten, and when one came to the wine vat to draw out fifty press measures, there were but twenty* (Hag. 2:15-16).

    B. Why does it not say in connection with wine, "Twenty measures, there were but ten," as in the case of the wheat, *when one came to a heap of twenty measures, there were but ten*?

    C. It is because the wine vat is a better omen [of what is to come] than wheat.

    D. So teaching you that so long as wine is smitten, it is a bad omen for the entire year to come.

E. The Israelites said to the Holy One, blessed be he, "Lord of the world, why did you do this to us?"

F. The Holy Spirit replied to them, "*You looked for much, and lo it came to little...because of my house, which lies waste, while you run every man for his own house* (Hag. 1:9).

G. "*Consider, I pray you...from the twenty-fourth day of the ninth month, even from the day that the foundation of the Lord's temple was laid...is the seed yet in the barn? Yes, the vine, and fig tree, pomegranate and olive tree have not you brought forth produce...from this day I will bless you* (Hag. 2:18-19)."

H. This teaches that there is no act of service more beloved before the Holy One, blessed be he, than is the Temple service.

The discourse on the second clause is coherent, since it makes a single point, given at the end. That point contradicts what has gone before, which gives higher ranking to study of the Torah, then second ranking to acts of supererogatory grace. The materials on Haggai's sayings stand separate from the foregoing and do not refer back to the preceding, which is why I treat them as a distinct unit.

IV:V

1. A. ...**on deeds of loving-kindness:** how so?

   B. Lo, Scripture says, *For I desire mercy and not sacrifice, [and the knowledge of God rather than burnt-offerings]* (Hos. 6:6).

   C. To begin with the world was created only on account of loving-kindness.

   D. For so it is said, *For I have said, the world is built with loving-kindness, in the very heavens you establish your faithfulness* (Ps. 89:3).

2. A. One time [after the destruction of the Temple] Rabban Yohanan ben Zakkai was going forth from Jerusalem, with R. Joshua following after him. He saw the house of the sanctuary lying in ruins.

   B. R. Joshua said, "Woe is us for this place which lies in ruins, the place in which the sins of Israel used to come to atonement."

   C. He said to him, "My son, do not be distressed. We have another mode of atonement, which is like [atonement through sacrifice], and what is that? It is deeds of loving-kindness.

   D. "For so it is said, *For I desire mercy and not sacrifice, [and the knowledge of God rather than burnt-offerings]* (Hos. 6:6)."

3. A. So we find in the case of Daniel, that most desirable man, that he carried out deeds of loving-kindness.

   B. And what are the deeds of loving-kindness that Daniel did?

   C. If you say that he offered whole-offerings and sacrifices, do people offer sacrifices in Babylonia?

   D. And has it not in fact been said, *Take heed that you not offer your whole-offerings in any place which you see but in the place which the Lord will select in the territory of one of the tribes. There you will offer up your whole offerings* (Deut. 12:13-14).

   E. When then were the deeds of loving-kindness that Daniel did?

F. He would adorn the bride and make her happy, join a cortege for the deceased, give a penny to a pauper, pray three times every day,

G. and his prayer was received with favor,

H. for it is said, *And when Daniel knew that the writing was signed, he went into his house – his windows were open in his upper chamber toward Jerusalem – and he kneeled upon his knees three times a day and prayed and gave thanks before his God as he did aforetime* (Dan. 6:11).

The exposition of the third of the three clauses invokes the same proof-text as the first, which is curious. For reasons already given, my view is that the basic thrust of the first exposition, **IV:I.1ff.**, is out of place and belongs here. That is almost certain, since **IV:V.3** is explicit on the matter of the bride and the deceased. No. 2, moreover, cites the proof-text to place acts of loving-kindness over the Temple service as well. In all, it appears to me that the exposition of Simeon's saying is slightly awry. Certainly the inclusion of the materials on charity in Chapter Three would be entirely out of place here.

IV:VI

1. A. Now when Vespasian came to destroy Jerusalem, he said to [the inhabitants of the city,] "Idiots! why do you want to destroy this city and burn the house of the sanctuary? For what do I want of you, except that you send me a bow or an arrow [as marks of submission to my rule], and I shall go on my way."

    B. They said to him, "Just as we sallied out against the first two who came before you and killed them, so shall we sally out and kill you."

    C. When Rabban Yohanan ben Zakkai heard, he proclaimed to the men of Jerusalem, saying to them, "My sons, why do you want to destroy this city and burn the house of the sanctuary? For what does he want of you, except that you send him a bow or an arrow, and he will go on his way."

    D. They said to him, "Just as we sallied out against the first two who came before him and killed them, so shall we sally out and kill him."

    E. Vespasian had stationed men near the walls of the city, and whatever they heard, they would write on an arrow and shoot out over the wall. [They reported] that Rabban Yohanan ben Zakkai was a loyalist of Caesar's.

    F. After Rabban Yohanan ben Zakkai had spoken to them one day, a second, and a third, and the people did not accept his counsel, he sent and called his disciples, R. Eliezer and R. Joshua, saying to them, "My sons, go and get me out of here. Make me an ark and I shall go to sleep in it."

    G. R. Eliezer took the head and R. Joshua the feet, and toward sunset they carried him until they came to the gates of Jerusalem.

    H. The gate keepers said to them, "Who is this?"

    I. They said to him, "It is a corpse. Do you not know that a corpse is not kept overnight in Jerusalem?"

    J. They said to them, "If it is a corpse, take him out," so they took him out and brought him out at sunset, until they came to Vespasian.

K. They opened the ark and he stood before him.

L. He said to him, "Are you Rabban Yohanan ben Zakkai? Indicate what I should give you."

M. He said to him, "I ask from you only Yavneh, to which I shall go, and where I shall teach my disciples, establish prayer [Goldin: a prayer house], and carry out all of the religious duties."

N. He said to him, "Go and do whatever you want."

O. He said to him, "Would you mind if I said something to you?"

P. [He said to him, "Go ahead."]

Q. He said to him, "Lo, you are going to be made sovereign."

R. He said to him, "How do you know?

S. He said to him, "It is a tradition of ours that the house of the sanctuary will be given over not into the power of a commoner but of a king, for it is said, *And he shall cut down the thickets of the forest with iron, and Lebanon* [which refers to the Temple] *shall fall by a mighty one* (Is. 10:34)."

T. People say that not a day, two or three passed before a delegation came to him from his city indicating that the [former Caesar had died and they had voted for him to ascend the throne.

U. They brought him a [Goldin:] catapult and drew it up against the wall of Jerusalem.

V. They brought him cedar beams and put them into the catapult, and he struck them against the wall until a breach had been made in it. They brought the head of a pig and put it into the catapult and tossed it toward the limbs that were on the Temple altar.

W. At that moment Jerusalem was captured.

X. Rabban Yohanan ben Zakkai was in session and with trembling was looking outward, in the way that Eli had sat and waited: *Lo, Eli sat upon his seat by the wayside watching, for his heart trembled for the ark of God* (1 Sam. 4:13).

Y. When Rabban Yohanan ben Zakkai heard that Jerusalem had been destroyed and the house of the sanctuary burned in flames, he tore his garments, and his disciples tore their garments, and they wept and cried and mourned.

2. A. Scripture says, *Open your doors, O Lebanon, that the fire may devour your cedars* (Zech. 11:1).

    B. That verse refers to the high priests who were in the sanctuary [on the day it was burned].

    C. They took their keys in their hands and threw them upward, saying before the Holy One, blessed be he, "Lord of the world, here are your keys which you entrusted to us, for we have not been faithful custodians to carry out the work of the king and to receive support from the table of the king."

3. A. Abraham, Isaac, and Jacob, and the twelve tribes were weeping, crying, and mourning.

4. A. Scripture says, *Wail, O cypress tree, for the cedar is fallen, because the glorious ones are spoiled, wail, O you oaks of Bashan, for the strong forest is come down* (Zech. 11:2).

B.   *Wail, O cypress tree, for the cedar is fallen* refers to the house of the sanctuary.

C.   *...because the glorious ones are spoiled* refers to Abraham, Isaac, and Jacob, and the twelve tribes [who were weeping, crying, and mourning].

D.   *...wail, O you oaks of Bashan* refers to Moses, Aaron, and Miriam.

E.   *...for the strong forest is come down* refers to the house of the sanctuary.

F.   *Hark the wailing of the shepherds, for their glory is spoiled* (Zech. 11:3) refers to David and Solomon his son.

G.   *Hark the roaring of young lions, for the thickets of the Jordan are spoiled* (Zech. 11:3) speaks of Elijah and Elisha.

The reason that this vast story is inserted surely is the reference at **IV:V.2** to Yohanan and the destruction of Jerusalem. Otherwise it is totally irrelevant, since it has no bearing on Simeon's saying and self-evidently does not allude to it.

IV:VII

1.   A.   In three aspects did the Holy One, blessed be he, distinguish people from one another, and these are they, in voice, [Goldin:] taste, and looks.

B.   In voice: how so?

C.   This teaches that the Holy One, blessed be he, gave people diverse voices, for if he had not done so, there would be a good bit of whoredom in the world. When someone would go out of his house [on a dark night], someone else would come in and ravish his wife in his house [since no one would have a voice different from anyone else's]. On that account the Holy One, blessed be he, gave people diverse voices, so that the voice of one person does not sound like the voice of another.

D.   In taste: how so?

E.   This teaches that the Holy One, blessed be he, gave people diverse tastes, for if he had not done so, there would be a great deal of envy in the world, [since everyone would want the same thing]. On that account the Holy One, blessed be he, gave people diverse tastes, so that the taste of one person is not like the taste of another.

F.   In looks: how so?

G.   This teaches that the Holy One, blessed be he, gave people diverse looks, for if he had not done so, Israelite women would not recognize their husbands, and the males would not recognize their wives.

H.   Therefore the Holy One, blessed be he, gave people diverse looks.

I have no idea why this item has been included. The only connection I can see is the reference to voice, around which the verse of Zechariah cited at **IV:VI.3** is built. I cannot imagine that the redactor saw in the reference to "three things" adequate basis for inserting the passage. The exposition of the opening statement is systematic, orderly, and formally cogent. If I could move this composition to an appropriate place, it would be Chapter Forty-One. And of course there we do deal with Simeon's three-crown saying – the other end of the matter of Simeon.

The Fathers According to Rabbi Nathan

Chapter Five

The chapter goes over Antigonus's saying, which is cited at the outset. It follows the following outline:

V:I

V:I.1 Citation and gloss of Antigonus's saying.

V:II

V:II.1 Story about what is at stake in that saying, with reference to the disciples, who formed two sects.

The passage forms a model of a commentary to a text.

V:I

1. A. Antigonus of Sokho received [the Torah] from Simeon the Righteous. He would say: Do not be like servants who serve the master on condition of receiving a reward, but [be] like servants who serve the master not on condition of receiving a reward. And let the fear of Heaven be upon you,
   B. so that your reward may be doubled in the time to come.

After the saying in Avot is cited, it receives a minor gloss.

V:II

1. A. Antigonus of Sokho had two disciples, who would repeat his teachings [and so memorize them].
   B. They would repeat the teachings to disciples, and the disciples to disciples.
   C. They went and criticized them, saying, "Why did our ancestors say this thing? Is it possible that a worker will do his work all day long and not receive his salary in the evening?
   D. "If, however, our ancestors had known that there is another world and the resurrection of the dead, they would never have made such a statement."
   E. They went and took their leave of the Torah and two breaches [in the fence of the Torah] were made of them, the Sadducees and the

Boethusians, the former in the name of Saddoq, and the latter after that of Boethus.

F. They would make use of silver and gold utensils all their lives, not that they were arrogant,

G. but the Sadducees said, "The Pharisees have a tradition that they inflict suffering on themselves in this world, but in the world to come, they will have nothing [while we, at least, enjoy this world]."

The account of the origin of the sects points to the difference of opinion as to the resurrection of the dead. The saying of Antigonus figures, because, in their view, it bears the implication that the ancestors of the Torah had no knowledge of the belief in the resurrection of the dead and the world to come, on which account such a belief is unfounded. And the rest follows. The amplification of the saying certainly attends to what has been said, and the tale directly responds to the saying. So the "commentary" to Avot here does serve the text and has been made up to address the saying at hand.

The Fathers According to Rabbi Nathan

Chapter Six

We work our way through the saying of Yose b. Yoezer:

> Yosé ben Yoezer of Zeredah and Yosé ben Yohanan of Jerusalem received [the Torah] from them. Yosé ben Yoezer says: Let your house be a gathering place for sages. And wallow in the dust of their feet, and drink in their words with gusto.

But we find ourselves moving far afield, as the following outline indicates:

VI:I

    VI:I.1 Citation and gloss of Yose b. Yoezer's saying.

VI:II

    VI:II.1-2 Same as above.

VI:III

    VI:III.1 Same as above.

VI:IV

    VI:IV.1 Prologue to stories about Aqiba and Eliezer, illustrative of wallowing in the dust of the feet of sages.

VI:V

    VI:V.1 Aqiba began studying at 40, knew nothing.

    VI:V.2 Simeon b. Eleazar: Parable on basic theme of foregoing.

    VI:V.3 Tarfon on Aqiba, in line with basic theme.

    VI:V.4 New theme: Aqiba supported himself in poverty.

    VI:V.5 Same as above.

    VI:V.6 Got rich.

VI:VI

VI:VI.1 Eliezer's beginnings in ignorance in mature years.

VI:VI.2 Starved, bad breath saying.

VI:VI.3 Same as above.

VI:VI.4 Got rich in the end: father gave him his whole estate.

VI:VII

VI:VII.1 The mention in **VI:VI.4** of three famous dignitaries leads to exposition of materials on all three of them.

VI:VIII

VI:VIII.1 As above.

VI:IX

VI:IX.1 As above.

VI:X

VI:X.1 As above.

As we see, once the sages are introduced at **VI:IV.1**, the entire composition moves in its own direction. **VI:IV.1** serves as a deftly constructed joining block, between the already-completed materials to follow on Aqiba, then Eliezer, and the rather pointed and germane exegesis of the statements of Avot. Clearly, the authorship has a powerful interest in including stories about sages' lives.

VI:I

1. A. Yosé ben Yoezer says: Let your house be a gathering place for sages. And wallow in the dust of their feet, and drink in their words with gusto.

   B. Let your house be a gathering place for sages: how so?

   C. This teaches that a person's house should be designated for sages and disciples and disciples of their disciples,

   D. such as when someone says to a friend, "Lo, I'll watch for you in such and such a place."

The house should be constantly available for the free use of sages and disciples. The passage then simply amplifies the base-saying.

VI:II

1. A. Another teaching: Let your house be a gathering place for sages: how so?

   B. When a disciple of a sage comes to you to say to you, "Repeat a tradition for me," if you have something to repeat for him, do so, and if not, bid him an immediate farewell.

2. A. And let a disciple sit before you not on a bench or on a pillow or a stool but in your presence let him sit on the ground.

B. And every word that comes out of your mouth let him accept upon himself in awe, fear, trembling, and signs of anguish,

C. just as our ancestors accepted [the Torah] at Mount Sinai in awe, fear, trembling, and signs of anguish,

D. so every word that comes out of your mouth let him take upon himself in awe, fear, trembling, and signs of anguish.

The second amplification of the base-saying shifts the meaning and the focus. Now we take up the attitude of the disciple, and the interest in the original saying seems to me nil. **VI:II.1,2** make the same point, which is that the transaction is to be focused and appropriate to the substance of what is taught.

VI:III

1. A. **And wallow in the dust of their feet:** how so?

B. When a disciple of a sage comes to town, do not say, "What do I need him for?" But go to him,

C. and do not sit before him on a bench or on a pillow or a stool but sit in his presence on the ground.

D. And every word that comes out of his mouth take upon yourself in awe, fear, trembling, and signs of anguish,

E. just as your ancestors accepted [the Torah] at Mount Sinai in awe, fear, trembling, and signs of anguish.

We go over familiar ground, assigning the same meaning to the second clause as to the first.

VI:IV

1. A. Another comment on the statement, **And wallow in the dust of their feet:**

B. This refers to R. Eliezer.

C. **...and drink in their words with gusto:**

D. This refers to R. Aqiba.

This pericope serves as a prologue to the vast stories to follow, first on Aqiba, then on Eliezer.

VI:V

1. A. How did R. Aqiba begin [his Torah-study]?

B. They say: He was forty years old and had never repeated a tradition. One time he was standing at the mouth of a well. He thought to himself, "Who carved out this stone?"

C. They told him, "It is the water that is perpetually falling on it every day."

D. They said to him, "Aqiba, do you not read Scripture? *The water wears away stones* (Job. 4:19)?"

E. On the spot R. Aqiba constructed in his own regard an argument *a fortiori*: now if something soft can [Goldin:] wear down something hard, words of Torah, which are as hard as iron, how much the more so should wear down my heart, which is made of flesh and blood."

F. On the spot he repented [and undertook] to study the Torah.

G. He and his son went into study session before a childrens' teacher, saying to him, "My lord, teach me Torah."

H. R. Aqiba took hold of one end of the tablet, and his son took hold of the other end. The teacher wrote out for him *Alef Bet* and he learned it, *Alef Tav* and he learned it, *the Torah of the Priests* [the books of Leviticus and Numbers] and he learned it. He went on learning until he had learned the entire Torah.

I. He went and entered study-sessions before R. Eliezer and before R. Joshua. He said to them, "My lords, open up for me the reasoning of the Mishnah."

J. When they had stated one passage of law, he went and sat by himself and said, "Why is this *alef* written? Why is this *bet* written? Why is this statement made?" He went and asked them and, in point of fact, [Goldin:] reduced them to silence.

2. A. R. Simeon b. Eleazar says, "I shall make a parable for you. To what is the matter comparable? To a stonecutter who was cutting stone in a quarry. One time he took his chisel and went and sat down on the mountain and started to chip away little sherds from it. People came by and said to him, 'What are you doing?'

B. "He said to them, 'Lo, I am going to uproot the mountain and move it into the Jordan River."

C. "They said to him, 'You will never be able to uproot the entire mountain.'

D. "He continued chipping away at the mountain until he came to a huge boulder. He quarried underneath it and unearthed it and uprooted it and tossed it into the Jordan.'

E. "He said to the boulder, 'This is not your place, but that is your place.'

F. "Likewise this is what R. Aqiba did to R. Eliezer and to R. Joshua."

3. A. Said R. Tarfon to him, "Aqiba, in your regard Scripture says, *He stops up streams so that they do not trickle, and what is hidden he brings into the light* (Job 28:11).

B. "Things that are kept as mysteries from ordinary people has R. Aqiba brought to light."

4. A. Every day he would bring a bundle of twigs [Goldin: straw], half of which he would sell in exchange for food, and half of which he would use for a garment.

B. His neighbors said to him, "Aqiba, you are killing us with the smoke. Sell them to us, buy oil with the money, and by the light of a lamp do your studying."

C. He said to them, "I fill many needs with that bundle, first, I repeat traditions [by the light of the fire I kindle with] them, second, I warm myself with them, third, I sleep on them."

5. A. In time to come R. Aqiba is going to impose guilt [for failing to study] on the poor [who use their poverty as an excuse not to study].

B. For if they say to them, "Why did you not study the Torah," and they reply, "Because we were poor," they will say to them, "But was not R. Aqiba poorer and more poverty-stricken?"

C. If they say, "Because of our children [whom we had to work to support]," they will say to them, "Did not R. Aqiba have sons and daughters?"

D. So they will say to them, "Because Rachel, his wife, had the merit [of making it possible for him to study, and we have no equivalent helpmates; our wives do not have equivalent merit at their disposal]."

6. A. It was at the age of forty that he went to study the Torah. Thirteen years later he taught the Torah in public.

B. They say that he did not leave this world before there were silver and golden tables in his possession,

C. and before he went up onto his bed on golden ladders.

D. His wife went about in golden sandals and wore a golden tiara of the silhouette of the city [Jerusalem].

E. His disciples said to him, "My lord, you have shamed us by what you have done for her [since we cannot do the same for our wives]."

F. He said to them, "She bore a great deal of pain on my account for [the study of] the Torah."

VI:VI

1. A. How did R. Eliezer ben Hyrcanus begin [his Torah-study]?

B. He had reached the age of twenty-two years and had not yet studied the Torah. One time he said, "I shall go and study the Torah before Rabban Yohanan ben Zakkai."

C. His father Hyrcanus said to him, "You are not going to taste a bit of food until you have ploughed the entire furrow."

D. He got up in the morning and ploughed the entire furrow.

E. They say that that day was Friday. He went and took a meal with his father in law.

F. And some say that he tasted nothing from the sixth hour on Friday until the sixth hour on Sunday.

2. A. On the way he saw a rock. He picked it up and took it and put it into his mouth.

B. And some say that what he picked up was cattle dung.

C. He went and spent the night at his hostel.

3. A. He went and entered study-session before Rabban Yohanan ben Zakkai in Jerusalem.

B. Since a bad odor came out of his mouth, Rabban Yohanan ben Zakkai said to him, "Eliezer my son, have you taken a meal today?"

C. He shut up.

D. He asked him again, and he shut up again.

E. He sent word and inquired at his hostel, and asked, "Has Eliezer eaten anything with you?"

F. They sent word to him, "We thought that he might be eating with my lord."

G. He said, "For my part, I thought that he might be eating with you. Between me and you, we should have lost R. Eliezer in the middle."

H. He said to him, "Just as the odor of your mouth has gone forth, so will a good name in the Torah go forth for you."

4. A. Hyrcanus, his father, heard that he was studying the Torah with Rabban Yohanan ben Zakkai. He decided, "I shall go and impose on Eliezer my son a vow not to derive benefit from my property."
    B. They say that that day Rabban Yohanan ben Zakkai was in session and expounding [the Torah] in Jerusalem, and all the great men of Israel were in session before him. He heard that he was coming. He set up guards, saying to them, "If he comes to take a seat, do not let him."
    C. He came to take a seat and they did not let him.
    D. He kept stepping over people and moving forward until he came to Ben Sisit Hakkesset and Naqdimon b. Gurion and Ben Kalba Sabua. He sat among them, trembling.
    E. They say, On that day Rabban Yohanan ben Zakkai looked at R. Eliezer, indicating to him, "Cite an appropriate passage and give an exposition."
    F. He said to him, "I cannot cite an appropriate passage."
    G. He urged him, and the other disciples urged him.
    H. He went and cited an opening passage and expounded matters the like of which no ear had ever heard.
    I. And at every word that he said, Rabban Yohanan ben Zakkai arose and kissed him on his head and said, "My lord, Eliezer, my lord, you have taught us truth."
    J. As the time came to break up, Hyrcanus his father stood up and said, "My lords, I came here only to impose a vow on my son, Eliezer, not to derive benefit from my possession. Now all of my possessions are given over to Eliezer my son, and all my other sons are disinherited and will have no share in them."

VI:IV.1 serves only as a preface to the autonomous materials collected on the theme of how two famous masters began their studies late in life, having had no prior education. Both figures, moreover, started off poor but got rich when they became famous. There is no clear connection between the materials and the original saying. Perhaps the reference to wallowing in the dust of their feet in connection with Eliezer is meant to link up to the detail that he put a piece of dirt or cow dung in his mouth, but that seems to me farfetched. We refer first to Eliezer, then to Aqiba, but tell the stories in reverse order. The diverse stories on Aqiba are hardly harmonious, since one set knows nothing of his wife, while the other introduces her as the main figure. The first set, No. 2ff., emphasizes how slow and steady wins the race. The lesson is that if one persists, one may ultimately best one's masters. No. 3 goes over the same matter, now with a parable to make the point that if one persists, he can uproot mountains. This seems to me appropriately joined to the foregoing, with the notion that Joshua and Eliezer are the mountains, as is made explicit.. Tarfon then goes over the same matter in yet another way, No. 4. No. 5 then goes over the theme of studying in poverty. No. 5 seems to me a rather pointless story, but it leads to No. 6, which presents its own message explicitly. I treat No. 6 as distinct from No. 5 because it introduces the distinct theme of Aqiba's wife, and that has nothing to do with studying in poverty, but rather, the wife's toleration of the husband's long absences. No. 7 then carries forward the second theme of the foregoing, Aqiba's wealth later on and how he lavished it on Rachel. I find puzzling the failure of the story-teller to take an interest in the source of Aqiba's great wealth. The sequence on Eliezer goes over a recurrent theme, but is as incoherent as the foregoing. No. 1 presents a number of problems of continuity, since 1.A-D are simply gibberish, there being no clear relationship between C and B. How E-F fit in I cannot say. One may make a good case for treating **VI:VI.1** and **VI:VI.2** as continuous. But because of the detail of 9.A, on the way he saw a rock, it seems to me that we are on good ground in treating the latter as a fragment of yet another story, rather than as a bridge. **VI:VI.3** is on its own coherent and complete, a cogent and readily comprehended statement on its own. **VI:VI.4** also works well, beginning to end. The details given in D then account for the appendix which follows, **VI:VII-X**.

VI:VI

1. A. Why was he called *Sisit Hakkesset*?

   B. Because he reclined on a silver couch at the head of all the great men of Israel.

We have nothing more than a gloss of the preceding story. What follows glosses the rest.

VI:VIII

1. A. They tell concerning the daughter of Naqdimon b. Gurion that she had a bed spread worth twelve thousand golden denars.

   B. She spent a Tyrian gold denar from Friday to Friday for [Goldin:] spice puddings.

   C. She was awaiting levirate marriage [and the levir was yet a minor].

No one has mentioned the daughter, but that does not stop the compiler from intruding whatever he has in hand on that uninvited theme.

VI:IX

1. A. Why was he called Naqdimon ben Gurion?

   B. Because the sun's rays penetrated for his sake [a play on the root NQD which occurs in both the name and in the verb for penetrate through].

   C. [Explaining the reference to the sun's shining for his sake, the following story is told:] One time the Israelites went up to Jerusalem for a pilgrim festival, but they had no water to drink. [Naqdimon b. Gurion] went to an official and said to him, "Lend me twelve wells of water from now until such-and-such a day. If I do not pay you back twelve wells of water, I shall pay you twelve talents of silver," and they agreed on a due date.

   D. When the time came, the official sent word to him, "Send me twelve wells of water or twelve talents of silver."

   E. He said to him, "There is still time today."

F. The official ridiculed him, saying, "This whole year it has not rained, and now is it going to rain?"

G. The official went into the bath house, rejoicing.

H. Naqdimon went to the study house.

I. He wrapped himself in his cloak and arose to pray, saying before him, "Lord of the world, it is perfectly clear to you that I did not act in my own behalf or in behalf of the house of father. I acted only in your behalf, so that there would be water for the pilgrims."

J. Forthwith the skies got thick with clouds, and it rained until the twelve wells were filled with water and overflowing.

K. He sent word to the official, "Pay me the value that I have coming to me from you of the excess water [since I have now returned more water than I took]."

L. He said to him, "The sun has already set, and the excess water now has come into my possession."

M. [Naqdimon] went back into the study house, wrapped himself in his cloak and arose to pray, saying before him, "Lord of the world, do it again for me, just like before."

N. Forthwith the wind blew, the clouds scattered, and the sun shone.

O. He came out and the two met one another. He said, "I know perfectly well that the Holy One, blessed be he, has shaken his world only on your account."

Once more we have an appendix on the theme of a detail introduced in the prior passage. The story on its own right is well composed and cogent, beginning to end. It makes its point through contrasts of details, e.g., G-H, and, in general, gives ample evidence of narrative care. No one has any interest in relating this story to the context of the earlier tales.

VI:X

1. A. Why was he called Ben Kalba Sabua [sated dog]?

   B. Because whoever came into his house hungry as a dog went out of his house sated.

2. A. When Caesar Vespasian came to destroy Jerusalem, the zealots wanted to burn up all of [Ben Kalba Sabua's] goods.

   B. Kalba Sabua said to them, "Why do you want to destroy this city and seek to burn up all those goods? Hold up for me until I can go into the house and see what I have in the house"

   C. He went in and found he had enough food to feed everybody in Jerusalem for twenty-two years.

   D. He immediately gave orders: "Heap it up, sort out the grain, sift and knead and bake and prepare food for twenty-two years for everybody in Jerusalem."

   E. But they paid no mind to him.

   F. What did the men of Jerusalem do? They brought the loaves of bread and bricked them into the walls and plastered them over with plaster.

3. A. [But ultimately] what did the men of Jerusalem have to do? They boiled straw and ate it.

B. And all the Israelites stationed near the walls of Jerusalem said, "Would that someone would give me five dates – I would go down and cut off five heads."

C. They would give him five dates, and he would go off and cut off five heads of Vespasian's troops.

D. Vespasian examined the excrement of the population and saw that there was not a trace of grain in it.

E. He said to his troops, "If these men, who are eating only straw can come out and kill off [our soldiers], if they had all the food that you are eating and drinking, how much the more so would they be wreaking havoc among you!"

The final gloss of the original story further enriches the materials on the third name on the list. The story, No. 2, is rather strange. It omits crucial details, e.g., an explanation for F. To the story-teller, it would appear, the contrast between the action at F and the fact at G makes the important point. The story-teller assumes that we know that the zealots burned the stores so as to encourage the resistance, a detail not in hand here. I is a secondary development of the story, which yields a very positive picture of the zealots. It seems to me that No. 3 forms a cogent statement, beginning to end. It surely can stand by itself. Still, the two elements – burning the stores, the courage of the starving soldiers – do explain one another, with the former accounting for the conditions of starvation, the latter accounting for the derring-do of the Israelite army. It goes without saying that the entire appendix to the original story has no more bearing on the exposition of the saying of Avot than did the stories about Aqiba and Eliezer.

The Fathers According to Rabbi Nathan

Chapter Seven

We proceed to the next saying in succession:

Yosé ben Yohanan of Jerusalem says: Let your house be open wide. And seat the poor at your table ["make the poor members of your household"]. And don't talk too much with women. He referred to a man's wife, all the more so is the rule to be applied to the wife of one's fellow. In this regard did sages say: So long as a man talks too much with a woman, he brings trouble on himself, wastes time better spent on studying Torah, and ends up an heir of Gehenna.

The chapter outline, which is as follows, shows us what a chapter meant to serve as a systematic amplification of a saying actually looks like:

VII:I
VII:I.1 **Let your house be wide open** -- north, south, etc., like Job.

VII:II
VII:II.1 **And seat the poor at your table,** like Job. But Abraham was a greater model for the perfect host than Job.

VII:III
VII:III.1 Teach the members of your household humility. [This is illustrated by reference to appropriate hospitality to the poor.]

VII:IV
VII:IV.1 Same as above. Now illustrated by importance of avoiding contention.

VII:V
VII:V.1 **Don't talk too much with women:** cited.

VII:VI

VII:VI.1 Foregoing is illustrated in terms of the life of the study house. Specifically, do not bring home the quarrels of the study house. It is demeaning to all concerned.

As we see, the chapter systematically and in a disciplined way expands on the pieces of advice, linking them all to a few main points about proper conduct with the poor and forming of the whole a coherent statement.

VII:I

1. A. Yosé ben Yohanan of Jerusalem says, Let your house be open wide. And seat the poor at your table ["make the poor members of your household"]. And don't talk too much with women.
    B. Let your house be open wide: how so?
    C. This teaches that a person's house should be open north, south, east, and west,
    D. just as Job made four doors to his house.
    E. And why did Job make four doors for his house [one in each direction]?
    F. So as not to trouble the poor to walk around the house.
    G. Whoever came from the north could enter as he went along, whoever came from the south could enter as he went along, and so in each direction.
    H. On that account Job made four doors for his house.

The explanation of the saying is rather fulsome, and the point is clear and pertinent. But no one in Avot has mentioned Job, so, once more, the principle of exegesis leads us far from the sayings at hand.

VII:II

1. A. **And seat the poor at your table:**
    B. Not really at your table, but make it possible for the poor to chatter about what they had eaten and drunk in your house, as the poor would chatter about what they had eaten and drunk in the house of Job.
    C. When they would meet with one another, one of them would say to the next, "Where are you coming from?
    D. "From Job's house."
    E. "And where are you going?"
    F. "To Job's house."
    G. But when the awful disaster came upon Job, he said before the Holy One, blessed be he, "Lord of the world, have I not given the hungry what to eat and the thirsty what to drink?"
    H. For it is written, *Or have I eaten my morsel myself alone, and the fatherless has not eaten of it?* (Job 31:17).
    I. "And did I not provide clothing for the naked?

J.   So it is said, *And if he were not warmed with the fleece of my sheep* (Job 31:20).

K.   Even so, the Holy One, blessed be he, said to Job, "Job, you have not yet reached half the measure of Abraham. You sit and waste time at home, while wayfarers come to you. The one who was accustomed to eat wheat bread you fed wheat bread, the one accustomed to eat meat you fed meat, to the one accustomed to drink wine you gave wine.

L.   "But that is not how Abraham did things. Rather, he would go forth and search the world, and when he would find wayfarers, he would bring them into his home. The one who was not used to eating wheat bread he fed wheat bread, the one not used to eating meat he fed meat, to the one not used to drinking wine he gave wine to drink. No only so, but he went and built way stations on the roads and left there food and drink, so that whoever came and entered could eat and drink, and then say a blessing to Heaven. Therefore he got satisfaction, and whatever anyone could ask was found in Abraham's home."

M.   For it is said, *And Abraham planted a tamarisk tree in Beer Sheba* (Gen. 21:33).

The same insistence on linking the sayings to Job accounts for the materials at hand, which illustrate the counsel to make the poor feel at home by an elaborate account of Job in comparison to Abraham.

VII:III

1.   A.   Teach the members of your household humility [in receiving the poor].

B.   When a householder is humble and the members of his household are humble, when a poor man comes and stands at the door of the household and says to the people there, "Is your father here", they will say to him, "Indeed so. Come in."

C.   Before he comes in, the table will be set before him. He comes in and eats and drinks and says a blessing for the sake of Heaven and [the householder thereby] derives much pleasure.

D.   But if the householder is not humble, then the members of the household will be surly. If then a poor man comes and stands at the door and says to them, "Is your father home," they will say to him, "No," and will show an angry face to him and nastily throw him out.

The exposition of the saying is clear and balanced. It would be inviting to suppose that A belongs with the sayings imputed to the authorities at hand.

VII:IV

1.   A.   Another interpretation of the statement, Teach the members of your household humility: how so?

B.   When a householder is humble and the members of his household are humble, if the householder goes overseas, he prays, "I give thanks before you, Lord my God, that my wife does not make fights with other people, and my children do not have quarrels with other people." He goes away with a steady heart and a serene mind until he comes home.

C. But when a householder is arrogant and the members of his household surly, when the householder goes overseas, he prays, "May it please you, Lord my God, that my wife will not make fights with other people, and my children will not have quarrels with other people." He goes away with an uncertain heart and a troubled mind until he comes home.

The exposition is essentially coherent with the foregoing.

VII:V

1. A. **And don't talk too much with women.** He referred to a man's wife, all the more so is the rule to be applied to the wife of one's fellow. For so long as a man talks too much with a woman, he brings trouble on himself, wastes time better spent on studying the Torah, and ends up an heir of Gehenna.

VII:VI

1. A. Another matter: **don't talk too much with women:** how so?
   C. When someone comes to the study house and people did not pay him the requisite courtesy, or he had an argument with his fellow, he should not go home and tell his wife, "Thus and so did I have words with my fellow, and this is what he said to me, and this is what I said to him."
   D. For in doing so he lowers himself, he lowers his wife, and he lowers his fellow.
   E. And his wife, who had treated him with respect, goes and ridicules him.
   F. And his fellow further hears and says, "Woe is me, the argument that was between him and me he has gone and reported to his wife."
   G. The man turns out to lower himself, his wife, and his fellow.

The clarification of the final clause links the matter of not talking too much with one's own wife of the affairs of the school house, and so joins the several clauses – brings trouble on himself, wastes time better spent on studying the Torah.

The Fathers According to Rabbi Nathan

Chapter Eight

The chapter follows the pattern of the foregoing:

> Joshua ben Perahyah and Nittai the Arbelite received [the Torah] from them.
>
> Joshua ben Perahyah says: Set up a master for yourself. And get yourself a companion-disciple. And give everybody the benefit of the doubt.

The outline shows that the pattern of systematic amplification of the clauses of the assigned saying is repeated. There is, however, a sizable appendix, tacked on because, in a general way, its point intersects with a minor detail of the foregoing.

VIII:I

VIII:I.1 Amplification of **Set up a master for yourself.** Have a single teacher for all subjects.

VIII:I.2 Same as above, parable.

VIII:II

VIII:II.1 Amplification of **Get yourself a companion-disciple.**

VIII:III.1-3 Special cases, if three, two, or one study by themselves, they get credit in heaven. Appendix on the same theme as the foregoing.

VIII:IV

VIII:IV.1 **And give everybody the benefit of the doubt** spelled out, example.

VIII:V

VIII:V.1 Same as above.

VIII:VI

VIII:VI.1-2 Appendix on what captives eat.

Apart from the concluding appendix, **VIII:VI.1-2,** every detail fits the main task at hand.

VIII:I

1. A. **Joshua ben Perahyah and Nittai the Arbelite received [the Torah] from them. Joshua ben Perahyah says: Set up a master for yourself. And get yourself a companion-disciple. And give everybody the benefit of the doubt.**

   B. **Set up a master for yourself: how so?**

   C. This teaches that he should make a permanent arrangement with his master [Goldin: provide himself with a single teacher] and study with him Scripture, Mishnah, exegesis, laws and narratives.

   D. [The advantage of having a single instructor in the sacred sciences is that] reasoning that he left out in connection with Scripture in the end he will tell him in connection with Mishnah-study, and reasoning that he left out in connection with Mishnah-study in the end he will tell him in connection with exegesis, reasoning that he left out in connection with exegesis in the end he will tell him in connection with laws, reasoning that he left out in connection with laws in the end he will tell him in connection with lore.

   E. What will come out is that person will stay in session in his own locale and be filled with good and blessing.

2. A. R. Meir says, "He who studies the Torah with a single master – to what may he be likened? To someone who had a single field, which he sowed partly in wheat, partly in barley, planted partly in olives, partly in fruit trees.

   B. "He will turn out to be filled with good and blessing.

   C. "When someone studies with two or three, he is like someone who owns many fields, one of which he sows with wheat, one with barley, one of which he plants in olives, one in fruit-trees.

   D. "That man turns out to be scattered among his plots, without good or blessing."

We open with an exposition of the meaning of the opening clause, which bears the meaning that one should establish a connection with only a single master. This point then is made explicit: one teacher may omit something at one stage, but he is sure to include it at a later stage. No. 2 then provides a parable to make the same point. It is that one should avoid the confusion involved in tending to a number of different fields – or viewpoints.

VIII:II

1. A. **And get yourself a companion-disciple: how so?**

   B. This teaches that one should get for himself a companion-disciple, with whom he will eat and drink and recite Scripture and repeat Mishnah-traditions, sleep and share all kinds of hidden things, secrets of the Torah and secrets having to do with worldly matters as well.

2. A. When two are in session occupied with study of the Torah and one of them makes an error in law or in a chapter beginning, or if one of them

should call what is unclean clean or what is clean unclean, or rule what is forbidden permitted or what is permitted forbidden, his fellow will correct him.

B. And how do we know on the basis of Scripture that, when his fellow corrects him and recites Scripture with him, they get a good reward from their shared labor?

C. As it is said, *Two are better than one, because they have a good reward for their labor* (Qoh. 4:9).

The exposition of the second clause stresses, once more, that there should be stability and order in the study-process – one master, one companion-disciple. The form is identical to the foregoing. Because of No. 2, we have a series of sayings about joint study among a number of disciples and how God is present with them.

VIII:III

1. A. In the case of three disciples in session and occupied with study of the Torah, the Holy One, blessed be he, credits it to them as if they formed a single band before him,

    B. as it is said, *He who builds his upper chambers in the heaven and has founded his band upon the earth, he who calls for the waters of the sea and pours them out upon the face of the earth, the Lord is his name* (Amos 9:6).

    C. Thus you have learned that in the case of three disciples in session and occupied with study of the Torah, the Holy One, blessed be he, credits it to them as if they formed a single band before him.

2. A. In the case of two disciples in session and occupied with study of the Torah, their reward is received on high,

    B. as it is said, *Then they who feared the Lord spoke one with another, and the Lord heard...and a book of remembrance was written before him for those who feared the Lord and who gave thought to his name* (Mal. 3:16).

    C. Who are those referred to as "they who feared the Lord"?

    D. They are the ones who reach a decision, saying, "Let us go and free those who are imprisoned and redeem those who have been kidnapped for ransom," and the Holy One, blessed be he, gave sufficient power in their hands to do so, and they go and do it right away.

    E. And who are those referred to as "they who gave thought to his name"?

    F. They are the ones who reckon in their hearts, saying, ""Let us go and free those who are imprisoned and redeem those who have been kidnapped for ransom," and the Holy One, blessed be he, did not give sufficient power in their hands to do so, so an angel came and beat them down to the ground.

3. A. In the case of an individual disciple in session and occupied with study of the Torah, his reward is received on high,

    B. as it is said, *Though he sit alone and keep silence, surely he has laid up [a reward] for him* (Lam. 3:28).

    C. The matter may be conveyed in a parable: to what is it comparable?

    D.   To someone who had a young child, whom he left at home when he went out to the market. The son went and took a scroll and set it between his knees and sat and meditated on it.

    E.   When his father came back from the market place, he said, "See my little son, whom I left when I went out to the market place. What has he done on his own! He has studied and taken the scroll and set it between his knees, going into session and meditating on it."

    F.   So you have learned that even an individual disciple who has gone into session and occupied with study of the Torah, receives his reward received on high.

The complement to **VIII:II.1**'s counsel to get a companion-disciple covers the ground of three, two, then one engaged in study. All three classifications receive a reward, an appropriate clarification, even though hardly demanded by the saying under discussion. Each entry follows the same pattern, and the secondary accretions at No. 2 and No. 3 are easily discerned. 2.C-F makes a point on its own, which is that the ones who act are better off than the ones who merely think of acting. Goldin, p. 185, n. 14: "The former are helped by God to carry out their decision; the latter are not helped and in the end an angel comes and strikes them down." The parable of No. 3 makes its own point as well.

VIII:IV

1. A.   **And give everybody the benefit of the doubt:** how so?

    B.   [By way of illustrating the importance of giving the benefit of the doubt, we tell] the case of a girl who was taken captive for ransom. Two pious men went after her to ransom her.

    C.   One of them went into the whore house. When he came out, he said to his fellow, "Of what did you suspect me?"

    D.   He said to him, "To find out how much was the going price for buying her back."

    E.   He said to him, "By the Temple service, that is just how it was!"

    F.   He said to him, "Just as you have given me the benefit of the doubt, so may the Holy One when he judges you give you the benefit of the doubt."

The illustration is apt and clear.

VIII:V

1. A.   [By way of illustrating the importance of giving the benefit of the doubt, we tell] another case of a girl who was taken captive for ransom. Two pious men went after her to ransom her.

    C.   One of them was arrested as a bandit and imprisoned.

    D.   Every day his wife brought him bread and water. One day he said to her, "Go to Mr. So-and-so and tell him that I am imprisoned on a charge of prostitution, while he is happily sitting at home and paying no mind to the girl."

E. She said to him, "Is it not enough for you that you are imprisoned, but you are getting involved in nonsense!"

F. She did not go, but she just kept herself busy with nonsense.

G. He said to her, "Please, please go and tell him."

H. She went and told him.

I. What did that man do? He went and brought silver and gold and reliable men with him and retrieved both [the man and the girl held for ransom].

J. When the man got out, he said to them, "Give me this girl, so that she will sleep with me in bed, but in her clothing."

K. In the morning, he said to them, "Allow me to immerse."

L. They immersed him. [Goldin: "Let her immerse herself." They had her immerse herself.]

M. He said to those who presided at the immersion, "As to this act of immersion of mine, on what account did you suspect me?"

N. They said to him, "We said to him, all the time you were in prison, you were hungry and thirsty [and therefore felt no sexual urge at all], and now that you have gotten out into the free air, you once again feel desire, on which account you may have produced a seminal emission."

O. He said to them, "As to the immersion of the girl, on what account did you suspect her?"

P. They said to him, "All that time that she was held among gentiles, she ate their food and drank their drink, now you have instructed us to immerse her so that she may regain a state of purity."

Q. He said to them, "By the Temple service, that is just how it was. Just as you have given me the benefit of the doubt, so may the Holy One, when he judges you, give you the benefit of the doubt."

The illustration is apt and clear. The detail about the wife's not believing the suspected man underlines the importance of the colleague's confidence in him. Otherwise the story seems to me a replay of the earlier one, only better told.

VIII:VI

1. A. Just as the righteous men in ancient times were pious, so their cattle were pious.

B. They say that the cattle of Abraham, our father, never went into a house which contained an idol,

C. as it is said, *For I have cleared the house and made room for the camels* (Gen. 24:31), meaning, *I have cleared the house of teraphim.*

D. And on what account does Scripture say, *And made room for the camels*?

E. This teaches that they would not enter Laban the Aramaean's house until they had cleared away all the idols from before them.

2. A. There was the case of the ass of R. Hanina b. Dosa, which bandits stole and tied up in the courtyard. They set before it straw, barley and water, but it would not eat or drink.

B. They said, "Why should we leave it here to die and make a stink for us in the courtyard? They went and opened the gate and sent it out, and it went along, braying, until it came to the house of R. Hanina b. Dosa.

C. When it got near the house, [Hanina's] son heard its braying.

D. He said to him, "Father, it appears to me that the braying is like the braying of our beast."

E. He said to him, "My son, open the gate for it, for it must be nearly dying of starvation."

F. He went and opened the gate for it, and put before it straw, barley and water, and it ate and drank.

G. Therefore they say: Just as the righteous men in ancient times were pious, so their cattle were pious.

I assume that the reason for including this odd composite is No. 2's reference to the ass's not eating the food and drink of the gentile bandits. That amplifies the detail of the girl's eating the ordinarily-unacceptable food and drink, then having to undergo an immersion to free herself of the uncleanness by which she had been affected. Otherwise I cannot imagine what impelled the compiler to include the item here. Goldin, p. 186, n. 28, adds, "This section on the saintliness of beasts was very likely added as a kind of climax to the discussion of judge everyone. In the previous comments some incidents in the lives of saintly folk had been reported; to these was later appended the present discussion on the saintliness of the very beasts of saints in ages past." This proposal would be more persuasive if the preceding item had mentioned Phineas b. Yair. Goldin further does not point to other examples of the same redactional principle (if indeed it is a principle).

The Fathers According to Rabbi Nathan

Chapter Nine

We proceed to the exposition of the following:

Nittai the Arbelite says: Keep away from a bad neighbor. And don't get involved with a bad person. And don't despair of retribution.

The outline shows that the bulk of the chapter is devoted to an appendix tacked on to the interpretation of a single item. But if we move the extraneous appendix, we find that pattern that is now familiar of a phrase by phrase exegesis of the whole.

IX:I

> **IX:I.1 Keep away from a bad neighbor,** because a bad neighbor may be the cause of having to tear down one's house. A bad neighbor, for example, may be a gossip and may therefore cause leprosy to develop on a wall that is shared both by him and by his fellow.

IX:II

> **IX:II.1** The evils of gossip.

IX:III

> **IX:III.1-5** The evils of gossip. Aaron and Miriam.

> **IX:III.6** Appendix: Moses was meek.

IX:IV

> **IX:IV.1** The evils of gossip and of arrogance. Gehazi and Hezekiah.

IX:V

> **IX:V.1 And don't get involved with a bad person:** three probative examples.

IX:VI

> **IX:VI.1 Don't get involved with a bad person:** minor
> clarification.

IX:VII

> **IX:VII.1** Don't despair of retribution: means to expect punishment at any
> time.

IX:VIII

> **IX:VIII.1** Same statement clarified in a different way.

The outline shows that, apart from the substantial interpolation of materials on
gossip, the redactor has systematically clarified the several clauses of the base-
saying.

IX:I

1. A. **Nittai the Arbelite says: Keep away from a bad neighbor.
   And don't get involved with a bad person. And don't give
   up hope of retribution.**
   B. **Keep away from a bad neighbor:** all the same are neighbor in the
   same house, a neighbor outside, and a neighbor in the field.
2. A. This teaches that leprosy-signs come only on account of the sin of a
   wicked person. The sins of a wicked person may cause the destruction of
   the wall of a righteous [neighbor, shared by both houses].
   B. How so? If there is a wall between the house of a wicked person and one
   of a righteous person, and a leprosy-sign appeared on the wall of the
   house of the wicked person that is shared with the house of the righteous
   person, it will result in tearing down that wall belonging to a righteous
   person on account of the sin of a wicked person.
   C. R. Ishmael son of R. Yohanan b. Beroqa says, "Woe to a wicked person,
   woe, too, to his neighbor. The sins of a wicked person may cause the
   destruction of the wall of a righteous [neighbor, shared by both houses]."

The illustration is apt, but rather special, as has often been the case. The
leprosy-signs mentioned in Lev. 14 under certain circumstances result in the
householders' having to tear down the walls of the house. Sages take the view
that these signs appear on account of sin (specified in the appendix to this unit,
at **IX:II.1ff.**). Consequently, the neighbor of the sinner is affected by the sin,
and the rest follows.

IX:II

1. A. Ten trials did our forefathers inflict upon the Holy One, blessed be he,
   and among them all they were penalized only on account of gossip.
   B. And these are the ten:

C. [Goldin: two] at the Red Sea, one at the beginning of the manna, one at the end, one at the appearance of the first quail, one at the end, one at the Bitter Water, one at Rephidim, one at Horeb, and one on the occasion of the spies [who gave an ill report of the land, hence the matter of gossip, as specified at F, below].

D. The one involving the spies was worst of all, as it is said, *And they have tried me these ten times and have not obeyed me* (Num. 14:22).

E. And also: *Even those men who brought up an evil report of the land died by the plague before the Lord* (Num. 14:37).

F. And does this not yield an argument *a fortiori*: if in behalf of the land, which has neither mouth with which to speak, nor face to feel shame, the Holy One, blessed be he, exacted a penalty for an insult done to it by the spies, one who speaks ill against his fellow and shames him – all the more so will the Holy One, blessed be he, exact a penalty for the insult done by him.

The "plague" mentioned in the foregoing is caused by gossip, and we now have a sizable anthology on the theme of gossip, tacked on in accord with the principle of thematic association.

IX:III

1. A. R. Simeon says, "Upon those who gossip plagues come, for so we find in the case of Aaron and Miriam, who gossiped against Moses, that punishment came on them.

   B. "For it is said, *And Miriam and Aaron spoke against Moses* (Num. 12:1)."

2. A. Why does Scripture give precedence to Miriam over Aaron? This indicates that Zipporah went and told Miriam, Miriam went and told Aaron, and then the two of them went and spoke ill of that righteous man.

   B. Because the two of them went and spoke ill of that righteous man, punishment came upon them, as it is said, *And the anger of the Lord was kindled against them and he departed* (Num. 12:9).

   C. Why does Scripture say, *and he departed*? This indicates that [the punishment] left Aaron but stuck to Miriam, for Aaron was not the principal in the matter, but since Miriam had been the principal in the matter, forthwith she bore the heavier punishment.

3. A. Miriam argued, "I too was subject to the word, and I did not cease having sexual relations with my husband."

   B. Aaron argued, "I too was subject to the Word, and I did not cease having sexual relations with my wife. So too our forefathers were subject to the Word, and they did not cease to have sexual relations with their wives.

   C. "But he [Moses], because he is arrogant, has ceased to have sexual relations with his wife."

   D. And they did not judge him in his presence but in his absence, and they did not judge him on the basis of certain knowledge but only on the basis of doubt.

   E. For it was a matter of doubt whether or not [he had refrained from having sexual relations with his wife merely because] he was arrogant.

F. Now this yields an argument *a fortiori*: if Miriam, who spoke only against her brother, and who spoke only behind Moses' back, was punished, an ordinary person, who speaks ill of his fellow in his presence and humiliates him, all the more so will his punishment be considerable.

4. A. At that time Aaron said to Moses, "Moses, my brother, is it your view that this leprosy afflicts only Miriam? It afflicts not her flesh alone but also our father, Amram.

B. "I shall give you a parable. To what may the matter be likened? It is like someone who put a coal into his hand. Even though he turns it this way and that, nonetheless his flesh is burned.

C. "For it is said, *Let her not, I ask, be as a corpse (Num.* 12:12)."

5. A. At that time Aaron began to appease Moses. He said to him, "My brother, Moses, have we ever done ill to anyone in the world?"

B. He said to him, "No."

C. He said to him, "Now if we have never done ill to anyone in the world, how should we do evil to you, our brother! But what can I do? It was a mistake on our side! We neglected the covenant between you and us, as it is said, *And they did not remember the covenant of brothers* (Amos 1:9).

D. "On account of the covenant that has been drawn up between us, which we have neglected, shall we now lose our sister?"

E. At that moment Moses drew a little circle and stood in it and sought mercy for her, saying, "I am not going to move from here until you heal Miriam my sister," as it is said, *Let her not, I ask, be as a corpse (Num.* 12:12).

F. At that moment the Holy One, blessed be he, said to Moses, "If a king had grown angry against her, if her father had grown angry with her, she would have had to bear the shame for seven days. I, the King of kings of kings, all the more so is it not proper that she should bear her shame for fourteen days? But on your account, it will be forgiven to her."

G. So it is said, *And the Lord said to Moses, if her father should spit in her face* (Num. 12:14).

6. A. *Now the man, Moses, was very meek, more than everyone on the face of the earth* (Num. 12:3):

B. Is it possible to suppose that he was meek in that he was a runt [lit.: not handsome and praiseworthy]?

C. Scripture says, *And he spread the tent of the tabernacle* (Ex. 40:19).

D. Just as the tabernacle was ten cubits high, so Moses was ten cubits tall.

E. Is it possible to suppose that he was [Goldin: more] meek than the ministering angels?

F. Scripture says, *...more than everyone on the face of the earth* (Num. 12:3).

G. They have said that he was more meek than men, not than ministering angels.

H. Is it possible to suppose that he was more meek than the ancients?

I. Scripture says, *...more than everyone on the face of the earth* (Num. 12:3), meaning, more than anyone in his generation, not more than the ancients.

J. There are three kinds of [Goldin:] furunculars created in the world, moist, dry, and the polypus-kind, and Moses was more humble than any of them.

Once the theme of gossip is introduced, we have the full conventional repertoire of cases that illustrate the same matter, namely, what is translated as leprosy, *saraat*, afflicts gossips. Miriam and Aaron spoke ill of Moses, and in the present standard statement, the matter is laid out. No. 1 begins the exposition, taking for granted the main point, which is only introduced in and spelled out in No. 3. Nos. 4, 5 then expand on the same matter. No. 6 proceeds to provide an exegesis of the nearby verse, but it has nothing to do with our topic. That shows that the redactors took clumps of completed materials, originally organized around the sequence of verses, and used them whole, without revision, when the thematic interest drew attention to something within the larger composition. We now move back to our main theme.

IX:IV

1. A. R. Simeon b. Eleazar says, "Also plagues come upon those who gossip, for so we find in the case of Gehazi, who gossiped against his master, that leprosy afflicted him until the day of his death."

    B. For it is said, *The leprosy therefore of Naaman shall cleave to you...and he went out from his presence a leper as white as snow* (2 Kgs. 5:27).

    C. He used to say, "Also plagues come upon those who are arrogant, for so we find in the case of Uzziah."

    D. For it is said, *But when he was strong, his heart was lifted up so that he did corruptly, and he trespassed against the Lord his God, for he went into the temple of the Lord to burn incense upon the altar of incense. And Azariah the priest went in after him, and with him eighty priests of the Lord, valiant men, and they opposed King Uzziah and said to him, It is not your task, Uzziah, to burn incense to the Lord, but it is the priests' task, that of the sons of Aaron, who are consecrated, to burn the incense. Go out of the sanctuary, for you have committed sacrilege, neither is it for your honor from the Lord God. Uzziah was angry, and he had a censer in his hand to burn incense, and while he was angry with the priests, leprosy broke out on his forehead* (2 Chr. 26:16-19).

    E. At that moment the sanctuary split in two, leaving a gap of twelve miles, and the priests quickly pushed him out: *Yes, he made haste to leave, because the Lord had smitten him. And he was a leper to the death of his death and dwelt in a house set apart as a leper, for he was cut off from the house of the Lord, and Jotham his son was in charge of the king's palace, judging the people of the land* (2 Chr. 26:20-21).

Simeon b. Eleazar continues the exposition of the theme of the anthology. We now return to the basic structure of the chapter.

IX:V

1. A. **And don't get involved with a bad person:** this teaches that one should not get involved with either a bad person or a wicked person.
   B. For so we find that Jehoshaphat got involved with Ahab and went up with him to Ramot Gilead, and the wrath of the Lord came forth on him.
   C. As it is said, *Should you help the wicked and love those who hate the Lord? for this thing wrath has come upon you from before the Lord* (2 Chr. 19:2).
   D. Further, he got involved with Ahaziah, and they built ships in Ezion Geber, and the Lord shattered what he had made.
   E. For it is said, *Because you have gotten involved with Ahaziah, the Lord has made a breach in your works, and the ships were broken* (2 Chr. 20:37).
   F. So we find in the case of Amnon, who got involved with Jonadab, and Jonadab gave him bad advice.
   G. As it is said, *But Amnon had a friend, named Jonadab, son of Shimeah, David's brother, and Jonadab was a very subtle person* (2 Sam. 13:3) – *subtle* in doing evil.

This is a rather effective amplification of the cited rule, because we are given facts of Scripture to back up the good advice. The three cases form a list of probative examples.

IX:VI

1. A. **And don't get involved with a bad person:** and even for purposes of study of the Torah.

The clarification is important.

IV:VII

1. A. **And don't despair of retribution:** how so?
   B. This teaches that a person's heart should be fearful every day, and one should say, "Woe is me, lest punishment come upon me today," "lest...tomorrow," and one will turn out to fear every day.
   C. As it is said, *The thing which I did fear is come upon me* (Job 3:25).

The "hope" of retribution is made to refer to expectation. The sense is now that one should expect every day for final punishment to come. The attitude of mind that one should cultivate is what is clarified.

IV:VIII

1. A. Another matter: **And don't despair of retribution:**
   B. How so? When someone sees his projects succeed, he should not say, "It is because I have attained merit that the Omnipresent has given me food and drink in this world, with the principle lasting for me in the world to come."

C. Rather he should say, "Woe is me, what if in my behalf only a single source of merit has been found before him, on which account he has given me food and drink in this world, so as to destroy me in the world to come."

The clarification carries forward the attitude of the foregoing. One should not assume that, because he thrives now, therefore he enjoys divine favor for all times. It may be just the opposite.

The Fathers According to Rabbi Nathan

Chapter Ten

Judah ben Tabbai and Simeon ben Shetah received [the Torah] from them.

Judah ben Tabbai says: Don't make yourself like one of those who advocate before judges [while you yourself are judging a case]. And when the litigants stand before you, regard them as guilty. But when they leave you, regard them as acquitted (when they have accepted your judgment).

Simeon ben Shetah says: Examine the witnesses with great care. And watch what you say, lest they learn from what you say how to lie.

The outline of the chapter obscures the simple fact that nothing before us clarifies the cited sayings. We have a sequence of observations of great merit, none of them having to do with not serving as an advocate when one is judging a case or with the attitude one is to have in court.

X:I

X:I.1 Listen to the reasoning of a ruling before replying to it.

X:I.2 Do not favor either the rich or the poor + Dt. 1:17.

X:I.3 Further comment on Dt. 1:17. Meir + Judah.

X:II

X:II.1 Further saying of Judah.

X:III

X:III.1 Simeon b. Shetah's saying is paraphrased.

We see that the formal structure derives from the base-saying, but the contents scarcely intersect in substance with that saying.

X:I

1. A. Judah ben Tabbai and Simeon ben Shetah received [the Torah] from them. Judah ben Tabbai says: Don't make

yourself like one of those who advocate before judges [while you yourself are judging a case]. And when the litigants stand before you, regard them as guilty. But when they leave you, regard them as acquitted when they have accepted your judgment.

B. Don't make yourself like one of those who advocate before judges: how so?

C. This teaches that if you come to the school house and hear a teaching or a law, do not rush headlong to refute it, but give it a fair hearing, asking on account of what reasoning someone has made the statement, or in what context the issue was raised, or what law had been brought for a ruling.

2. A. When two litigants come before you, one poor, one rich, do not say, "How can I ever acquit the poor man and impose liability on the rich, how can I ever acquit the rich man and impose liability on the poor.

B. "For if I impose liability on the poor man, the poor man will end up my enemy, and if I acquit the poor man, the rich man will be my enemy."

C. And do not say, "How shall I take money from this one and give it to that one."

D. The Torah has said, *You will not show favor in judgment* (Deut. 1:17).

3. A. R. Meir would say, "What is the meaning of the statement of the Torah, *You shall hear the small and the great alike* (Deut. 12:17)?

B. "The meaning is that one should not stand while the other sits, one should not have a full hearing, while to the other you say, 'Make it quick.'"

C. R. Judah says, "I have heard that if the judge wanted to allow both parties to sit, they may seat them.

D. "What is forbidden is for one to stand while the other sits.

E. "The ruling of *small and great alike* means a judgment involving a penny should have the same probity of judgment as one involving a hundred *minas*."

The main point of **X:I.1** is to emphasize the importance of giving a balanced hearing, in context, to an opinion that is new. That does not seem to me the subject of the saying that is subject to amplification. **X:I.2** seems to me equally remote from the saying at hand. No. 3 is an appendix to **X:I.2.D.**

X:II

1. A. He used to say, "Before I took up high office, if someone had said to me, 'Go on up,' I should have wanted to fight him to the death.

B. "Now that I have taken high office, if anyone says to me, 'Get out,' I'd like nothing more than to pour a pot of boiling water on him.

C. "For as to high office, it is hard to go up to it, but just as it is hard to go up to it, so it is hard to descend from it.

D. "For so we find in the case of Saul, when someone said to him, 'Stand for the kingship,' he hid, as it is said, *And the Lord answered, behold he hid himself among the baggage* (1 Sam. 10:22). But when they said to him, 'Go down,' he hunted out David to kill him."

The continuation of the foregoing has no more bearing on the base-statement than does **X:I.3**.

X:III

1. A. **Simeon ben Shetah says: Examine the witnesses with great care.** [**And watch what you say, lest they learn from what you say how to lie.**]

   B. And when you are examining them, watch what you say, lest from what you say those who hear will carry forward what you say through lying, on account of those who deceive.

This appears to me a paraphrase of Simeon's statement, nothing more.

The Fathers According to Rabbi Nathan

Chapter Eleven

Shemaiah and Avtalyon received [the Torah] from them.
Shemaiah says: Love work. Hate authority. Don't get
friendly with the government.

Avtalyon says: Sages, watch what you say, lest you
become liable to the punishment of exile, and go into
exile to a place of bad water, and disciples who follow
you drink bad water and die, and the name of Heaven be
thereby profaned.

Shemaiah's saying introduces the theme of work, which receives a sizable
exemplification. The other two clauses are given excellent clarification.
Avtalyon's saying is merely glossed.

XI:I

XI:I.1 Love work, and do not hate work. Work involves a covenant.

XI:I.2 Work may save one's life.

XI:I.3 If one does not work six days, he may end up working seven days.

XI:I.4 The first man had to work to eat.

XI:I.5 Israel had to work before the presence of God came to rest in it.

XI:I.6 Any sort of work is better than idleness.

XI:I.7 One dies of idleness.

XI:I.8 Complement to foregoing.

XI:II

XI:II.1 Hate authority: Do not honor yourself, let others do so.

XI:II.2 Same point as above, now with special reference to teachings of
Torah.

XI:II.3 As above.

XI:III

> **XI:III.1** Do not get friendly with the government means do not become known to the government, because they will take away everything you have.

XI:IV

> **XI:IV.1** As above.

XI:V

> **XI:V.1** As above.

XI:VI

> **XI:VI.1** As above.

XI:VII

> **XI:VII.1** Gloss of Avtalyon's statement.

While some of the materials do not serve the base-saying so well as the compiler would have liked, the program is essentially a familiar one: citation and explanation of the base-saying, with some appendices.

XI:I

1. A. Shemaiah and Avtalyon received [the Torah] from them. Shemaiah says: Love work. Hate authority. Don't get friendly with the government.
    B. Love work: how so?
    C. This teaches that a person should love work and not hate work.
    D. For just as the Torah has been given as a covenant, so work has been given as a covenant.
    E. For so it is written, *Six days will you labor and do all your work, and the seventh day is a Sabbath to the Lord your God* (Ex. 20:10).
2. A. R. Aqiba says, "There are occasions on which a person does work and so escapes from death, and times that a person does not do work and becomes liable to death at the hands of Heaven.
    B. "How so?
    C. "If a man sits out the whole week and does no work, on Friday he has nothing to eat. He had in the house some coins set aside for the purposes of the sanctuary and took them and bought food with them and ate it, so becoming liable [on the count of sacrilege] to the death penalty inflicted at the hands of Heaven.
    D. "But if he had worked through the week in the [upkeep of the] building of the sanctuary, even though he was paid in coins that had been set aside for the purposes of the sanctuary as his wage, if he took them and bought food and ate it, he would have escaped the death penalty."
3. A. R. Dosetai says, "How do we know that if someone did no work on all six days, he [will end up] working on all seven days?

B. "Lo, if he sat home all week and did no work, on Friday he ends up with nothing to eat. If then he went and joined a gang of bandits and was caught and put into chains, then he will be put to work even on the Sabbath.

C. "All this because he did not work on all of the six days of the week."

4. A. R Simeon b. Eleazar says, "Even the first Man tasted nothing before he had performed work.

B. "For it is said, *And he put him into the Garden of Eden to tend it and to keep it; of every tree of the garden you may freely eat [having worked]* (Gen. 2:15-16)."

5. A. R. Tarfon says, "Also the Holy One, blessed be he, did not bring his Presence to rest on Israel before they had carried out work.

B. "For it is said, *They shall make a sanctuary for me, then I shall dwell in their midst* (Ex. 25:5)."

6. A. R. Judah b. Batera says, "If someone has no work to do, what should he do? If he has a neglected courtyard or field, he should go and keep himself busy puttering in it.

B. "For it is said, *Six days will you labor and do all your work.*

C. "Why does Scripture say, *all your work?*

D. "It means to encompass one who has a neglected courtyard or field, indicating that he should go and keep himself busy puttering in it."

7. A. R. Yose says, "A person dies only out of idleness.

B. "For it is said, *And he expired and was gathered unto his people* (Gen. 49:33).

C. "Lo, if someone was smitten and fell at his furrow and died, lo, he will have died only out of idleness.

D. "If he was standing on his roof top or on the bank of the stream and fell and died, he will have died only out of idleness."

E. [These cases serve to prove the case] only for men, but how may we provide examples of the same fact for women?

F. As it is said, *Let neither man nor woman make any more work for the offering of the sanctuary* (Ex. 36:6).

G. And as to children? *And the people [inclusive of children] was restrained from bringing* (Ex. 36:6).

8. A. Said R. Nathan, "When Moses was engaged in the work of the tabernacle, he did not wish to take counsel with the heads of Israel, and the heads of Israel sat silently.

B. "They thought, 'Now Moses is going to need us.'

C. "When they heard the announcement in the camp, The stuff they had was sufficient (Ex. 36:7), they thought, 'Woe is us, for we do not have a share in the work of the tabernacle.'

D. "They went and added a major donation on their own part, as it is said, *And the rulers brought the onyx stones* (Ex. 35:27)."

Once the theme of work is introduced, the anthologizing instincts of our compilers are aroused to full force. The result is a sizable repertoire of statements on the theme, none of which makes a striking or fresh point. The effort of Nos. 1, 2 is to link work to religious duties, a point which will have surprised the people who maintained that study of the Torah takes precedence.

No. 3 goes over essentially the same ground. Nos. 4, 5 then make a second and separate point. No. 6 goes on to a minor detail. Work involves the actual doing, not necessarily employment. No. 7 is somewhat less successful in making its own point. It seems to me No. 8 is attached only as an appendix to Ex. 36:6, cited at **XI:I.7.G.**

XI:II

1. A. **Hate authority: how so?**
   B. This teaches that a person should not place the crown on his own head, but that others should put it on his head.
   C. So it is said, *Let another person praise you and not your own mouth, a stranger and not your own lips* (Prov. 27:2).
2. A. Said R. Aqiba, "Whoever raises himself over teachings of the Torah – to what is such a one to be compared? To a carcass left lying on the road.
   B. "Whoever passes by holds his nose and steps away from it.
   C. "For it is said, *If you have done foolishly in lifting yourself up or if you have planned devices put your hand on your mouth* (Prov. 30:32)."
   D. Said to him Ben Azzai, "Interpret the passage in its own context. If a person humbles himself for the sake of the teachings of the Torah, eating dried dates and wearing dirty clothing and sitting and watching at the door of sages, whoever passes by will say, 'This one is a fool,' but in the end you will find that the whole of the Torah is with him."
3. A. R. Yose says, "Going down is going up, and going up is coming down.
   B. "Whoever raises himself over teachings of the Torah in the end will be thrown down, and whoever lowers himself over teachings of the Torah in the end will be raised up."

The point of hating authority has nothing to do with the government. "Authority" here bears the meaning of importance, and Goldin's translation, lordship, has much to recommend it. The point at No. 1 is straightforward and is stated twice, B, C. What is interesting, then, is that it has no bearing on Torah-study, but No. 2, repeated in substance by No. 3, immediately calls attention to people who aggrandize themselves through Torah-study. Aqiba's version has a person raise himself over Torah-teachings, while Yose's is more to the point. The entire complex assuredly serves the base-saying quite nicely.

XI:III.

1. A. **Don't get friendly with the government: how so?**
   B. This teaches that a person should not make his name known to the sovereign. Once he becomes known to the sovereign, in the end they will pay attention to him and kill him and take over his entire estate.
   C. How [would such a thing happen]? If one's fellow sits in the market and says, "The Holy One, blessed be he, shows grace to Mr. So-and-so. Today a hundred oxen have come forth from his household, a hundred sheep, a hundred goats."

D. A local official may hear and go and report the matter to the local authority, who goes and surrounds the entire establishment and takes everything from the man.

E. Concerning such a case Scripture says, *He who blesses his friend with a loud voice—it shall be counted a curse to him* (Prov. 27:14).

The point of the story is not quite germane, since the story has someone made known by a third party, while B says that one should not do so on his own. The point of C-D is certainly appropriate, but the story C-D serve to illustrate E, not A-B. Yet C-E are thematically relevant, even if they make a different point.

XI:IV

1. A. Another matter: **Don't get friendly with the government:**

B. If one's fellow sits in the market and says, "The Holy One, blessed be he, shows grace to Mr. So-and-so. Today he brought into his storehouse how many *kors* of wheat, how many *kors* of barley," a bandit hears and comes and surrounds the entire household, taking from him all his wealth.

C. In the morning he has nothing left.

D. Concerning such a case Scripture says, *He who blesses his friend with a loud voice—it shall be counted a curse to him* (Prov. 27:14).

The same story is repeated with slightly different details.

XI:V

1. A. Another matter: **Don't get friendly with the government:**

B. How so?

C. This teaches that someone should not imagine announcing, "I am the prince of this city" or "...the [Goldin:] viceroy,"

D. for [holders of such offices merely] rob the Israelites.

I do not see the relevance of C-D to the saying at hand. How proclaiming one's power involves robbing from the Israelites I cannot say.

XI:VI

1. A. Another matter: A person should not have the intent of gaining authority [Goldin: resorting to the ruling powers].

B. For at first they open the door for someone and accompany him, but in the end it goes hard on him.

This seems to me a clear statement of the intent of the saying under discussion. One should avoid all contact with the government.

XI:VII

1. A. Avtalyon says: Sages, watch what you say, lest you teach something which is not in accord with the correct teaching of the Torah, and therefore become liable to the punishment of exile, and go into exile to a place of bad water, and disciples who follow you may also teach something which is not in accord with the correct teaching of the Torah, and therefore become liable to the punishment of exile, and go into exile to a place of bad water.

   B. What is bad water? One must say: *And they mingled themselves with the nations and learned their works* (Ps. 106:35).

   C. Another matter: **Bad water** is precisely what it says.

   D. And some say, Perhaps **they may go into exile** to hard work.

The saying of Avtalyon is nicely glossed.

The Fathers According to Rabbi Nathan

Chapter Twelve

The sayings are worked out, with the usual appendices attached as well:

Hillel and Shammai received [the Torah] from them. Hillel says: Be disciples of Aaron, loving peace and pursuing peace, loving people and drawing them near to the Torah.

He would say [in Aramaic]: A name made great is a name destroyed, and one who does not add, subtracts.

And who does not serve as disciple to sages is liable to death. And the one who uses the crown, passes away.

He would say: If I am not for myself, who is for me? And when I am for myself, what am I? And if not now, when?

Overall the chapter works its way through these sayings, but it includes statements attributed to Hillel in other documents, and, as usual, the anthological principle accounts for the inclusion of diverse materials with no direct relevance to what is before us, as the following outline indicates:

I:I

    I:I.1 Loving peace: how so?

    I:I.2 What does it mean to love peace as Aaron did? Amplification of proof-text in foregoing.

    I:I.3 Mourning for Aaron exceeded that of Moses: why?

    I:I.4 Same as above.

    I:I.5 Same as above.

XII:II

    XII:II.1 Continues foregoing.

    XII:II.2 Continues foregoing.

    XII:II.3 Continues foregoing.

    XII:II.4 Continues foregoing.

    XII:II.5 Continues foregoing.

XII:III

> **XII:III.1 and pursuing peace:** how so?
>
> **XII:III.2** What it means to pursue peace.
>
> **XII:III.3** God does the same.

XII:IV

> **XII:IV.1 Loving people:** how so?

XII:V

> **XII:V.1 And drawing them near to the Torah:** how so?

XII:VII

> **XII:VII.1 He would say: If I am not for myself, who is for me?**

XII:VI

> **XII:VI.1-2** Illustrate the foregoing and are presently out of place.

XII:VIII

> **XII:VIII.1** He would say, "If you will come to my house, I shall come to your house. To the place which my heart loves, there my feet lead me."

XII:IX

> **XII:IX.1** If I am here, all are here...in accord with the pain is the gain: illustrated.

XII:X

> **XII:X.1** Skull floating on the water.

XII:XI

> **XII:XI.1** Name made great.

XII:XII Amplification of foregoing.

XII:XIII

> **XII:XIII.1 And who does not serve as disciple to sages is liable to death:** how so?

XII:XIV

> **XII:XIV.1** One who does not add subtracts: how so?

XIV:XV

XIV:XV.1 One who makes worldly use of the crown: how so?

There is a simple redactional form: citation of a base-clause plus **how so?** This then carries amplification in the form of appendices found pertinent on account of theme.

XII:I

1. A. Hillel and Shammai received [the Torah] from them. Hillel says: Be disciples of Aaron, loving peace and pursuing peace, loving people and drawing them near to the Torah.

   B. He would say [in Aramaic]: A name made great is a name destroyed, and one who does not add subtracts.

   C. And who does not learn is liable to death. And the one who uses the crown, passes away.

   D. He would say: If I am not for myself, who is for me? And when I am for myself, what am I? And if not now, when?

   E. Loving peace: How so?

   F. This teaches that a person should love peace among Israelites as Aaron did,

   G. as it is said, *The Torah of truth was in his mouth, and unrighteousness was not found in his lips; he walked with me in peace and uprightness and did turn away many from iniquity* (Mal. 2:6).

2. A. R. Meir says, "Why does the cited verse state, *did turn away many from iniquity?*

   B. "When Aaron would go along, he might meet a bad man or a wicked one. He greeted him. The next day the same man might want to commit a transgression. But he thought to himself, 'Woe is me, how can I raise my eyes afterward and look at Aaron? I should be ashamed on his account, for he has now greeted me.' That person would then keep himself from committing a transgression.

   C. "So too, if there were two people quarreling with one another, Aaron went and took a seat near one of them and said to him, 'My son, see your friend – what is he saying? His heart is torn, he rips his garments, saying, "Woe is me, how can I raise my eyes afterward and see my friend? I should be ashamed on his account, for I am the one who [Goldin:] treated him foully."'

   D. "He would sit with him until he had removed the envy from his heart.

   E. "Then Aaron would go to his fellow and take a seat near him, and say to him, 'My son, see your friend – what is he saying? His heart is torn, he rips his garments, saying, "Woe is me, how can I raise my eyes afterward and see my friend? I should be ashamed on his account, for I am the one who [Goldin:] treated him foully."'

   F. "He would sit with him until he had removed the envy from his heart.

   G. "Then, when the two met, they hugged and kissed one another.

   H. "Therefore it is said, *And every member of the house of Israel wept for Aaron for thirty days* (Num. 20:20)."

3. **A.** Another comment on the same verse: Why did all the Israelites mourn for Aaron for thirty days [Goldin: while only the men wept for Moses]?

B. Because [following Goldin's insertions] Moses gave a strict judgment in accord with the truth, while [following Goldin:] Aaron never said to someone, "You have committed an offense," or to a woman, "You have committed an offense."

C. That is why *every member of the house of Israel wept for Aaron for thirty days* .

D. But of Moses, who rebuked the people with harsh words, it is said, *And the sons of Israel mourned for Moses* (Deut. 34:8).

E. And how many thousands of Israelites are called Aaron, for were it not for Aaron['s principles], this one would not have come into the world.

4. **A.** And there are those who say that for this reason it is said *every member of the house of Israel wept for Aaron for thirty days:*

B. Whoever can see our lord, Moses, standing and weeping and not join in the weeping?

5. **A.** And there are those who say that for this reason it is said *every member of the house of Israel wept for Aaron for thirty days:*

B. Whoever can see Eleazar and Phineas, sons of high priests, standing and weeping, and not join in the weeping?

Once, at No. 1, we have cited the pertinent statement of Avot, we proceed to work on some of its clauses. The disciples of Aaron love peace, and that theme forms the exposition to follow. But, as we see, as soon as the theme turns to Aaron, then his loving peace precipitates the introduction of other sayings not on the subject of loving peace at all. The specific verse cited as a proof-text, Mal. 2:6, is itself subjected to exegesis, in line with the larger theme of Aaron's bringing peace among people, No. 2. Then No. 3 – interpreted as Goldin rightly insists – contrasts the description of the mourning for Aaron, involving all Israel, and of that for Moses, involving only the males. That contrast is drawn at C-D. Nos. 4, 5 then move still further away from the original theme, since they explain why everyone wept for Aaron for thirty days but do not appeal to the issue of his bringing peace. In all, we see a kind of moving, or dialectical, discourse, in which one thing leads to the next, with the original point of departure not entirely forgotten, but also not paramount. The unit to follow continues this same line of thought about Aaron's death.

XII:II

1. **A.** At that moment Moses asked for a death like the death of Aaron,

B. for he saw the bier of Aaron lying in state in great honor, with bands of ministering angels lamenting for him.

C. But did he ask for such a death in the presence of some other person? Was it not in the privacy of his own heart? But the Holy One, blessed be he, heard what he had whispered to himself.

D. And how do we know that Moses asked for a death like the death of Aaron and [the Holy One, blessed be he,] heard what he had whispered to himself?

E. As it is said, *Die in the mountain to which you go up, and be gathered to your people as Aaron your brother died in Mount Hor* (Deut. 32:50).

F. Thus you have learned that Moses asked for a death like the death of Aaron.

2. A. At that time [the Holy One, blessed be he,] said to the angel of death, "Go, bring me the soul of Moses."

B. The angel of death went and stood before him, saying to him, "Moses, give me your soul."

C. Moses grew angry with him and said to him, "Where I am sitting you have no right even to stand, yet you have said, 'Give me your soul'!" He threw him out with outrage.

D. Then the Holy One, blessed be he, said to Moses, "Moses, you have had enough of this world, for lo, the world to come is readied for you, for a place is prepared for you from the first six days of creation."

E. For it is said, *And the Lord said, Behold a place by me, and you shall stand upon the rock* (Ex. 33:21).

F. The Holy One, blessed be he, took the soul of Moses and stored it away under the throne of glory.

G. And when he took it, he took it only with a kiss, as it is said, *By the mouth of the Lord* (Deut. 34:5).

3. A. It is not the soul of Moses alone that is stored away under the throne of glory, but the souls of the righteous are stored away under the throne of glory,

B. as it is said, *Yet the soul of my Lord shall be bound in the bundle of life with the Lord your God* (1 Sam. 25:29).

C. Is it possible to imagine that that is the case also with the souls of the wicked?

D. Scripture says, *And the souls of your enemies, those he shall sling out as from the hollow of a sling* (1 Sam. 25:29).

E. For even though one is tossed from place to place, it does not know on what to come to rest.

F. So too the souls of the wicked go [Goldin:] roving and fluttering about the world and do not know where to come to rest.

4. A. The Holy One, blessed be he, further said to the angel of death, "Go, bring me the soul of Moses."

B. The angel of death went in search of him in his place but did not find him. He went to the Great Sea and said to it, "Has Moses come here?"

C. The sea replied, "From the day on which the Israelites passed through me, I have not seen him."

D. He went to the mountains and hills and said to them, "Has Moses come here?"

E. They replied, "From the day on which Israel received the Torah on Mount Sinai, we have not seen him."

F. He went to Sheol and Destruction and said to them, "Has Moses come here?"

G. They said to him, "His name we have heard, but him we have never seen."

H. He went to the ministering angels and said to them, "Has Moses come here?"

I. They said to him, "*God understands his way and knows his place* [Goldin: cf. Job 28:23]. God has hidden him away for the life of the world to come, and no one knows where."

J. So it is said, *But wisdom, where shall it be found? and where is the place of understanding? Man does not know its price, nor is it found in the land of the living. The deep says, It is not in me, and the sea says, It is not with me....Destruction and death say, We have heard a rumor thereof with our ears* (Job.28:13-15, 22).

5. A. Joshua too was seated and grieving for Moses,

   B. until the Holy One, blessed be he, said to him, "Joshua, why are you grieving for Moses? *Moses, my servant, is dead* (Joshua 1:2)."

From the theme of Aaron's death, we move quite naturally to that of Moses – simply by the transition, "Moses wanted to die in the same way." From that point, at No. 1, we simply follow the theme along its own lines. But the materials do not correspond to that theme, and in fact contradict it. For the death by a kiss is hardly at issue in No. 2, where it does not occur, or at No. 3, which continues No. 2, and No. 4 has its own, extraordinarily powerful interest in identifying Moses with Wisdom in the cited verse of Job, which is subjected to paraphrase. The conclusion is anticlimactic. But the main point, from the redactional angle, is that as soon as the transition is accomplished, it is ignored, and the materials, ready at hand, are introduced within their own logic. That constitutes the principle of agglutination of this document, so far as the authorship moves beyond the exegesis and amplification of the base-statements.

XII:III

1. A. ...and pursuing peace: how so?

   B. This teaches that a person should pursue peace in Israel between one person and the next, just as Aaron pursued peace in Israel between one person and the next.

   C. So it is said, *Depart from evil and do good, seek peace and pursue it* (Ps. 34:15).

2. A. R. Simeon b. Eleazar says, "If someone stays in his own place and keeps silent, how is he going to pursue peace in Israel between one person and the next?

   B. "But he has to go forth from his place and circle around the world and pursue peace in Israel."

   C. "So it is said, *...seek peace and pursue it* (Ps. 34:15).

   D. "How so? Seek it in your own locale, pursue it in another locale."

3. A. So too the Holy One, blessed be he, made peace on high.

   B. What is the peace that the Holy One, blessed be he, made on high?

   C. That he did not call ten [angels] by the name of Gabriel, ten Michaels, ten Uriels, ten Raphaels, as people may use the name Reuben for ten different people, or Simeon, or Levi, or Judah.

   D. For if he had done things the way mortals do, if he then called one of them, all of those bearing that name would come before him and express jealousy of one another.

E. So he called only one angel by the name of Gabriel, one Michael, and when he calls one of them, only that one comes and stands before him, and he sends him wherever he wishes.

F. How, then, do we know that they fear and honor one another and exhibit greater humility than do mortals?

G. When they open their mouths and recite a song, this one says to his fellow, "You start, for you are greater than I am," and that one says, "You start, for you are greater than I am."

H. This is not the way of mortals, for this one says to his fellow, "I am greater than you are," and that one says to his fellow, "I am greater than you are."

I. Some say that they form groups, and one group says to its fellow, "You start, for you are greater than I am."

J. For so it is said, *"And this calls to that"* (Is. 6:3).

No. 1 provides a good amplification of the base-statement, and so does No. 2, which explains what is required when it is said to go in pursuit of peace. No. 3 then invokes the model of God in the same matter. So the entire composition is devoted to the exposition of the theme at hand.

XII:IV

1. A. **Loving people:** how so?

B. This teaches that someone should show love to others and not hate them.

C. For so we find of the men of the Generation of the Dispersion [who built the tower of Babel] that, because they showed love to one another, the Holy One, blessed be he, did not want to destroy them from the world, but he merely scattered them in the four corners of the world.

D. But the men of Sodom, because they hated one another, did the Holy One, blessed be he, destroy from this world and from the world to come.

E. For it is said, *And the men of Sodom were evil, sinning greatly against the world* (Gen. 13:13).

F. *...evil* against one another,

G. *...sinful* in fornication,

H. *...against the Lord* in the profanation of the divine name,

I. *...greatly*, that they sinned through malice.

J. Lo, you have learned that because they hated one another the Holy One, blessed be he, destroyed from this world and from the world to come.

The well established form is followed, a citation of the base-clause, followed by the reference to a biblical fact or precedent to amplify that virtue.

XII:V

1. A. **And drawing them near to the Torah:** how so?

B. This teaches that a person should [Goldin:] bend to others and so draw them under the wings of the Presence of God,

C. just as Abraham, our father, bent to others and drew them under the wings of the Presence of God.

D. And it was not Abraham alone who did so, but Sarah did so as well,

E. for it is said, *And Abram took Sarai, his wife, and Lot, his brother's son, and all their substance that they had gathered and the souls that they had made in Haran* (Gen. 12:5).

F. Now is it not the fact that no creature in the world can create even a gnat, so why does Scripture say, *The souls that they had made in Haran?*

G. This teaches that the Holy One, blessed be he, credited it to them as if they had made them.

The amplification ends at C+D. The remaining part is not entirely to the point, since the exegesis of F-G is meant to prove that Abram and Sarai made converts, not that Sarai, in addition to Abram, did so. That is tangential to the focus of the exegesis of the verse, which therefore does not contribute to the amplification of the base-clause.

XII:VI

1. A. Just as a person does not share in the wage of his fellow in this world, so he does not share in the wage of his fellow in the world to come,

   B. as it is said, *And behold the tears of such as are oppressed and have no comforter, and on the side of their oppressors there is power, and they have no comforter* (Qoh 4:1).

   C. Why does it say twice, *and they have no comforter?*

   D. This refers to people who eat and drink and enjoy success in sons and daughters in this world, while in the world to come they have nothing.

   E. *And they have no comforter:* Now if something is stolen from someone, or if he suffers a bereavement, his sons and brothers come and comfort him. Is it possible that also in the world to come, things are the same?

   F. Scripture says, *Yes, he has neither son nor brother* (Qoh. 4:8).

2. A. So too if someone commits a transgression and produces a *mamzer* [the child of parents who can legally never wed, e.g., mother and son, such a classification of person being beyond all remedy in his lifetime], people say to him, "Empty head! you have hurt yourself, you have hurt him."

   B. For that *mamzer*-son wanted to study Torah with those who are in session and repeating Torah-traditions in Jerusalem, and that fellow went with them until they came to Ashdod. He stood there and said, "Woe is me, for if I were not a *mamzer*, I should have been able to go into session and repeat Torah-traditions among those disciples with whom I have studied up to now. But since I am a *mamzer*, I am not going to go into session and repeat Torah-traditions among the disciples, for a *mamzer*-child cannot enter Jerusalem at all."

   C. For it is said, *And a mamzer will dwell in Ashdod and I will cut off the pride of the Philistines* (Zech. 9:6).

I am puzzled by the introduction here of **XII:VI.1.A**, which seems to me to have no relevance to the context of drawing people to the Torah. No. 2 maintains that one's actions have far-reaching effects upon his *mamzer*-son. The entire composition therefore strikes me as parachuted down for reasons that will be obvious, as I shall presently specify.

XII:VII

1. A. He would say: If I am not for myself, who is for me?
   B. If I do not acquire merit for myself [in my lifetime], who will acquire merit for me?
   C. And when I am for myself, what am I?
   D. If I do not acquire merit for myself, who will acquire merit for me?
   E. And if not now, when?
   F. If I do not acquire merit for myself in my own lifetime, who will acquire merit for me after my death?
   G. For so it says, *For a living dog is better off than a dead lion* (Qoh. 9:4):
   H. *For a living dog is better off::* this refers to a wicked person who makes out well in this world.
   I. *...than a dead lion :* even than Abraham, Isaac, and Jacob, who lie in the dust.

XII:VII

1. A. Another matter: *For a living dog is better off than a dead lion* refers to a wicked person, who makes out well in this world.
   B. If he repents, the Holy One, blessed be he, will accept him.
   C. But as to the righteous, once he has died, he cannot acquire further merit.

The glossing of **XII:VII.1**'s base-clause works out rather well, with no problems and a cogent message imputed to the whole. If we look back at **XII:XI.1-2** we find a remarkably cogent message, namely, what "wage" or reward one attains is accomplished in this life, and no one can add to that of another in the life to come. Translate wage into merit, and we have the entire story. No one can help anyone else in the world to come. That is the very point of **XII:VII**'s saying, what merit one is going to acquire has to be gotten in the here and now. Then No. 2, above, adds a pertinent qualification, which is that while one cannot acquire merit, one has got the power to do permanent damage to others, specifically by begetting a mamzer, who will suffer even after the father is dead. If **XII:VI** were located after **XII:VII**, therefore, we should have slight difficulty in explaining the inclusion of **XII:VI**, even though, overall, it is still not tightly linked to the composition that does belong in the amplification of clauses in the sayings assigned to Hillel. In the proper sequence, however, the relevance of the first to the second would not have posed any question whatsoever.

XII:VIII

1. A. He would say, "If you will come to my house, I shall come to your house. To the place which my heart loves, there my feet lead me."
   B. If you will come to my house, I shall come to your house: how so?
   C. This refers to people who get up early in the morning and stay late in the evening to attend the sessions of synagogues and study houses.
   D. The Holy One, blessed be he, blesses them for the world to come.

E. That accords with the following verse: *In every place where I cause my name to be mentioned I will come to you and bless you* (Ex. 20:21).

F. To the place which my heart loves, there my feet lead me.

G. How so? This refers to people who leave [at home] their silver and gold and go up for the pilgrim-festival to greet the face of the Presence of God in the sanctuary.

H. The Holy One, blessed be he, protects them in their camps [at home, so no one will steal their money], as it is said, *Neither shall any one covet your land when you go up to appear before the Lord your God* (Ex. 34:24).

The saying, which could as well have occurred in Avot, receives a fine and systematic explanation, with both parts cogent and harmonious to the whole.

XII:IX

1. A. He would say, "If I am here, all are here. If I am not here, who is here? Turn it over again and again, because everything is in it, and in all ways, in accord with the pain is the gain."

2. A. There is the case of Hillel the Elder, who was going along the way and met people carrying wheat.

B. He said to them, "How much is a *seah* of wheat?"

C. They said to him, "Two *denars*."

D. He met others, saying to them, "How much for a *seah* of wheat?"

E. They said to him, "Three *denars*."

F. He said to them, "But the ones who came by before asked two."

G. They said to him, "Dumb Babylonian! Don't you know that in accord with the pain is the gain?"

H. He said to them, "You miserable louts! To what I say to you do you answer me in that way?"

I. What did Hillel the Elder do to them? He brought them back to the right way.

The story, No. 2, is introduced only because the *in accord with*-saying is included. The ending is anticlimactic. Otherwise it has no bearing on the amplification of what is before us. The principle of aggregation is once more not propositional or thematic but merely formal.

XII:X

1. A. So he saw a skull floating on the water.

B. He said to it, "Because you drowned others, they drowned you, and those who drowned you will be drowned."

The saying is introduced without any amplification whatsoever.

XII:XI

1. A. Further, in the Babylonian language he says four things: **He would say [in Aramaic]: A name made great is a name destroyed, and one who does not add subtracts.**

   B. **And who does not serve as disciple to sages is liable to death. And the one who uses the crown, passes away.**

The saying is introduced without any amplification, which now follows.

XII:XII

1. A. **A name made great is a name destroyed:** how so?

   B. This teaches that one should not make himself known to the government, for once one makes himself known to the government, in the end they look upon him with cupidity and take away all his money.

The amplification is identical with materials already given.

XII:XIII

1. A. **And who does not serve as disciple to sages is liable to death:** how so?

   B. How so?

   C. There was the case of someone who lived in Beth Ramah, who applied to himself the rules of piety.

   D. Rabban Yohanan ben Zakkai sent a disciple to him to investigate his character. The disciple came and found that he took oil and put it on the stove and took it from the stove and put it into the bean-soup.

   E. He said to him, "What are you doing?"

   F. He said to him, "I am in the status of a high priest, and I am preparing in a condition of cultic purity to eat my food in the status of priestly rations."

   G. He said to him, "Is this stove in a state of cultic cleanness or uncleanness? [Can the stove become cultically unclean, or is it neutral and perpetually in a state of insusceptibility?]"

   H. He said to him, "And in the Torah do we have a rule covering the cultic uncleanness of a stove? [A stove, in the man's view, simply cannot become cultically unclean at all, the uncleanness pertaining solely to an oven, while the stove is a neutral object.] For it is said, *Whatever is in [the oven] shall be unclean* (Lev. 11:33). [The stress on the oven means an oven can become cultically unclean but the stove remains perpetually insusceptible.]"

   I. He said to him, "Just as the Torah has given the rule that an oven can become cultically unclean, so the Torah has given the rule that a stove can be cultically unclean, for it is said, *Whether oven or stove for pots, it shall be broken in pieces, they are unclean* (Lev. 11:35) [hence as much as an oven falls into the classification of cultic uncleanness, if it is subjected to a source of uncleanness, so a stove falls into that same category]."

J.   "If, therefore, this is how you have been doing things, you have never in your life eaten your priestly rations in a state of cultic cleanness."

The story shows that the man had not served sufficiently as a disciple to sages even to know the rules made explicit in the Torah. Eating heave-offering or priestly ration in a state of cultic uncleanness imposes liability to death, so the story provides a fine illustration of the cited rule.

XII:XIV

1. A.   **And one who does not add subtracts:** how so?
    B.   This teaches that if one has studied a tractate or two or three but does not add to those [by studying more tractates], he loses what he has already studied.

The amplification makes explicit what is clear in the original statement.

2. A.   **And the one who uses the crown, passes away:** how so?
    B.   Whoever makes use of the fully spelled out name of God has no portion in the world to come.

The worldly use is of God's fully-expressed name.

The Fathers According to Rabbi Nathan

Chapter Thirteen

The brief saying of Shammai is expounded clause by clause:

Shammai says: Make your learning of Torah a fixed obligation. Say little and do much. Greet everybody cheerfully.

The chapter follows a simple outline:

XIII:I

XIII:I.1 Shammai cited: Make your study of Torah a fixed obligation.

XIII:II

XIII:II.1 Say little and do much. Example of Abraham.

XIII:II.2 Continuation of foregoing.

XIII:II.3 Continuation of foregoing.

XIII:II.4 Continuation of foregoing.

XIII:III

XIII:III.1 Greet everybody cheerfully.

XIII:I

1. A. **Shammai says: Make your learning of Torah a fixed obligation. Say little and do much. Greet everybody cheerfully.**

   B. **Shammai says: Make your learning of Torah a fixed obligation:** how so?

   C. This teaches that if someone has heard something from a sage in the school house, he should not treat it casually but should turn it into a fixed obligation [for close study].

   D. And what someone learns he should do and teach to others so that they may do it too.

   E. For it is said, *That you may learn them and observe to carry them out* (Deut. 5:1).

   F. And so in the book of Ezra it says, *For he had set his heart to seek the Torah of the Lord and to do it*, and then: *and to teach in Israel statutes and ordinances* (Ezra 7:10).

The clarification at C is cogent. The use of fixed obligation in Shammai's saying finds its corresponding point at C, and that seems to me to justify the interpretation given at C to what Shammai has said. I do not see the close tie between C and D-F, though one may claim that *doing much* involves exactly the viewpoint of D-F.

XIII:II

1. A **Say little and do much:** How so?

   B. This teaches that righteous people say little but do much, while wicked people say much and even a little bit they scarcely accomplish.

   C. How do we know that righteous people say little but do much?

   D. We find in the case of our father, Abraham, that he said to the angels, "You shall eat bread with me today," for it is said, *And I will fetch a morsel of bread and satisfy your hunger* (Gen. 18:5).

   E. But in the end see what Abraham did for the ministering angels! He went and prepared for them three oxen and nine *seahs* of fine flour.

2. A. And how do we know that he prepared for them nine *seahs* of fine flour?

   B. As it is said, And Abraham made haste to the tent, to Sarah, and said, *Make haste and prepare three seahs of fine flour.*

   C. *Three* – in the plain sense of the word,

   D. *fine [flour]* – six,

   E. *flour* – lo, nine in all.

   F. And how do we know that he prepared for them three oxen?

   G. As it is said, *And Abraham ran to the herd and fetched a calf, tender and good* (Gen. 18:7).

   H. *The herd* – one,

   I. *a calf* – two,

   J. *tender* – three.

   K. Some add: *Good* – four.

   L. *And he gave it to the servant, and he hastened to dress it* (Gen. 18:7):

   M. He gave it over to Ishmael, his son, to educate him to carry out religious duties [such as hospitality to wayfarers].

3. A. So too the Holy One, blessed be he, said little but did much.

   B. For it is said, *And the Lord said to Abram, Know with certainty that your seed will be a stranger in a land that does not belong to them and shall serve them and they shall afflict them four hundred years and also that nation whom they shall serve will I punish and afterward they shall come out with great substance* (Gen. 15:13f.).

   C. He said to them only [following Goldin, p. 73:] [that he would punish them] by means of his D and N name,

   D. but in the end, when the Holy One, blessed be he, exacted punishment from Israel's enemies, he exacted punishment only with the name of seventy-two letters.

   E. For it is said, *Or has God tried to go and take him a nation from the midst of another nation, by trials, by signs, and by wonders...and by great terrors* (Deut. 4:34).

F. Lo we learn that when the Holy One, blessed be he, exacted punishment from Israel's enemies, he exacted punishment only with the name of seventy-two letters.

4. A. And how do we know that wicked people say much and even a little bit they scarcely accomplish?

B. So we find in the case of Ephron, who said to Abraham, *A land worth four hundred silver shekels* (Gen. 23:15), but in the end, when it came to weighing out the money, *And Abraham obeyed Ephron, and Abraham weighed to Ephron* (Gen. 23:16).

The clarification of the first clause is worked out at B and then give ample exemplification with Abraham, **XIII:II.1**, then with God, **XIII:II.3**. Abraham's case, moreover, bears in its wake a secondary exegesis at **XIII:II.2**. Then we find the converse at No. 4, a complete and systematic work of formal elegance.

XIII:III

1. A. **Greet everybody cheerfully:** how so?

B. This teaches that if someone gave to his fellow every good gift in the world, but with a stolid face, Scripture treats it as if he gave nothing.

C. But he who receives his fellow cheerfully, even if he gave him nothing, is credited by Scripture as if he had given him every good gift in the world.

The clarification presents no problems. It is balanced and complete, as before.

The Fathers According to Rabbi Nathan

Chapter Fourteen

The exposition of the saying at hand provides systematic glosses, but at the end an additional piece answers what seems to me an interesting question left open by the construction of Avot, specially, with its repeated claim that Eleazar b. Arakh is at the climax of Yohanan's tradition.

Rabban Yohanan ben Zakkai received [the Torah] from Hillel and Shammai. He would say: If you have learned much Torah, do not puff yourself up on that account, for it was for that purpose that you were created. He had five disciples, and these are they: Rabbi Eliezer ben Hyrcanus, Rabbi Joshua ben Hananiah, Rabbi Yosé the Priest, Rabbi Simeon ben Nethanel, and Rabbi Eleazar ben Arakh.

He would list their good qualities: Rabbi Eliezer ben Hyrcanus – a plastered well, which does not lose a drop of water. Rabbi Joshua happy is the one who gave birth to him. Rabbi Yosé – a pious man. Rabbi Simeon ben Nethanel a man who fears sin. And Rabbi Eleazar ben Arakh a surging spring.

He would say: If all the sages of Israel were on one side of the scale, and Rabbi Eliezer ben Hyrcanus were on the other, he would outweigh all of them.

Abba Saul says in his name: If all of the sages of Israel were on one side of the scale, and Rabbi Eliezer ben Hyrcanus was also with them, and Rabbi Eleazar [ben Arakh] were on the other side, *he* would outweigh all of them.

He said to them: Go and see what is the straight path to which someone should stick.

Rabbi Eliezer says: A generous spirit. Rabbi Joshua says: A good friend. Rabbi Yosé says: A good neighbor. Rabbi Simeon says: Foresight. Rabbi Eleazar says: Good will.

He said to them: I prefer the opinion of Rabbi Eleazar ben Arakh, because in what he says is included everything you say.

He said to them: Go out and see what is the bad road, which someone should avoid. Rabbi Eliezer says: Envy. Rabbi Joshua says: A bad friend. Rabbi Yosé says: A bad neighbor. Rabbi Simeon says: A loan. All the same is a loan owed to a human being and a loan owed to the Omnipresent, the blessed, as it is said, *The wicked borrows and does not pay back, but the righteous person deals graciously and hands over [what is owed]* (Ps. 37:21).

Rabbi Eleazar says: Ill will.

He said to them: I prefer the opinion of Rabbi Eleazar been Arakh, because in what he says is included everything you say.

The outline of the chapter follows:

XIV:I

XIV:I.1 Yohanan received the Torah from Hillel and Shammai.

XIV:I.2 Identification of Yohanan ben Zakkai.

XIV:II

XIV:II.1 Gloss of Yohanan's saying.

XIV:III

XIV:III.1 As above.

XIV:IV

XIV:IV.1 Story about death of Yohanan's son. Eleazar's departure.

The framer has glossed the sayings and added a story.

XIV:I

1. A. **Rabban Yohanan ben Zakkai received [the Torah] from Hillel and Shammai.**
   B. Hillel the Elder had eighty disciples. Thirty of them were worthy of having the Presence of God rest on them like our lord, Moses, but the generation in which they lived was not worthy of such a thing. Thirty of them were worthy of intercalating the year. And twenty of them were mediocre.
   C. The greatest of the lot was Jonathan b. Uzziel, the least of the lot was Rabban Yohanan ben Zakkai.
2. A. They say concerning Rabban Yohanan ben Zakkai that he did not neglect a single passage of Scripture, the Mishnah, Gemara, laws and exegesis and supplements, fine points of the Torah and fine points of the scribal tradition, and all of the exegetical principles of sages.
   B. And there was not a single matter that is in the Torah that he neglected to learn.
   C. To carry out what is in Scripture: *That I may cause those that love me to inherit substance and that I may fill their treasuries* (Prov. 8:21).

Both units complement the saying by identifying Yohanan ben Zakkai. I see no marked tendency, though calling him the least of the mediocrities on the surface is hardly a compliment.

XIV:II

1. A. He would say: If you have learned much Torah, do not puff yourself up on that account, for it was for that purpose that you were created.
   B. For people were created only on the stipulation that they should occupy themselves with the Torah.

Yohanan's saying is lightly glossed.

XIV:III

1. A. He had five disciples, and he called each a name.
   B. Rabbi Eliezer ben Hyrcanus he called a plastered well, which does not lose a drop of water, a pitch-lined flask that holds its wine.
   C. Rabbi Joshua he called a three fold cord, not quickly broken.
   D. Yose the Priest he called the pious man of the generation.
   E. Rabbi Simeon ben Nethanel he called [following Goldin, p. 74:] oasis in the wilderness, which holds its waters. Happy is the disciple whose master praises him and testifies to his [excellence].
   F. And Rabbi Eleazar ben Arakh he called an overflowing stream and a surging spring, whose waters overflow, thus carrying out this statement: *Let your springs be dispersed abroad and courses of water in the streets* (Prov. 5:16).
   G. He would say, "If all the sages of Israel were on one side of the scale, and Rabbi Eliezer ben Hyrcanus were on the other, he would outweigh all of them."
   H. Abba Saul says in his name, "If all of the sages of Israel were on one side of the scale, and Rabbi Eliezer ben Hyrcanus was also with them, and Rabbi Eleazar [ben Arakh] were on the other side, he would outweigh all of them."
   I. He said to them, "Go and see what is the straight path to which someone should stick so as to enter the world to come."
   J. Entered Rabbi Eliezer and said: A generous spirit. Entered Rabbi Joshua and said: A good friend. Entered Rabbi Yosé and said: A good neighbor, a good impulse, and a good wife. Entered Rabbi Simeon and said: Foresight. Entered Rabbi Eleazar and said: Good will toward Heaven and good will toward other people.
   K. He said to them, "I prefer the opinion of Rabbi Eleazar ben Arakh, because in what he says is included everything you say."
   L. He said to them: "Go out and see what is the bad road, which someone should avoid so as to enter the world to come."

M. Entered **Rabbi Eliezer and said: Envy.** Entered **Rabbi Joshua
and said: A bad friend.** Entered **Rabbi Yosé and said: A bad
neighbor,** an evil impulse, and a bad wife. Entered **Rabbi Simeon
and said: He who takes out a loan and does not pay it
back.** All the same is a loan owed to a human being and a
loan owed to the Omnipresent, the blessed, as it is said,
*The wicked borrows and does not pay back, but the
righteous person deals graciously and hands over [what is
owed]* (Ps. 37:21). Entered **Rabbi Eleazar and said: Ill**
will toward Heaven, ill-will toward the religious duties, and ill-will
toward other people.

N. **He said to them: I prefer the opinion of Rabbi Eleazar
been Arakh, because in what he says is included
everything you say.**

Yohanan's saying is lightly glossed.

XIV:IV

1. A. When the son of Rabban Yohanan ben Zakkai died, his disciples came in
to bring him comfort.

B. R. Eliezer came in and took a seat before him and said to him, "My lord,
with your permission, may I say something before you."

C. He said to him, "Speak."

D. He said to him, "The first Man had a son who died, and he accepted
comfort in his regard. And how do we know that he accepted comfort in
his regard?

E. "As it is said, *And Adam knew his wife again* (Gen. 4:25). You, too, be
comforted."

F. Said he to him, "Is it not enough for me that I am distressed on my own
account, that you should mention to me the distress of the first Man?"

G. R. Joshua came in and said to him, "My lord, with your permission, may
I say something before you."

H. He said to him, "Speak."

I. He said to him, "Job had sons and daughters who died, and he accepted
comfort in their regard. And how do we know that he accepted comfort
in their regard?

J. "As it is said, *The Lord gave and the Lord has taken away, blessed be the
name of the Lord* (Job 1:21). You too, be comforted."

K. Said he to him, "Is it not enough for me that I am distressed on my own
account, that you should mention to me the distress of the Job?"

L. R. Yose came in and took a seat before him and said to him, "My lord,
with your permission, may I say something before you."

M. He said to him, "Speak."

N. He said to him, "Aaron had two grown-up sons who died on the same
day, and he accepted comfort in their regard.

O. "For it is said, *And Aaron held his peace* (Lev. 10:3), and silence means
only comfort. You too, be comforted."

P   Said he to him, "Is it not enough for me that I am distressed on my own
account, that you should mention to me the distress of Aaron?"

Q. R. Simeon came in and said to him, "My lord, with your permission, may I say something before you."

R. He said to him, "Speak."

S. He said to him, "King David had a son who died, and he accepted comfort in his regard. You too, be comforted. And how do we know that he accepted comfort in his regard?

T. "As it is said, *And David comforted Bath Sheba his wife and went in unto her and lay with her and she bore a son and called his name Solomon* (2 Sam. 12:24). You too, be comforted."

U. Said he to him, "Is it not enough for me that I am distressed on my own account, that you should mention to me the distress of King David?"

V. R. Eleazar b. Arakh came in. When he saw him, he said to his servant, "Take my clothes and follow me to the bathhouse [so that I can prepare to accept consolation], for he is a great man and I shall not be able to resist his arguments."

W. He came in and took a seat before him and said to him, "I shall draw a parable for you. To what may the matter be compared? To the case of a man with whom the king entrusted a treasure. Every day he would weep and cry, saying, 'Woe is me, when shall I get complete and final relief from this treasure that has been entrusted to me.'

X. "You too, my lord, had a son, he recited from the Torah, Prophets and Writings, Mishnah, laws, lore, and has departed from this world without sin. You have reason, therefore, to accept consolation for yourself that you have returned your treasure, entrusted to you, whole and complete."

Y. He said to him, "R. Eleazar b. Arakh, my son, you have given comfort to me in the right way in which people console one another."

XIV:IV

1. A. When they took their leave of him, he said, "I shall go to [following Goldin:] Emmaus, a pleasant place with good and sweet water," while the others said, "Let us go to Yavneh, the place in which numerous disciples [of] sages love the Torah."

    B. The name of him who went to Emmaus, a pleasant place with good and sweet water, became less in the Torah, while the names of those who went to Yavneh, the place in which numerous disciples [of] sages love the Torah, became great in the Torah.

The elegant construction, repeating the same pattern three times and then ending with Eleazar as the climax, is an appropriate conclusion. For it sets the balance right with regard to Eleazar. Now the point is made that despite his excellence -- superiority over the other disciples -- Eleazar lost out because he abandoned the collegiality of the others. Perhaps the great praise assigned to Eleazar in the earlier materials -- all of them in fact in Avot -- precipitated the question of why, in the legal writings overall, he takes so slight a role. But that seems to me farfetched.

The Fathers According to Rabbi Nathan

Chapter Fifteen

As usual, we have a mixture of amplification of words and phrases, on the one side, and an appendix of thematically intersecting material, on the other.

> They [each] said three things. Rabbi Eliezer says: Let the respect owing to your companion .be as precious to you as the respect owing to yourself. And don't be easy to anger. And repent one day before you die. And warm yourself by the fire of the sages, but be careful of their coals, so you don't get burned — for their bite is the bite of a fox, and their sting is the sting of a scorpion, and their hiss is like the hiss of a snake, and everything they say is like fiery coals.

The outline shows the layout of the materials:

XV:I

XV:I.1 Amplification of **respect owing to companion**-saying.

XV:II

XV:II.1 Same as above.

XV:III

XV:III.1 Don't be easy to anger + prologue to Hillel-Shammai stories.

XV:IV

XV:IV.1 Patience of Hillel the Elder.

XV:V

XV:V.1 Impatience of Shammai the Elder.

XV:V.2 As above.

XV:VI

XV:VI.1 Amplification of **Repent**-saying.

XV:VII

XV:VII.1 Chain of tradition tied to Eliezer's sayings.

There is no variation on the familiar pattern.

XV:I

1. A. They [each] said three things.   Rabbi Eliezer says: Let the respect owing to your companion be as precious to you as the respect owing to yourself.   And don't be easy to anger.   And repent one day before you die.
    B. Let the respect owing to your companion be as precious to you as the respect owing to yourself: how so?
    C. This teaches that just as someone sees to the honor owing to himself, so he should see to the honor owing to his fellow.
    D. And just as a person does not want a bad name to circulate against his honor, so he should not want to circulate a bad name against the honor owing to his fellow.

As before, we observe what is clearly the standard form, namely, citation of a clause of a saying, then *how so?* followed by an amplification.   The clarification here stays within the limits of the saying under discussion, which is simply paraphrased.

XV:II

1. A. Another explanation of the statement, **Let the respect owing to your companion be as precious to you as the respect owing to yourself:** how so?
    B. [Following Goldin's interpretation:] when a person has a myriad and all his money is taken away from him, he should nonetheless not lower himself for something worth a mere penny [but should retain his dignity].   [Goldin: Let him not discredit himself over so much as a *perutah*'s worth.]

The amplification is formally identical with the foregoing.

XV:III

1. A. **And don't be easy to anger:** how so?
    B. This teaches that one should be humble, like Hillel the Elder, and not captious, like Shammai the Elder.

What has already been said applies here too.   The pericope forms a prologue to most of the rest of the chapter, an anthology on the stated theme of Hillel's patience contrasted to Shammai's captiousness.

XV:IV

1. A. What characterized the patience of Hillel the Elder?
   B. They tell the following case, concerning two people, who went and made a bet with one another for four hundred *zuz*.
   C. They stipulated, "Whoever can go and infuriate Hillel will get the four hundred *zuz*.
   D. One of them went [to try]. That day was a Friday, toward nightfall, and Hillel was washing his hair. The man came and knocked on the door, saying, "Where is Hillel, where is Hillel?"
   E. Hillel wrapped himself up in his cloak and came to meet him. He said to him, "Speak."
   F. He said to him, "Why are the eyes of the people of Palmyra [Tadmor] bleary?"
   G. He said to him, "Because they live in the sands of the desert and the winds blow and scatter the sand into their eyes. Therefore their eyes are bleary."
   H. He went and waited a while and came back and knocked on the door.
   I. He said, "Where is Hillel, where is Hillel?"
   J. He wrapped himself up in his cloak and come out.
   K. He said to him, "My son, what do you need?"
   L. He said to him, "I need to ask a matter of law."
   M. He said to him, "Go ahead."
   N. He said to him, "Why are the feet of the Africans flat?"
   O. He said to him, "Because they live by swamps, and every day walk in water, therefore their feet are flat."
   P. The man went his way, waited a while, came back, and knocked on the door.
   Q. He said, "Where is Hillel? where is Hillel?"
   R. He wrapped himself in his cloak and went out.
   S. He said to him, "What do you need to ask?"
   T. He said to him, "I have to ask a matter of law."
   U. He said to him, "Ask." He then wrapped himself in his garment and sat down before him.
   V. He said to him, "What do you need to ask?"
   W. He said to him, "Is this the way princes reply? May people like you not become many in Israel."
   X. He said to him, "God forbid! Watch yourself. What do you want?"
   Y. He said to him, "On what account are the heads of the Babylonians long?"
   Z. He said to him, "My son, you have asked an important 'law.' It is because over there they do not have smart midwives. When the baby is born, the ones who deal with it are slave-boys and slave-girls. Therefore their heads are long. But here, where we have smart midwives, when a baby is born, they raise it in a cradle and rub its head. Therefore their heads are round."
   AA. He said to him, "You have cost me four hundred *zuz*."
   BB. He said to him, "Hillel is worth your losing four hundred *zuz* without Hillel's losing his temper."

Once the issue of humility is introduced, the compilers of the text gather relevant exemplary tales. It will be some time before Eliezer reappears. The story obviously is a set-piece account, in no way reframed to fit the present setting (but what such a revision would have consisted of is hardly clear).

XV:V

1. A. What characterized the impatience of Shammai the Elder?
   B. They say, there was the case of a man who stood before Shammai. He said to him, "My lord, how many Torahs do you have?"
   C. He said to him, "Two, one in writing, one memorized."
   D. He said to him, "As to the one in writing, I believe you. As to the memorized one, I do not believe you."
   E. He rebuked him and threw him out.
   F. He came before Hillel. He said to him, "My lord, how many Torahs were given?"
   G. He said to him, "Two, one in writing, one memorized."
   H. He said to him, "As to the one in writing, I believe you. As to the memorized one, I do not believe you."
   I. He said to him, "My son, sit."
   J. He wrote for him, *Alef, bet.*
   K. He said to him, "What is this?"
   L. He said to him, "An *alef.*"
   M. He said to him, "This is not an *alef* but a *bet.*"
   N. He said to him, "What is this?
   O. He said to him, "*Bet.*"
   P. He said to him, "This is not a *bet* but a *gimmel.*"
   Q. He said to him, "How do you know that this is an *alef* and this a *bet* and this a *gimmel*? But that is what our ancestors have handed over to us – the tradition that this is an *alef*, this a *bet*, this a *gimmel*. Just as you have accepted this teaching in good faith, so accept the other in good faith."

2. A. There was the case of a gentile who was passing behind a synagogue and heard a child reciting in Scripture: *This is the clothing which they shall make: a breast plate, ephod, and robe* (Ex. 28:4).
   B. He came before Shammai and said to him, "My lord, all this honor – for whom is it designated?"
   C. He said to him, "It is for the high priest who stands and carries out the service at the altar."
   D. He said to him, "Convert me on the stipulation that you make me high priest so that I may carry out the service at the altar."
   E. He said to him, "Is there no priesthood in Israel, and do we not have high priests to stand and carry out the acts of service at the altar assigned to the high priest, so that a mere convert who has come only with his staff and wallet may come and take up the service of the high priest?"
   F. He threw him out.
   G. He came before Hillel and said to him, "My lord, convert me, on the stipulation that you make me high priest so that I may carry out the service at the altar."

H. He said to him, "Sit, and I shall tell you something [of the rules of the office you propose to enter]. For if someone proposes to greet a mortal king, is it not logical that he should learn the rules of going in and coming out?"

I. He said to him, "Yes."

J. "You, who wish to greet the King of kings of kings, the Holy One, blessed be he, surely should learn how to enter the house of the Holy of Holies, how to set up the lamps, how to offer an offering on the altar, how to arrange the table, how to set out the wood."

K He said to him, "Do what you think appropriate."

L. He first wrote for him, "*Alef, bet,*" and the man learned the letters.

M. Then he presented the *Torah of the Priests* [the books of Leviticus and Numbers], and the man went on learning the words until he came to the verse, *The non-priest who draws near [the altar] shall die* (Num. 1:51).

N. The proselyte constructed an argument *a fortiori* concerning himself: if an Israelite, who is called a son of the Omnipresent, and concerning whom the Presence of God has said, *And you shall be mine as a kingdom of priests and a holy people* (Ex. 19:6), nonetheless is subject to Scripture's admonition, *The non-priest who draws near [the altar] shall die* (Num. 1:51), I, who am a mere proselyte, who has come only with my wallet, all the more so!"

O. The proselyte was reconciled on his own.

P. He came before Hillel the Elder and said to him, "May all the blessings that are in the Torah rest on your head, for if you had been like Shammai the Elder, you would have wiped me out of this world and of the world to come. Your humility has brought me into this world and the coming one."

Q. They say that to that proselyte two sons were born. One he called Hillel, and one he called Gamaliel, and they called them, Hillel's converts.

The story focuses, of course, not on Shammai but on Hillel, but the point is made, just as before.

XV:VI

1. A. **And repent one day before you die:**
   B. The disciples of R. Eliezer asked him, "But does someone know on what day he is going to die, that that is the day on which he should repent?"
   C. He said to them, "All the more so that one should repent today, lest he die tomorrow, and tomorrow, lest he day the day afterward.
   D. "One will turn out to spend all his days in repentence."

The amplification of Eliezer's statement asks the necessary question and elicits the inevitable answer.

XV:VII

1. A. R. Yose bar Judah says in the name of R. Judah bar Ilai, who said in the name of R. Ilai, his father, who said in the name of R. Eliezer the Elder,

"And repent one day before you die. And warm yourself by the fire of the sages, but be careful of their coals, so you don't get burned — for their bite is the bite of a fox, and their sting is the sting of a scorpion, and their hiss is like the hiss of a snake, and everything they say is like fiery coals."

The attributive clause is amplified, but otherwise there is no contribution.

The Fathers According to Rabbi Nathan

Chapter Sixteen

Rabbi Joshua says: Envy, the evil impulse [desire of bad things], and hatred for people push a person out of the world.

The exposition of the stated theme works its way through the three principal clauses, with a long appendix on the evil impulse as well. The outline thus shows conformity with the familiar pattern:

XVI:I

    XVI:I.1 Envy: how so?

XVI:II

    XVI:II.1 Same as above.

XVI:III

    XVI:III.1 Evil impulse: how so?

XVI:III Same as above.

XVI:IV

    XVI:IV.1-4 Examples of those whc have resisted the evil impulse.

XVI:V

    XVI:V.1-4 More on the evil impulse.

XVI:VI

    XVI:VI.1-2 Hatred for people, how so?

XVI:I

1. A. Rabbi Joshua says: Envy, desire of bad things, and hatred for people push a person out of the world.
   B. Envy: how so?
   C. This teaches that in the way in which someone sees to his own household, so should he see to the household of another person.

D. And just as a person does not want a bad name to circulate against his wife and children, so he should not want to circulate a bad name against the honor owing to his fellow's wife and children.

The exposition follows the pattern in the preceding: an example deriving from the Golden Rule.

XVI:II

1. A. Another matter concerning **envy**: how so?
   B. A person should not [Goldin:] begrudge another person the learning that that person has achieved.
   C. There is the case of someone who envied the learning of his fellow. His life was shortened, he died and went his way.

This is identical in form to the counterpart in Chapter Fifteen.

XVI:III

1. A. **Desire of bad things:** how so?
   B. The impulse to do evil is thirteen years older than the impulse to do good.
   C. From the mother's womb it grows and develops with a person.
   D   If one began to profane the Sabbath, it does not stop him. If he wanted to kill, it does not stop him. If he goes to commit a transgression [of a sexual character], it does not stop him.
   E. After thirteen years the impulse to do good is born. When the man then violates the Sabbath, it says to him, "Empty head, lo, Scripture says, *Those who profane it will surely die* (Ex. 31:11)."
   F. When the man then kills, it says to him, "Empty head, lo, Scripture says, *One who sheds man's blood by man his blood will be shed* (Gen. 9:6)."
   G. When he goes to commit a transgression, it says to him, "Empty head, lo, Scripture says, *The adulterer and the adulteress will surely die* (Lev. 20:10)."
2. A. When a man arouses himself and goes to commit fornication, all of his limbs obey him, because the impulse to do evil is king over the two hundred and forty-eight limbs.
   B. But when he goes to carry out a religious duty, all his limbs [Goldin:] begin to drag, because the impulse to do evil from the womb is king over the two hundred and forty-eight limbs that are in a man.
   C. The impulse to do good is only like one who is imprisoned, as it is said, *For out of prison he came forth to be king* (Qoh. 4:14), referring to the impulse to do good.

The exposition makes the same powerful point two times, that the impulse to do evil is more deeply seated than the impulse to do good. We now give the example of a biblical hero who came forth from prison to rule, namely, Joseph.

XVI:IV

1. A. Now there are those who say that this [verse] refers to Joseph, the righteous man.
   B. When that wicked woman [Potiphar's wife] came, she disturbed him by her words, saying to him, "I shall lock you up in prison [if you do not go to bed with me]."
   C. He said to her, *The Lord loosens prisoners* (Ps. 146:7).
   D. She said to him, "I shall put out your eyes."
   E. He said to her, *The Lord opens the eyes of the blind* (Ps. 146:8).
   F. She said to him, "I shall force you to stoop."
   G. He said to her, *The Lord raises up those who are bowed down* (Ps. 146:8).
   H. She said to him, "I shall make you wicked."
   I. He said to her, *The Lord loves the righteous* (Ps. 146:8).
   J. She said to him, "I shall make you into an Aramaean."
   K. He said to her, *The Lord preserves strangers* (Ps. 146:9).
   L. Finally he said, *How shall I commit this great evil* (Gen. 39:9).

2. A. And do not take as surprising the case of Joseph, the righteous man, for lo, R. Sadoq was the greatest saint of his generation. When he was taken captive in Rome, a certain noble lady took him and sent a beautiful slave-girl to him [to mate with him and produce more slaves].
   B. When he saw her, he turned toward the wall, so as not to lay eyes on her, and he went into session repeating [Mishnah-sayings] all night long.
   C. In the morning the girl went and complained to her mistress, saying to her, "I'd rather die than have you give me back to that man."
   D. She sent and called him, saying to him, "Why did not you do with that woman what men naturally do?"
   E. He said to her, "What can I do, for I am of the high priesthood, and I am from an important family. I thought to myself, if I have sexual relations with her, I shall increase the number of *mamzer*-children in Israel."
   F. When she heard his statement, she gave orders concerning him and freed him with great dignity.

3. A. And do not take as surprising the case of R. Sadoq, for lo, R. Aqiba was still greater than he. When he went to Rome, he was [Goldin:] slandered before an authority. He sent to him two beautiful women, washed, anointed, and outfitted like brides, who threw themselves at him all night long.
   B. This one said, "Turn toward me," and that one said, "Turn toward me."
   C. He lay between them [Goldin:] in disgust and did not turn to them.
   D. When morning came the women went and greeted the authority, saying to him, "We'd rather die than be given to that man."
   E. He sent and called him, saying to him, "Why did not you do with those women what man naturally do with women? Are they not pretty? Are they not ordinary folk like you? Did not the same God who made you make them?"
   F. He said to him, "What could I do? Their odor reached me, from the meat of carrion and *terefah*-meat and swarming things that they have eaten."

4. A. And do not take as surprising the case of R. Aqiba, for lo, there is R. Eliezer the Elder, who is still greater than he, who raised the daughter of his sister for thirteen years with him in the same bed, until the puberty signs appeared.

B. He said to her, "Go, marry a man."

C. She said to him, "Am I not your slave girl, a handmaiden there to wash the feet of your disciple[s]?"

D. He said to her, "My daughter, I am an old man. Go and marry a youngster like yourself."

E. She said to him, "Have I not said to you, Am I not your slave girl, a handmaiden there to wash the feet of your disciple[s]?"

F. When he had heard what she said, he asked permission of her, betrothed her, and had sexual relations with her [as his bride].

We have four statements, joined in a clear and effective pattern to make the same point. The anthology is inserted, of course, in line with **XVI:III**. But it makes its own point, which is not the same as the point introduced in exposition of the base-saying at hand.

XVI:V

1. A. R. Reuben b. Astrobuli says, "How can someone [Goldin:] escape from the evil impulse in his guts, for the very first drop [of semen] that a man puts into a woman is the evil impulse.

   B. "And the impulse to do evil is located only at the gates of the heart. For it is said, *Sin crouches at the door* (Gen. 4:7).

   C. "It says to a person while still an infant in the cradle, 'Someone wants to kill you,' [and] the infant wants to pull out his hair.

   D. "When an infant in the cradle puts its hand on a snake or a scorpion and gets bitten, is it not the impulse to do evil that is the cause?

   E. "[If the infant] puts its hand on coals and is burned, is it not the evil impulse in his guts that is the cause?

   F. "For the evil impulse is what [Goldin:] drives him headlong.

   G. "But come and see the case of a kid or a lamb: when it sees a well, it jumps backward, because there is no evil impulse in a beast.

2. A. R. Simeon b. Eleazar says, "I shall draw a comparison, to what is the impulse to do evil to be likened? To iron that one tossed into the fire.

   B. "So long as it is in the fire, people can shape it any way they want.

   C. "So is the impulse to do evil: its remedy lies only in teachings of the Torah, which are like fire,

   D. "For it is said, *If your enemy is hungry, give him bread to eat, and if he is thirsty, give him water to drink, for you will heap coals of fire upon his head, and the lord will reward you* (Prov. 25:21f).

   E. "In place of the letters that read *will reward you*, read *will put him at peace with you*."

3. A. R. Judah the Patriarch says, "I shall give you a parable. To what is the impulse to do evil to be compared? To the case of two men who went to an inn. One of them was arrested as a bandit. They said to him, 'Who is with you?'

   B. "He could have said, 'No one is with me.

   C. "But he says, 'If I am going to be put to death, let my fellow be put to death with me.'

   D. So it is with the impulse to do evil: 'Since I am going to perish in the world to come, so I shall make the entire body perish with me.'"

4. A. R. Simeon b. Yohai said, "How do we know that the Israelites are never going to see the face of Gehenna? The matter may be stated in a parable. To what is it comparable?

B. "To the case of a mortal king who had a field of no value. People came and rented it out for a fee of ten *kors* of wheat a year. They fertilized the field, fenced it in, watered it, cleared it, but brought in from it only one *kor* of wheat.

C. "The king said to them, 'What's going on?'

D. "They said to him, 'Our lord, O king, you know of this field that you handed over to us that to begin with you never brought in any crop at all from it, and now that we have fertilized it and cleared it and watered it, we have brought in only a single *kor* of wheat.'

E. "So the Israelites are destined to say before the Holy One, blessed be he, 'Lord of the world, you know of the impulse to do evil that it incites us, as it is said, *For he knows our impulse* (Ps. 103:14). [At least we have done as well as we have done.]'"

We have a sequence of impulse-to-do-evil materials, relevant in a general way to the base-clause subject to amplification. I see no common principle, only the shared theme.

XVI:VI.

1. A. **And hatred for people:** how so?

B. This teaches that a person should not have the plan of saying, "Love sages and hate disciples," "love disciples and hate common folk," but rather, "Love them all, and hate heretics, apostates and informers."

C So did David say, *Do I not hate those, Lord, that hate you? And do I not strive with those who rise up against you? I hate them with utmost hatred, I regard them as my enemies* (Ps. 139-21-22)."

D. But does Scripture not say, *You shall love your neighbor as yourself, I am the Lord* (Lev 19:18)?

E. Why so? Because I have created him, and if he does a proper deed with you [Goldin: if he acts as thy people do, thou shalt love him], you should love him too, but if not, you should not love him.

2. A. R. Simeon b. Eleazar says, "By a great oath this matter was stated: *You shall love your neighbor as yourself, I am the Lord* (Lev 19:18).

B. "*I the Lord* have created him. If you love him, I shall be faithful to pay you a just reward, and if not, I am a just God to exact a penalty."

No. 1 spells out the final clause. It balances the love with hatred of appropriate parties. Once Lev. 19:18 is introduced, No. 2 proceeds to present its own exegesis of that passage, essentially out of phase with No. 1. No. 2 treats the matter as unconditional, and No. 1 wishes to introduce conditions.

The Fathers According to Rabbi Nathan

Chapter Seventeen

The fixed pattern – gloss or amplification of the base-saying, joined to a sizable appendix on a theme tangentially introduced by that gloss – is repeated without variation.

> Rabbi Yosé says: Let your companion's property be as precious to you as your own. And get yourself ready to learn Torah, for it does not come as an inheritance to you. And may everything you do be for the sake of Heaven.
>
> Rabbi Simeon says: Be meticulous about the recitation of the Shema and the Prayer. And when you pray, don't treat your praying as a matter of routine; but let it be a [plea for] mercy and supplication before the Omnipresent, the blessed, as it is said, *For He is gracious and full of compassion, slow to anger and full of mercy, and repents of the evil* (Joel 2:13). And never be evil in your own eyes.
>
> Rabbi Eleazar says: Be constant in learning of Torah; know what to reply to an Epicurean; and do not forget a single teaching of the Torah; know before whom you work, for your employer can be depended upon to pay your wages for what you do.

The chapter-outline is as follows:

XVII:I

XVII:I.1 **Let your companion's property be as precious to you as your own**: how so?

XVII:I.2 Another comment on the same.

XVII:II

XVII:II.1 **And get yourself ready to learn Torah:** Moses' sons did not inherit, Joshua did. Proof-text: Song 1:8.

XVII:III

XVII:III.1 Story of impoverished girl, connected to Song 1:8.

XVII:IV

XVII:IV.1 Story on girl taken captive.

XVII:V

XVII:V.1 As above. All thus added because of Song 1:8 and its
extenuation.

XVII:VI

XVII:VI.1 **And may everything you do be for the sake of
Heaven:** how so?

XVII:VII

XVII:VII.1 Sayings of Simeon and Eleazar cited without comment.

XVII:I

1. A. **Rabbi Yosé says: Let your companion's property be as
precious to you as your own.** And get yourself ready to
learn Torah, for it does not come as an inheritance to you.
And may everything you do be for the sake of Heaven.
   B. **Let your companion's property be as precious to you as
your own:** how so?
   C. This teaches that just as someone looks out for his own property, so he
should look out for the property of his fellow,
   D. and just as a person does 'not want a bad name to circulate concerning his
property, so he should not want a bad name to circulate concerning the
property of his fellow.
2. A. Another comment on **Let your companion's property be as
precious to you as your own:** how so?
   B. When a disciple of a sage comes to you, saying, "Teach me," if you have
something to teach him, repeat the tradition, and if not, send him away
right off, and do not take his money.
   C. For it is said, *Do not say to your neighbor, Go and come again, and
tomorrow I will give; when you have it with you all along* (Prov. 3:28).

The exegesis of the base-clause follows what is now an established pattern.
The opening comment simply reads the saying in light of the Golden Rule, and
the second rereads it in light of sages' own setting.

XVII:II

1. A. **And get yourself ready to learn Torah, for it does not
come as an inheritance to you:** how so?
2. A. When Moses, our master, saw that his sons had no knowledge of the
Torah which would qualify them to succeed him in the leadership, he
cloaked himself and stood in prayer.
   B. He said before him, "Lord of the world, tell me who will go in [and] who
will come out at the head of all this people?"

C. For it is said, *And Moses spoke to the Lord, saying, Let the Lord, the God of the spirits of all flesh, set a man over the congregation, who may go out before them and who may come in before them* (Num. 27:15ff.).

D. Said the Holy One, blessed be he, to Moses, *Moses, take Joshua* (Num. 27:15).

E. Said the Holy One, blessed be he, to Moses, "Go and act as his voice so that he may give an exposition in your presence at the head of all the great men of Israel [and that will signify that he is heir]."

F. At that moment Moses said to Joshua, "Joshua, as to this people that I am handing over to you, I am giving you not goats but kids, not sheep but lambs, for as yet they are not much experienced in the practice of religious duties, and they have not yet reached the growth of goats and sheep."

G. So it is said, *If you do not know, O you fairest among women, go your way forth by the footsteps of the flock and feed your kids beside the shepherds' tents* (Song 1:8).

The base-clause is illustrated by the case of Moses' sons, but only in a rather general way. For the focus of the story is Moses' leaving the people in Joshua's hands and warning Joshua that the people is still in an immature state. This story has nothing to do with the exposition of the notion that the Torah is no one's inheritance, although the story does intersect with that notion. What follows is tacked on because it invokes the proof-text, Song 1:8.

XVII:III

1. A. One time Rabban Yohanan ben Zakkai was walking in the market place. He saw a young girl gathering barley from under the hooves of the cattle of Arabs. He said to her, "My daughter, who are you?"

B. She kept silent.

C Again he said to her, "My daughter, who are you?"

D. She kept silent.

E. She said to him, "Hold it a minute." Then she covered herself with her hair and sat down before him. She said to him, "My lord, I am the daughter of Nakdimon b. Gurion."

F. He said to her, "My daughter, what ever became of the wealth of your father's house?"

G. She said to him, "My lord, is it not an apophthegm in Jerusalem: [Goldin:] 'Money will keep if you don't keep it,' and some say, '...if you give charity.'"

H. He said to her, "What ever happened to your father-in-law's money?"

I. She said to him, "My lord, this came and took the other along with it."

J. At that moment said Rabban Yohanan ben Zakkai to his disciples, "For my entire life I have been reciting this verse of Scripture, *If you do not know, O you fairest among women, go your way forth by the footsteps of the flock and feed your kids beside the shepherds' tents* (Song 1:8).

K. "But I never learned what it meant until I came to this day and I have now learned what it means.

L.   "For the Israelites have fallen subject to the most despicable of all nations, and not only to that despicable nation alone, but even to the dung of their cattle."

M.   The girl further said to him, "My lord, do you remember when you inscribed your seal on my marriage-contract?"

N.   He said to her, "Yes I do," and he said to the disciples, "By the Temple service! I inscribed my seal on this girl's marriage-contract, and in it was written the sum of a thousand thousand golden *denars* in Tyrian coinage.

O.   "In the time of this girl's father's household they never went from their houses to the house of the sanctuary before woolen rugs were spread out [for them to walk on]."

The appearance of the proof-text accounts for the inclusion of this story, which does not intersect in any direct way with the base-clause. Still, the theme that one generation does not succeed in leaving as an inheritance knowledge of the Torah is matched by the point that a generation does not leave wealth as a secure inheritance either. This same theme continues in the sizable anthology on the theme of captive girls of rich families, and that makes it virtually certain that the anthological principle is pointed – the instability of money – and not merely topical – captive Israelite women.

XVII:IV

1.   A.   There was the case of a girl who was taken captive with her ten slave-girls, and a Greek bought her, and she was growing up in his house.

B.   One day he gave her a pitcher and said to her, "Go, bring me water."

C.   One of her slave girls went and took it from her.

D.   He said to her, "What's this?"

E.   She said to him, "By the life of your head, my lord, I was one of the five hundred slave-girls of this girl."

F.   When the man heard what she said, he set the girl free, along with her ten slave-girls.

The story in this context is inane, but it does carry forward the (newly-) established theme.

XVII:V

1.   A.   There was another case involving a girl who was taken captive, and a Greek bought her, and she was growing up in his household.

B.   The master of dreams appeared to him and said to him, "Send this girl out of your house."

C.   His wife said to him, "Do not send her out."

D.   The master of dreams appeared to him again and said to him, "If you do not send her out, lo, I shall kill you."

E.   He went and sent her out, and he followed her.

F.   He said, "I shall go and see what will come of this girl."

G.   As she was going along the way, she became thirsty and went down to drink water at a spring. When she put her hand on the wall, a snake came out and bit her and she died, and her corpse floated on the water.

H.   He went down and picked her up and brought her back and buried her and he came and said to his wife, "With such as this, whom you see, only their father in heaven can be angry!"

The story is included because it is part of a larger thematic anthology. It would fit well into a collection of stories on the implacable punishment meted out by God to Israel after the destruction of the Temple.

XVII:VI

1. A.   And may everything you do be for the sake of Heaven: how so?

   B.   that is, for the sake of the Torah,

   C.   as it is said, *In all your ways know him and he will direct your paths* (Prov. 3:6).

The next base-clause is lightly glossed.

XVII:VII

1. A.   Rabbi Simeon says: Be meticulous about the recitation of the Shema and the Prayer. And when you pray, don't treat your praying as a matter of routine; but let it be a [plea for] mercy and supplication before the Omnipresent, the blessed, as it is said, *For He is gracious and full of compassion, slow to anger and full of mercy, and repents of the evil* (Joel 2:13). And never be evil in your own eyes.

   B.   Rabbi Eleazar says: Be constant in learning of Torah; know what to reply to an Epicurean; and do not forget a single teaching of the Torah; know before whom you work, for your employer can be depended upon to pay your wages for what you do.

The sayings are copied without comment.

The Fathers According to Rabbi Nathan

Chapter Eighteen

The outline shows a carefully drafted chapter.

XVIII:I

XVIII:I.1 Nicknames of Judah the Prince for Tarfon, Aqiba, Eleazar b. Azariah, Yohanan b. Nuri, and Yose the Galilean.

XVIII:I.2 Tarfon.

XVIII:I.3 Aqiba.

XVIII:I.4 Eleazar b. Azariah.

XVIII:II

XVIII:II.1 Appendix on Eleazar b. Azariah.

XVIII:II.1-2 Yohanan b. Nuri and Yose the Galilean.

XVIII:III

XVIII:III.1-2 Isi b. Judah would assign nicknames to sages.

XVIII:I

1. A. [Corresponding to the nicknames assigned by Yohanan ben Zakkai to his disciples], R. Judah the Patriarch would tote up the good qualities of sages: R. Tarfon, R. Aqiba, R. Eleazar b. Azariah, R. Yohanan b. Nuri, and R. Yose the Galilean.
2. A. R. Tarfon he called a pile of stones.
   B. There are those who say it was a pile of nuts.
   C. Once one removes one of the stones, all of them come tumbling down after one another.
   D. So was R. Tarfon: when a disciple of a sage came to him and said to him, "Repeat a tradition for me," he would produce for him a verse of Scripture, a passage of the Mishnah, an exegesis of a legal passage and of a narrative passage of Scripture.
   E. When the disciple left him, he would go out filled with blessing and goodness.
3. A. R. Aqiba he called [Goldin:] a well-stocked store-house.
   B. To what is R. Aqiba to be compared? To a worker who took his basket and went out. If he found wheat, he put it in the basket, if he found barley, he put it in, so too with spelt, and lentils.

C. When he got home, he sorted out the wheat by itself, the barley by itself, the beans by themselves, the lentils by themselves.

D. That is what R. Aqiba accomplished, and he turned the entire Torah into well-ordered rings. [He established appropriate classifications for diverse data.]

4. A. R. Eleazar b. Azariah he called a peddler's basket.

B. To what is R. Eleazar b. Azariah to be compared? To a peddler who took his basket and went to town, and the people of the town came and said to him, "Do you have good oil? do you have ointment? do you have balsam?"

C. That is what R. Eleazar b. Azariah was like. When the disciples of sages came to him, they would ask a question concerning Scripture, and he would give the answer, so too concerning the Mishnah, exegesis, laws, narratives.

D. When someone left his presence, he would be filled with goodness and blessing.

I am puzzled by the inclusion of this composition, which seems to me to have slight bearing on any passage of Avot. But I assume that the composition involving Yohanan b. Zakkai and his disciples has precipitated including a counterpart, with its own formal merits.

XVIII:II

1. A. When R. Joshua got old, his disciples came to visit him. He said to them, "My sons, what was the new point that you had today in school?"

B. They said to him, "We are your disciples, and your water [alone] do we drink."

C. He said to them, "God forbid! it is impossible that there is a generation of sages that is orphaned [and without suitable guidance]. Whose week was it to teach?"

D. They said to him, "It was the week of R. Eleazar b. Azariah."

E. He said to them, "And what was the topic of the narrative today?"

F. They said to him, "It was the passage that begins, *Assemble the people, the men and the women and the children* (Deut. 31:12)."

G. He said to them, "And what did he expound in that connection?"

H. They said to him, "This is how he interpreted it. The men come to learn, the women to listen, but why do the children come? It is to provide the occasion for the gaining of a reward for those who bring them.'"

I. He said to them, "You had a good pearl in your hands, and you wanted to make me lose it! If you had come only to let me hear this one thing, it would have been enough for me."

2. A. They said to him, "There was another exposition today, concerning the following verse: *The words of the wise are as goads and as nails well fastened are those that sit together in groups; they are given from one shepherd* (Qoh. 12:11)."

B. "[This is what he said:] 'Just as a goad guides the cow in its furrow, so the words of the Torah guide a person to the ways of life.

C. "'Is it possible to argue that just as a goad may be removed, so the words of the Torah may be moved?

D. "'Scripture states, *and as nails well fastened.* Just as nails are well fastened and do not move, so words of the Torah will not be moved.

E. *"'those that sit together in groups* are those disciples of sages that go in in groups. These declare prohibited what those declare permitted, these declare unclean what those declare clean, these declare unsuitable what those declare suitable..

F. "'Might one then conclude to refrain from learning [since there is so much dissension]?

G. "'Scripture says, *they are given from one shepherd* .

H. "'One God created them, one responsible authority gave them, the master of all deeds said them.

I. "'So you, make your ears like a [Goldin:] hopper and draw into them the words of those who prohibit and the words of those who permit, the words of those who declare unclean and the words of those who declare clean.'"

The appendix on Eleazar b. Azariah finds its natural place in the composition at large. The second address is worked out without reference to the context, which is why I distinguish it from the narrative setting.

XVIII:II

1. A. R. Yohanan ben Nuri he called a basket of laws.

2. A. R. Yose the Galilean: "One who gathers well, without arrogance, who has seized the good quality of sages received from Mount Sinai and would praise all the sages of Israel [for the same].

The original list is now completed. The established pattern is violated.

XVIII:III

1. A. Isi b. Judah would assign nicknames to sages.

B. R. Meir he called "sage and scribe."

C. R. Judah: "a sage when he wants."

D. R. Eliezer b. Jacob: "little but unblemished."

E. R Yose: "his reasoning goes with him."

F. R. Yohanan b. Nuri: "a basket of laws."

G. R. Yose the Galilean: "one who gathers well, without arrogance."

H. R. Simeon b. Gamaliel: "a store full of good purple yarn."

I. R. Simon: "learns much and forgets little."

2. A. R. Simeon came upon Isi b. Judah later on. He said to him, "On what account do you treat my words [at 1.I] as trivial before disciples of sages?"

B. He said to him, "What did I say about you, but that you learn much and forget little, and what you forget is the chaff of your knowledge."

We end up with a counterpart list, a neat composition in all.

The Fathers According to Rabbi Nathan

Chapter Nineteen

The chapter provides a systematic and orderly exposition of the following:

Aqabya ben Mehallel says, Whoever reflects on four things will never again sin: whence he comes, where he goes, what he is going to become, and who is his judge.

XIX:I

XIX:I.1-2 Clause by clause gloss.

XIX:I.3 Same, now with proof-text.

XIX:I.4 Same, now with parable.

XIX:II

XIX:II.1 Eliezer's death scene. Intersects with **who is his judge.**

XIX:III

XIX:III.1 More on Eliezer's death scene.

XIX:I

1. A. Aqabya ben Mehallel says, Whoever reflects on four things will never again sin: whence he comes, where he goes, what he is going to become, and who is his judge.
2. A. Whence he comes: from a place of darkness,
   B. ...where he goes, to a place of darkness and gloom,
   C. what he is going to become, dust and worm and maggot,
   D. and who is his judge, the King of kings of kings, the Holy One, blessed be he.
3. A. R. Simeon says, "He comes from a place of darkness and returns to a place of darkness, he comes from a rotting drop of liquid, from a place which no eye can see, and what he is destined to become is dust and worm and maggot.
   B. "For it is said, *Surely man is a worm, and the son of man a maggot* (Job 25:6)."
   C. R. Eliezer b. Jacob says, "*He is a worm* in his lifetime, *and the son of man is a maggot* after death.
   D. "What is *a worm while alive?* Vermin.

E. "*And the son of man is a maggot* after death? This refers to the fact that one creates worms in death."

4. A. R. Simeon b. Eleazar says, "I shall tell you a parable. To what is the matter likened? To the case of a king who built a great palace and took up residence [following Goldin:] in it. But the sewer pipe of a tannery flowed through it and emptied out at its gate.

B. "Whoever passed by would say, 'What a beautiful palace this would be, were it not for the sewer pipe of the tannery that flows through it!'

C. "So is man. Now, if at this time his intestines produce a flood of rot, yet he takes such pride in himself over all other creatures, if he produced [from his bowels] a spring of good oil, balsam, and ointment, how much the more so would he take pride over all other creatures!"

The exposition of the base-statement is systematic and orderly, with each of the clauses nicely expounded, then assigned a proof-text which itself is worked out, and, finally, given a parable for the sense of the whole. I cannot imagine a more disciplined program of exegesis.

XIX:II

1. A. When R. Eliezer fell ill, his disciples came in to see him and took seats before him. They said to him, "Our lord, teach us something."

B. He said to them, "This is what I shall teach you: go forth and let each take responsibility for the honor owing to his fellow.

C. "And when you say your prayers, know before whom you are standing up to pray.

D. "And on account of this teaching, you will gain the merit to enter the world to come."

What is added is a secondary explanation of the final clause, *know before whom you are going to be judged.*

XIX:III

1. A. Said R. Eleazar b. Azariah, "There are five things that we learned from R. Eliezer [on that occasion], and we got more pleasure from them than we got from them when he was alive.

B. "And these are the topics: the rule, as to uncleanness, covering a round cushion, ball, shoe last, amulet, and phylactery that was torn.

C. "[We said to him,] 'In these matters concerning which you gave rules for us, what is the law?'

D. "He said to us, 'They are subject to uncleanness, and [should they contract uncleanness] be careful in their regard to immerse them just as is, for these are absolutely firm rulings that were stated to Moses at Mount Sinai.'"

The continuation of the foregoing completes discourse.

The Fathers According to Rabbi Nathan

Chapter Twenty

The base saying – which is not in Avot – is worked out in an orderly and systematic way, as usual.

XX:I

XX:I.1 Hananiah's saying + Deut. 28:46-8.

XX:I.2 Exposition of Deut. 28:46-8 in its own terms.

XX:II

XX:II.1 He would interpret Song 1:6.

XX:III

XX:III.1 Further interpretation of Song 1:6.

XX:IV

XX:IV.1-2 Continuation of above.

XX:V

XX:V.1 Further interpretation of Song 1:6.

XX:VI

XX:VI.1-2 As above.

XX:VII.1 Reversion to the theme of Deut. 28:46-8.

The composition is totally cogent, a systematic and completely coherent statement, beginning to end.

XX:I

1. A. R. Hananiah, prefect of the priests, says, "Whoever places the teachings of the Torah upon his heart is relieved of many [Goldin:] preoccupations:
   B. "Those of hunger, silliness, libido, impulse to do evil, a bad woman, idle nonsense, the yoke of mortals.

C. "For so it is written in the book of Psalms by King David of Israel: *The precepts of the Lord are right, rejoicing the heart, the commandment of the Lord is pure, enlightening the eyes* (Ps. 19:9).

D. "And whoever does not place the teachings of the Torah upon his heart is burdened by many [Goldin:] preoccupations:

E. "those of perpetual hunger, silliness, libido, the evil impulse, a bad woman, idle nonsense, the yoke of mortals.

F. "For so it is written in the Repetition of the Torah [the book of Deuteronomy] by Moses, our lord, *And they shall be upon you for a sign and for a wonder, and upon your descendants forever, because you did not serve the Lord your God with joyfulness, and with gladness of heart, by reason of the abundance of all things, therefore you shall serve your enemy whom the Lord shall send against you, in hunger and in thirst and in nakedness and in want of all things* (Deut. 28:46-48).

2. A. "*...in hunger:* how so? When someone craves to eat a piece of barley-bread and does not find it, the nations of the world will demand from him white bread and fat meat.

B. "*...and in thirst:* How so? When someone wants to drink merely a drop of vinegar or a drop of beer and cannot find it, the nations of the world will demand from him a glass of world-class vintage wine.

C. "*...and in nakedness:* How so? when a person [Goldin: is in need of clothing and cannot find] a wool or linen shirt, the nations of the world ask him for silk and the best fabric in the world.

D. "*...and in want of all things:* without a lamp, a knife, or a table."

E. Another interpretation of *...and in want of all things:* without vinegar and salt.

F. For this is a curse people address to one another: "May you have neither vinegar nor salt in your house."

The base saying does not occur in Avot, but the passage fits in with everything that does, and the composition as a whole accords with the general plan of our document. Once the proof-text is introduced, F, the systematic exposition of the clauses of that text takes over. But the elements of the verse, hunger, thirst, and so on, are not then linked to the foregoing. That is why I treat the exposition of the verse as essentially distinct from the proposition of No. 1.

XX:II

1. A. He would say, "*Do not look on me, that I am dark, that the sun has tanned me, my mother's sons were angry against me, they made me keeper of the vineyards, but my own vineyard have I not kept* (Song 1:6).

B. "*Do not look on me, that I am dark, that the sun has tanned me, my mother's sons were angry against me,* – this refers to the councils of Judea, who broke off the yoke of the Holy One, blessed be he, from upon themselves and accepted upon themselves the dominion of a mortal king."

We now work on a further verse of Scripture systematically expounded in Hananiah's name. But the exposition of the verse then takes over in its own terms, and Hananiah's sense of matters is left behind.

XX:III

1. A. Another interpretation of the statement, *my mother's sons were angry against me* : this refers to Moses, who killed the Egyptian.
   B. For it is said, *And it came to pass in those days, when Moses had grown up, that he went out to his brethren and looked on their burdens. And he looked this way and that, and when he saw that there was no man, he killed the Egyptian and hid him in the sand* (Ex. 2:11).
   C. Why does Scripture say, *there was no man* ? It teaches that Moses called into session sanhedrin-courts made up of ministering angels, and he said to them, "Shall I kill this man?"
   D. They said to him, "Kill him."
   E. Did he kill him with a sword?
   F. Was it not merely by a spoken word that he killed him?
   G. For it is said, *Do you speak to kill me, as you killed the Egyptian* (Ex. 2:14).
   H. This teaches that he killed him by invoking the divine name.

Once the verse or Scripture is introduced, further interpretations are provided, in a sizable anthology.

XX:IV

1. A. Another interpretation of the statement, *my mother's sons were angry against me:* this refers to Moses, who fled to Midian.
   B. For it is said, *Now when Pharaoh heard this thing, he sought to slay Moses. But Moses fled from Pharaoh and settled in the land of Midian, and he sat down by a well. The priest of Midian had seven daughters...and the shepherds came and drove them away, but Moses stood up and helped them and watered their flock* (Ex. 2:15-17).
   C. Moses came and went into session as a court in judgment over them. He said to them, "It is the way of the world that men draw the water and women water the flocks, but here the women draw the water and the men water the flocks. [Goldin:] Justice is perverted in this place!"
2. A. Some say, so long as Moses was standing at the rim of the well, the water would continually leap up to meet him.
   B. When he turned away, the waters dropped back.
   C. At that moment he said, "Woe is me that I have abandoned my people and have come to dwell with the nations of the world."

The further exposition of the verse leads to yet another irrelevant entry.

XX:V

1. A. Another interpretation of the statement, *my mother's sons were angry against me* : this refers to the Israelites, who made the golden calf.

B. For to begin with they said, *Whatever the Lord says we shall do and obey* (Ex. 24:5).
C. But they went and said, *These are your gods Israel* (Ex. 32:4).

As before, we rework the given verse.

XX:VI

1. A. Another interpretation of the statement, *my mother's sons were angry against me:* this refers to the spies, who produced a bad report concerning the land and caused the Israelites to die:
   B. *In this wilderness your carcasses will fall* (Num. 14:29).
2. A. *They made me keeper of the vineyards:*
   B. Said the Holy One, blessed be he, "What is it that made me do good for the nations of the world? It was Israel.
   C. "For so long as the nations of the world enjoy prosperity, Israel is afflicted, driven out, driven from place to place."

We begin the road back to the verse of Deuteronomy with which the composition got under way.

XX:VII

1. A. Another explanation of the verse, *they made me keeper of the vineyards, but my own vineyard have I not kept* :
   B. This refers to the Israelites, who went into exile to Babylonia.
   C. The prophets that were among them arose and said to them, "Designate a portion of your crop for priestly rations and for tithes."
   D. They said to them, "The exile from our land itself is solely on account of our not designating portions of the crops as priestly rations and tithes, and now do you tell us to designate a portion of the crop as priestly rations and as tithes?"
   E. That is the point of the statement: *they made me keeper of the vineyards, but my own vineyard have I not kept.*

The connection to Deut. 28:46-48, with its reference to serving the enemy, is now complete, and the goal of discourse, the reference to priestly rations and tithes, has been accomplished. The entire composition must be regarded as unitary. Furthermore, the final link, to Hananiah's statement, is readily to be seen, since many, though not all, of items on the list of blessings and curses, have been covered. If I had to give a model of the principles of conglomeration and composition of the authorship before us, I would cite this chapter. For it is, in fact, in ultimate conception utterly cogent.

The Fathers According to Rabbi Nathan

Chapter Twenty-One

A simple pattern serves for the exposition of Dosa's statement, phrase by phrase, with some appendices that clearly belong.

> R. Dosa b. Harkinas says, Sleeping late in the morning, drinking wine at noon, chatting with children, and attending the synagogues of the ignorant drive a man out of the world.

XXI:I

XXI:I.1 Citation of Dosa + sleeping late in the morning – how so? It teaches, etc.

XXI:II

XXI:II.1 Drinking wine at noon – how so?

XXI:II.2 Secondary explanation of proof-text.

XXI:III

XXI:III.1 Chatting with children: how so?

XXI:IV

XXI:IV.1 Attending the synagogues of the ignorant: how so?

XXI:IV.2 Meir clarifies language of proof-text cited above.

XXI:V

XXI:V.1 Pertinent case of Aqiba.

XXI:I

1. A. R. Dosa b. Harkinas says, Sleeping late in the morning, drinking wine at noon, chatting with children, and attending the synagogues of the ignorant drive a man out of the world.
   B. Sleeping late in the morning: how so?
   C. This teaches that a person should not intend to sleep until the time of reciting the *Shema* has passed.

D. For when someone sleeps until the time for reciting the *Shema* has passed, he turns out to waste time that should be spent studying the Torah.

E. As it is said, The lazy one says, *There is a lion in the way, yes, a lion is in the streets. The door is turning on its hinges and the lazy man is still in bed* (Prov. 26:13-14).

The pattern is simple and clear: an amplification that links the cited saying to Torah-study. The pattern is now repeated.

XXI:II

1. A. **Drinking wine at noon**: how so?

   B. This teaches that someone should not plan to drink wine at noon.

   C. For when someone drinks wine at noon, he turns out to waste time that should be spent studying the Torah.

   D. As it is said, *Woe to you, O land, when your king is a boy and your princes feast in the morning* (Qoh. 10:16).

   E. And further: *Happy are you, O land, when your king is a free man, and your princes eat in due season, in strength and not in drunkenness* (Qoh. 10:17).

2. A. What is the meaning of *in due season*? One must say, this refers to the coming age, as it is said, *I the Lord will hasten it in its time* (Is. 60:22).

   B. And further: *After a lapse of time like this shall it be said of Jacob and of Israel, O what God has done* (Num. 23:23).

   C. So did the Holy One, blessed be he, say to the wicked Balaam, "After a period of time *like this* – but not now, not while you are standing among them, but at the time that I am going to carry out redemption for Israel [Goldin: will their king be free and prophecy be restored]."

We see the same excellent pattern as before. No. 2 carries forward the secondary explanation of language used in No. 1.

XXI:III

1. A. **Chatting with children**: how so?

   B. This teaches that a person should not plan to sit by himself and repeat traditions at home.

   C. For if someone sits by himself and repeats traditions at home, he chats with his children and dependents and turns out to waste time that should be spend in the study of the Torah.

   D For it is said, *This book of the Torah shall not depart out of your mouth, but you shall meditate in it day and night* (Josh. 1:8).

The established pattern recurs yet again. The power of the exegesis is to say the same thing about many things. Whatever the practices one should avoid, the reason is consistent: one wastes time better spent in studying the Torah.

XXI:IV

1. A. And attending the synagogues of the ignorant drive a man out of the world: how so?

   B. This teaches that a person should not plan to join with the idle in the corners of the market place.

   C. For if someone sits around with the idle in the corners of the market place, he turns out to waste time that he should spend in studying the Torah.

   D. For so it is said, *Happy is the one who has not walked in the counsel of the wicked, stood in the way of the sinners, or sat in the seat of the scornful...But his delight is in the Torah of the Lord* (Ps. 1:1-2).

2. A. R. Meir says, "What is the meaning of the statement, *sat in the seat of the scornful?*

   B. "This refers to the theaters and circuses of the gentiles, in which people are sentenced to death,

   C. "as it is said, *I hate the gathering of evil doers and will not sit with the wicked* (Ps. 26:5).

   D. "The word *evil doers* refers only to the wicked, as it is said, *For the evil doers shall be cut off, and yet a little while and the wicked is no more* (Ps. 37:9-10).

   E. "And what will be the form of the punishment that is coming to them in time to come?

   F. "*For behold the day comes, it burns as a furnace, and all the proud and all that do wickedness shall be stubble* (Ma. 3:19).

   G. "And the proud are only the scorners, as it is said, *A proud and haughty man — scorner is his name* (Prov. 21:24)."

After the replication of the base form, No. 1, we proceed to a sizable secondary expansion, developing the proof-text and showing how it leads us right to the point at which we began.

XXI:V

1. A. There was the case of R. Aqiba who was in session and repeating teachings for his disciples. He remembered something that he had done in his youth.

   B. He said, "I give thanks for you, O Lord my God, that you have placed my portion among those who sit in the house of study and have not placed my portion with those who sit idly in the market place."

This is a final appendix on the established topic.

The Fathers According to Rabbi Nathan

Chapter Twenty-Two

Hanina's saying on the importance of deeds even over Torah-study is amplified not only in the usual way but also by the citation, as proof-texts, of materials that occur in Avot itself.

> R. Hanina b. Dosa says, For anyone whose fear of sin takes precedence over his wisdom, his wisdom will endure. And for anyone whose wisdom takes precedence over his fear of sin, wisdom will not endure."
>
> He would say, Anyone whose deeds are more than his wisdom – his wisdom will endure. And anyone whose wisdom is more than his deeds – his wisdom will not endure.

XXII:I

XXII:I.1 Hanina cited, lightly glossed with scriptural proof-texts.

XXII:II

XXII:II.1 Story about Yohanan ben Zakkai that contains the same ideal as in Hanina's saying: that is, the importance of deeds as well as learning.

XXII:III-XXII:V Sayings in Avot that make the same point.

XXII:I

1. A. R. Hanina b. Dosa says, For anyone whose fear of sin takes precedence over his wisdom, his wisdom will endure. And for anyone whose wisdom takes precedence over his fear of sin, wisdom will not endure, as it is said, *The beginning of wisdom is the fear of the Lord* (Ps. 111:10).
   B. He would say, Anyone whose deeds are more than his wisdom – his wisdom will endure. And anyone whose wisdom is more than his deeds – his wisdom will not endure, as it is said, *We will do and then we will listen* (Ex. 24:7).

The base-saying is lightly glossed with proof-texts.

XXII:II

1. A. People said before Rabban Yohanan ben Zakkai, "A sage who fears sin – to what is [he comparable]?"
   B. He said to them, "Lo, such a one is a craftsman with his tools in hand."
   C. "A sage who does not fear sin?"
   D. He said to them, "Lo, this is a craftsman without his tools."
   E. "One who fears sin but is no sage?"
   F. "This is not a craftsman, but he has tools in hand."

The original saying is now given a case by way of illustration.

XXII:III

1. A. R. Eleazar b. Azariah says, If there is no learning of Torah, there is no proper conduct, if there is no proper conduct, there is no learning in 'Torah. If there is no wisdom, there is no reverence. If there is no reverence, there is no wisdom.
   B. He would say, A person who has good works and has studied much Torah – to what is he likened? To a tree that stands by water, with few branches but deep roots. Even though the four winds of the world come, they cannot move it from its place,
   C. as it is said, *He shall be as a tree planted by the waters, and that spreads out its roots by the river, and shall not fear when heat comes, and his leaf shall be green, and shall not be careful in the year of drought, neither shall cease from yielding fruit* (Jer. 17:8).
   D. A person in whom are no good deeds but who has studied much Torah – to what is he compared? To a tree that stands in the wilderness, with abundant branches but shallow roots. When the winds blow, they will uproot it and blow it down,
   E. as it is said, *He shall be like a tamarisk in the desert and shall not see when good comes, but shall inhabit the parched places in the wilderness* (Jer. 17:6).

XXII:IV

1. A. Rabban Gamaliel says, Set up a master for yourself, avoid doubt, don't tithe too much by guesswork.

XXII:V

1. A. Simeon, his son, says, All my life I have grown up among the sages and I have found nothing better for a person than silence, and not the learning is the thing but the doing, and whoever takes too much causes sin.

My best guess on why the materials from Avot are inserted here derives from Eleazar b. Azariah's and Simeon's sayings about not learning but doing being more important. That ties in with the opening saying and may represent the reason that the redactor has inserted here the entire composite at hand.

The Fathers According to Rabbi Nathan

Chapter Twenty-Three

The sayings are systematically cited and glossed, then enriched with an appendix that goes over the same ground.

> Ben Zoma says, "Who is a sage? He who learns from everybody, as it is said, *From all my teachers I have gotten understanding* (Ps. 119:99).
>
> "Who is strong? He who overcomes his desire, as it is said, *He who is slow to anger is better than the mighty, and he who rules his spirit than he who takes a city* (Prov. 16:32).
>
> "Who is rich? He who is happy in what he has, as it is said, *When you eat the labor of your hands, happy will you be, and it will go well with you* (Ps. 128:2). *Happy will you be* – in this world, *and it will go well with you* – in the world to come."
>
> "Who is honored? He who honors everybody, as it is said, *For those who honor me I shall honor, and they who despise me will be treated as of no account* (I Sam. 2:30)."
>
> R. Nehorai says, "Go into exile to a place of the Torah, and do not suppose that it will come to you. For your fellow-disciples will make it solid in your hand. And on your own understanding do not rely."

We find a paraphrase and expansion of Ben Zoma's sayings, rather than a systematic citation and gloss.

XXIII:I

XXIII:I.1 Ben Zoma cited and glossed with verses of Scripture.

XXIII:II

XXIII:II.1 Nehorai cited.

XXIII:III

XXIII:III.1 Nehorai cited and glossed.

XXIII:IV

XXIII:IV.1-2 Study the Torah in your youth sayings.

XXIII:IV.3-5 Appendix: *Study the Torah in your youthsayings* by other authorities.

XXIII:I

1. A. Ben Zoma says, "Who is a sage? He who learns from everybody, as it is said, *From all my teachers I have gotten understanding* (Ps. 119:99).

   B. "Who is the humblest of the humble? One who is as humble as our lord, Moses: *The man Moses was most modest* (Num. 12:33).

   C. "Who is the richest of the rich? He who is happy in what he has, as it is said, *When you eat the labor of your hands, happy will you be, and it will go well with you* (Ps. 128:2).

   D. "Who is the strongest of the strong? He who overcomes his desire, as it is said, *He who is slow to anger is better than the mighty, and he who rules his spirit than he who takes a city* (Prov. 16:32).

   E. "Whoever overcomes his desire is credited [by Scripture] as if he had conquered a city full of heroes, as it is said, *A wise man scales the city of the mighty and brings down the stronghold in which it trusts* (Prov. 21:22).

   F. "The mighty are only the mighty in Torah-learning, as it is said, *You mighty in strength, who carry out his word, obeying the voice of his word* (Ps. 103:20)."

   G. And some say it refers to the ministering angels, as it is said, *His angels are mighty heroes* (Ps. 103:20).

   H. And some say it is one who turns his enemy into his friend.

The wording assigned to Ben Zoma's saying varies somewhat and bears a few glosses, but the essential purpose is simply to lay out his statement and add a few biblical proof-texts.

XXIII:II

1. A. R. Nehorai says, "Go into exile to a place of the Torah, and do not suppose that it will come to you. For your fellow-disciples will make it solid in your hand. And on your own understanding do not rely."

Ben Zoma's saying is simply repeated without comment.

XXIII:III

1. A. He used to say, Do not treat anyone contemptuously, and do not regard [paraphrasing Goldin:] anything as impossible,

B. as it is said, *Whoever despises the word shall suffer from it, but whoever fears the commandment shall be rewarded* (Prov. 13:13).

XXIII:IV

1. A. He used to say, "He who studies the Torah in his youth – to what is he likened? To a calf subdued when young, as it is said, *Ephraim is a heifer well broken, that loves to thresh* (Hos. 10:11).
   B. "But he who studies the Torah in his old age – to what is he likened? To a full-grown cow that has been subdued only in its old age, as it is said, *For Israel is stubborn as a rebelling old beast* (Hos. 4:16)."
2. A. He used to say, "He who studies the Torah in his youth is like a woman who kneads using hot water. And one who studies the Torah in his old age is like a woman who kneads using cold water."
3. A. R. Eliezer b. Jacob says, "**One who studies the Torah in his youth is like writing incised on clean paper. One who studies the Torah in his old age is like writing incised on used paper.**"
   B. Rabban Gamaliel adds to his statement: "He who studies the Torah in his youth is like a youngster who married a virgin who is suitable for him and he for her, and she [Goldin:] is drawn to him and he to her.
   C. "He who studies the Torah in his old age is like an old man who married a virgin. She is suitable for him, but he is not suitable for her. She is drawn to him, but he is repelled from her,
   D. "as it is said, *Like arrows in the hand of a hero are the children of one's youth* (Ps. 127:4), and immediately afterward: *Happy is the man who has his quiver full of them, and they shall not be put to shame when they speak with their enemies in the gate* (Ps. 127:5)."
4. A. He who repeats Mishnah-traditions and forgets them is like a woman who gives birth and then buries her children,
   B. as it is said, *Yes, though they bring up their children, yet I will bereave them that there be not a man left* (Hos. 9:12).
   C. Read the letters that are pronounced *I will bereave them* to sound like *I will cause them to forget*.
5. A. R. Simeon b. Eleazar says, "He who studies the Torah in his youth is like a physician to whom people present a wound for which he has a scalpel for cutting and also drugs for healing.
   B. "He who studies the Torah in his old age is like a physician to whom people present a wound who has a scalpel for cutting but no drugs for healing.
   C. "So should the teachings of the Torah be clearly distinguished for you from one another,
   D. "clearly distinguished for you beside one another.
   E. "For it is said, *Bind them on your fingers, write them on the table of your heart* (Prov. 7:3), and also, *Bind them continually upon your heart, tie them around your neck* (Prov. 6:21)."

Nehorai's saying is cited and then glossed, and further sayings, in the style of Avot, are then added and glossed. A series of sayings on the same subject as Nehorai's is tacked on as an amplificatory appendix.

The Fathers According to Rabbi Nathan

Chapter Twenty-Four

The materials in this chapter carry forward the general theme of the contrast of good deeds and study of the Torah. The connection to the foregoing is clear at **XXIV:V.1**, and for that reason the entire chapter has to be regarded as an appendix to the foregoing. Elisha's sayings before us are not in Avot.

XXIV:I.1-XXIV:IV.1 Both good deeds and Torah-learning are necessary. Four parables that make the same point.

XXIV:V

XXIV:V.1 Studying Torah in one's youth is better than doing so in one's old age, because in the former case the teachings are absorbed in one's blood.

XXIV:VI

XXIV:VI.1 Hard to learn Torah-teachings and easy to lose them.

XXIV:VII.1 Same as above.

XXIV:VIII

XXIV:VIII.1 One should get his fellow to carry out religious duties, and if he does, he gets the credit too.

XXIV:I

1. A. Elisha b. Abuyah says, "One who has good deeds to his credit and has studied the Torah a great deal – to what is he to be likened?

   B. "To someone who builds first with stones and then with bricks. Even though a great flood of water comes and washes against the foundations, the water does not blot them out of their place.

   C "One who has no good deeds to his credit but has studied the Torah – to what is he to be likened?

   B. "To someone who builds first with bricks and then with stones. Even if only a little water comes and washes against the foundations, it forthwith overturns them."

The saying serves as a parable to expound a saying that is not before us. But if we go back to Chapter Twenty-Two, we find a comfortable niche for this saying. That suggests the probability that Elisha's chapter was worked out on its own and then situated in a suitable place, where it serves as an appendix on themes amply introduced in the two prior chapters.

XXIV:II

1. A. He used to say, "One who has good deeds to his credit and has studied the Torah a great deal – to what is he to be likened?
   B. "To lime spread over stones. Even if vast rain storms come down on them, they do not stir the lime from its place.
   C. "One who has no good deeds to his credit but has studied the Torah a great deal – to what is he to be likened?
   D. "To lime spread over bricks. Even if a sporadic rain falls on the lime, it is forthwith melted and disappears."

XXIV:III

1. A. He used to say, "One who has good deeds to his credit and has studied the Torah a great deal – to what is he to be likened?
   B. "To a cup with a base.
   C. "One who has no good deeds to his credit but has studied the Torah a great deal – to what is he to be likened?
   D. "To a cup with no base. When the cup is filled, it turns on its side and whatever is in it pours out."

XXIV:IV

1. A. He used to say, "One who has good deeds to his credit and has studied the Torah a great deal – to what is he to be likened?
   B. "To a horse that has a bridle.
   C. "One who has no good deeds to his credit but has studied the Torah a great deal – to what is he to be likened?
   D. "To a horse without a bridle. When someone rides on the horse, it throws him off with a toss of the head [Goldin: headlong]."

We go on with the same exercise. Now we come to the point of the insertion of the entire composition.

XXIV:V

1. A. He used to say, "He who studies the Torah in his youth – the words of the Torah are absorbed in his blood and come out of his mouth fully spelled out.
   B. "He who studies the Torah in his old age – the words of the Torah do not get absorbed in his blood and do not come out of his mouth fully spelled out.
   C. "And so is the apophthegm: 'If in your youth you did not want them, how will you get them in your old age?'"

The Torah-sayings move from the match of deeds to learning to a new point, and from here other Torah-sayings follow. The composition is thematic, but the inclusion in the present site entirely cogent with the larger document's plan.

XXIV:VI

1. A. He used to say, "The teachings of the Torah are as hard to acquire as golden vessels and as easy to destroy as glass ones.

   B. "For it is said, *Gold and glass cannot equal it, neither shall the exchange for it be vessels of fine gold* (Job 28:17).

   C "Gold is compared to glass. Just as golden utensils, once broken, can be fixed, while glass utensils have no remedy when broken except to be melted down [so teachings of Torah are as hard to acquire as golden vessels and easy to destroy as glass ones]. [Goldin: Scripture compares gold to glass – even as gold vessels can be mended after they have been broken, and glass vessels cannot be mended when they are broken unless they are restored to their original state.]

   D. "And what is the sense of the words *neither shall the exchange for it be vessels of fine gold* ?

   E. "This indicates that whoever works hard at them and does what they say – his face glows like gold.

   F. "But whoever works hard at them but does not do what they say – his face turns dark like glass.

The earlier theme, the importance of doing the teachings of the Torah, not merely studying them, returns. The composite on its own is thematic and not an orderly exposition of an idea concerning that theme.

XXIV:VII

1. A. He used to say, "A person can study the Torah for ten years and forget it in two years.

   B. "How so? If someone goes for six months without reviewing his learning, he turns out to declare that the unclean is clean and the clean unclean. If he goes for twelve months without reviewing, he turns out to confuse one sage with another. If he goes for eighteen months without reviewing, he turns out to forget the chapter-headings. If he goes for twenty-four months without reviewing, he turns out to forget even the tractate-headings.

   C. "Once he calls the unclean clean and the clean unclean, confuses the names of sages with one another, forgets the chapter-headings and then the tractate-headings, in the end he sits in utter silence.

   D. "In his regard, Solomon said, *I went by the field of the lazy and by the vineyard of the man void of understanding, and lo, it was all grown over with thistles, its face was covered with nettles, and its stone wall was broken down* (Prov. 24:30-31).

   E. "When the wall of the vineyard falls, the whole vineyard is ruined."

The Torah-saying-set moves on to the importance of reviewing what one knows.

XXIV:VIII

1. A. He used to say, "Whoever prevails on his fellow to carry out a religious duty is credited by Scripture as if he himself had done it personally.
   B. "The matter may be compared to the case of a mortal king who hunted a bird and gave it to one of his servants and said to him, 'Take care of this bird, and if you are careful with it, well and good, but if not, I shall take your life in its stead.'
   C. "So the Holy One, blessed be he, said to the Israelites, 'As to the words of the Torah which I have given to you, if you keep them, well and good, but if not, I shall take your life in their stead.
   D "For it is said, *Only take care of yourself and keep your soul diligently, lest you forget the things which your eyes saw, but teach them to your sons,* and it says, *For it is no vain thing for you, because it is your life* (Deut. 32:47)."

Learning and doing leads to a third category: getting someone else to do the same thing. And that completes the matter.

The Fathers According to Rabbi Nathan

Chapter Twenty-Five

The exposition of Ben Azzai's sayings begins with those not in Avot and concludes with those that are.

> Ben Azzai says, Run after the most minor religious duty as after the most important, and flee from transgression. For doing one religious duty draws in its wake doing yet another, and doing one transgression draws in its wake doing yet another. For the reward of doing a religious duty is a religious duty, and the reward of doing a transgression is a transgression.

The chapter works its way through the theme of one's demeanor at death and then proceeds to Ben Azzai's saying:

XXV:I
XXV:I.1 Ben Azzai: Omens on the death bed.

XXV:II
XXV:II.1 Death-scene of Yohanan ben Zakkai.

XXV:II.2-3 Secondary expansions of No. 1.

XXV:II.4 Conclusion of No. 1.

XXV:III
XXV:III.1 More omens on the death-bed.

XXV:IV
XXV:IV.1-5 Eliezer b. Hyrcanus"s death scene.

XXV:V-IX Further sayings of Ben Azzai.

XXV:I
1. A. Ben Azzai says, "Whoever has a serene mind on account of his learning has a good omen for himself, and who does not have a serene mind on account of his learning has a bad omen for himself.

B. "Whoever has a serene mind on account of his impulse, has a good omen for himself, but [Goldin:] if his mind is distressed because of his impulse, it is a bad sign for him.

C. "For him with whom the sages are satisfied at the hour of death it is a good sign, and for him with whom sages are not satisfied at the hour of death it is a bad sign.

D. "For whoever has his face turned upward [at death] it is a good sign, and for whoever has his face turned toward the bed it is a bad sign.

E. "If one is looking at people, it is a good sign, at the wall, a bad sign.

F. "If one's face is glistening, it is a good sign, glowering, a bad one."

The saying will now be extensively amplified with stories about sages on their death bed. But the details before us – the direction of the face and the like – are ignored; the stories are a set-piece and not made up for the larger composite before us.

XXV:II

1. A. At the time that Rabban Yohanan ben Zakkai was departing from this life, he raised up his voice and wept. His disciples said to him, "Lord, tall pillar, eternal light, mighty hammer, why are you weeping?"

B. He said to them, "Now am I going to appear before a mortal king, who, should he be angry with me, is angry only in this world, and if he should imprison me, imposes imprisonment only in this world, and if he should put me to death, imposes death only in this world, and not only so, but whom I can appease with words and bribe with money?

C. "Lo, I am going to appear before the King of kings of kings, the Holy One, blessed be he, who, should he be angry with me, is angry both in this world and in the world to come, whom I cannot appease with words or bribe with money.

D. "And furthermore, before me are two paths, one to the Garden of Eden, the other to Gehenna, and I do not know on which road, whether I shall be drawn down to Gehenna or whether I shall be brought into the Garden of Eden."

E. And in this regard it is said, *Before him shall be sentenced all those who go down to the dust, even he who cannot keep his soul alive* (Ps. 22:30).

2. A. In regard to Moses Scripture says, *And I will take away my hand and you shall see my back, but my face shall not be seen* (Ex. 33:23).

B. And further, *And he spread it before me and it was written on its face and on its back* (Ez. 2:10).

C. *Its face* refers to this world, *its back*, to the world to come.

D. Another interpretation: *its face* refers to the distress of the righteous in this world and the prosperity of the wicked in this world, *its back*, to the reward given to the righteous in the world to come, and the punishment inflicted on the wicked in Gehenna.

3. A. *And there was written therein lamentations and jubilant sound and woe* (Ez. 2:10):

B. *Lamentations* refers to the penalty inflicted on the wicked in this world, as it is said, *This is the lamentation with which they shall lament, the daughters of the nations shall lament with it* (Ez. 32:16).

C.   ...*and jubilant sound and woe* refers to the reward of the righteous in the world to come, as it is said, *With an instrument of ten strings and with the psaltery, with a jubilant sound on the harp* (Ps. 92:4).

D.   ...*and woe*: refers to the punishment that is coming to the wicked in the world to come, as it is said, *Calamity shall come upon calamity, and rumor upon rumor* (Ez. 7:26).

4.   A.   [Yohanan ben Zakkai] would say, "Clear the house on account of uncleanness and prepare a throne for King Hezekiah of Judah."

The introduction of Ben Azzai's statement on one's attitude at death triggers the insertion of death-scenes, together with secondary materials associated with them. No. 1 provides Yohanan b. Zakkai's, and that story surely does not illustrate any of the good omens Ben Azzai has mentioned. No. 2 goes on to Moses, though I see no evidence that his death scene is at hand, and the secondary development through No. 4 gives no indication that the compiler has death-scenes in mind at all in his treatment of the cited base-verses. So I cannot account for the inclusion of Nos. 2-4.

XXV:III

1.   A.   [Ben Azzai] would say, "If one dies in a serene mind, it is a good omen from him, in derangement, it is a bad omen.

B.   "...while speaking, it is a good omen, in silence, a bad omen.

C.   "...in repeating words of the Torah, it is a good omen for him, in the midst of discussing business, it is a bad omen.

D.   "...while doing a religious duty, it is a good omen, while involved with a trivial matter, it is a bad omen.

E.   "...while happy, it is a good omen, while sad, a bad omen.

F.   "...while laughing, a good omen, while weeping, a bad omen.

G.   "...on the eve of the Sabbath, a good omen, at the end of the Sabbath, a bad omen.

H.   "...on the eve of the Day of Atonement a bad omen, at the end of the Day of Atonement a good omen.

After the sizable interruption illustrating the first unit of the sayings, we revert to the completion of Ben Azzai's statement on this theme. A mark of the end of a systematic list is the change in the established pattern, as at H.

XXV:IV

1.   A.   When R. Eliezer was dying – they say it was the eve of the Sabbath [toward dusk] – R. Aqiba and his colleagues came in to see him, and he was dozing in the room, sitting back [Goldin:] on a canopied couch. They took seats in the waiting room. Hyrcanus his son came in to remove his phylacteries [which are worn on week days but not on the Sabbath, about to begin]. But he did not let him do so, and he was weeping.

B.   Hyrcanus went out and said to the sages, "My lords, it appears to me that my father is deranged."

C [Eliezer] said to him, "My son, I am not the one who is deranged, but you are the one who is deranged. For you have neglected to light the lamp for the Sabbath, on which account you may become liable to death penalty inflicted by heaven, but busied yourself with the matter of the phylacteries, on account of which liability is incurred, at worst, merely on the matter of violating the rules of Sabbath rest."

D. Since sages saw that he was in full command of his faculties, they came in and took up seats before him, but at a distance of four cubits [as was required, because Eliezer was in a state of ostracism on account of his rejection of the decision of the majority in a disputed case]. [Bringing up the case subject to dispute, so to determine whether he had finally receded to the decision of the majority,] they said to him, "My lord, as to a round cushion, a ball, [a shoe when placed on] a shoe maker's last, an amulet, and phylacteries that have been torn, what is the law as to their being susceptible to uncleanness? [Are they regarded as completed and useful objects, therefore susceptible, or as useless or incomplete and therefore not susceptible?]"

E. [Maintaining his earlier position,] he said to them, "They remain susceptible to uncleanness, and should they become unclean, immerse them as is [without undoing them, e.g., exposing their contents to the water], and take great pains in these matters, for these represent important laws that were stated to Moses at Sinai."

F. They persisted in addressing to him questions concerning matters of insusceptibility and susceptibility to uncleanness as well as concerning immersion-pools, saying to him, "My lord, what is the rule on this matter?"

G. He would say to them, "Clean."

H. And so he went, giving the answer of susceptible to uncleanness to an object that could become unclean, and insusceptible to one that could not become unclean.

I. After a while R. Eliezer said to sages, "I am amazed at the disciples of the generation, perhaps they are liable to the death penalty at the hand of Heaven."

J. They said to him, "My lord, on what account?"

K. He said to them, "Because you never came and performed the work of apprenticeship to me."

L. Then he said to Aqiba b. Joseph, "Aqiba, on what account did you not come before me and serve as apprentice to me?"

M. He said to him, "My lord, I had no time."

N. He said to him, "I shall be surprised for you if you die a natural death."

O. And some say, He said nothing to him, but when R. Eliezer spoke as he did to his disciples, forthwith [Aqiba's] [Goldin:] heart melted within him.

P. Said to him R. Aqiba, "My lord, how will I die?"

Q. He said to him, "Aqiba, yours will be the worst."

2. A. R. Aqiba entered and took a seat before him and said to him, "My lord, now repeat traditions for me."

B. He opened a subject and repeated for him three hundred rules concerning the bright spot [to which Lev. 13:1ff. refers in connection with the skin ailment translated as leprosy].

C. Then R. Eliezer raised his two arms and folded them on his breast and said, "Woe is me for these two arms, like two scrolls of Torahs, which now are departing from the world.

D. "For were all the oceans ink, all the reeds quills, all men scribes, they could not write down what I have learned in Scripture and repeated in Mishnah-traditions, and derived as lessons from my apprenticeship to sages in the session.

E. "Yet I have taken away from my masters only as much as does a person who dips his finger into the ocean, and I have taken away for my disciples only so much as a paintbrush takes from a paint tube.

F. "And furthermore, I can repeat three hundred laws on the rule: *You shall not permit a sorceress to live*."

G. Some say, "Three thousand."

3. A. "But no one ever asked me anything about it, except for Aqiba b. Joseph.

B. "For one time he said to me, 'My lord, teach me how people plant cucumbers and how they pull them up.'

C. "I said something and the entire field was filled with cucumbers.

D. "He said to me, 'My lord, you have taught me how they are planted. Teach me how they are pulled up.'

E. "I said something, and all of the cucumbers assembled in a single place."

4. A. Said R. Eleazar b. Azariah to him, "My lord, as to a shoe that is on the shoemaker's last, what is the law? [Is it susceptible to uncleanness, as a useful object, or insusceptible, since it is not fully manufactured and so finished as a useful object?]"

B. He said to him, "It is insusceptible to uncleanness."

C. And so he continued giving answers to questions, ruling of an object susceptible to uncleanness that it is susceptible, and of one insusceptible to uncleanness that it is permanently clean, until his soul went forth as he said the word, "Clean."

D. Then R. Eleazar b. Azariah tore his clothes and wept, going forth and announcing to sages, "My lords, come and see R. Eliezer, for he is not in a state of purity as to the world to come, since his soul went forth with the word pure on his lips."

5. A. After the Sabbath R. Aqiba came and found [Eliezer's corpse being conveyed for burial] on the road from Caesarea to Lud. Then he tore his clothes and ripped his hair, and his blood flowed, and he fell to the earth, crying out and weeping, saying, "Woe is me for you, my Lord, woe is me, my master, for you have left the entire generation orphaned."

B. At the row of mourners he commenced [the lament,] saying, "*My father, my father, chariot of Israel and its horsemen!* I have coins but no expert money-changer to sort them out."

The snippets of death-scenes of Eliezer are sewn together, but the distinct components are fairly easy to recognize, through the repetitions, on the one side, and the shifts in setting and premise as to the location of authorities, on the other. But the flow is smooth, beginning to end, a credit to the compiler. The detail of No. 1 becomes a main point later on, that is, the ruling on objects Eliezer had held subject to uncleanness, sages taking the opposite view. No. 1

moves along to the complaint of Eliezer that the disciples had kept their distance from him. No. 2 picks up at this point, but by introducing Aqiba, suggests that the tale is distinct from the foregoing, which already has him on the scene. The same happens later with Eleazar b. Azariah's paragraph. No. 3 then goes back over the matter of No. 2 – the distance of the disciples – and goes over its own point. No. 4 does not appear to know anything about much that has gone before, as I said, and No. 5 is independent as well, since up to now we have had Aqiba at the death scene, while here Aqiba finds out about the death only after the Sabbath and on a different set. The story serves as a good illustration for some of the positive omens Ben Azzai has listed, though not many of them, and I think that is a minor consideration.

XXV:V

1. A. **Ben Azzai says, Run after the most minor religious duty** and flee from a transgression."

We have a light gloss of the next relevant saying.

XXV:VI

1. A. He would say, "If you have fulfilled one religious duty and do not regret it, in the end it will bring about the doing of many more religious duties, and if you have done one transgression and do not worry about that transgression, in the end it will cause the doing of many more transgressions,

   B. "for doing one religious duty draws in its wake doing yet another, and doing one transgression draws in its wake doing yet another. For the reward of doing a religious duty is a religious duty, and the reward of doing a transgression is a transgression."

The matter is somewhat restated, but the basic point is clear.

XXV:VII

1. A. He would say, "On your own refrain [from sinning] [following Goldin], and there will be a reward for your restraint.

   B. "But do not wait for other people to make you refrain and get the reward for holding you back."

XXV:VIII

1. A. He would say, "Go two or three steps below the place suitable for you and take your seat there.

   B. "It is better for people to say to you, 'Go up,' than that they should say to you, 'Go down.'

   C. "For so it is said, *For it is better that it should be said to you, Come up hither, than that you should be put lower in the presence of the prince, whom your eyes have seen* (Prov. 25:7)."

The further saying is given its own amplification, as though it had appeared in Avot.

XXV:IX

1. A. There are three whose lives are no life, and these are they: one who depends on the table of his fellow, one who lives in a cramped attic, and one whose wife runs his life.

   B. And some say, "One whose suffering controls his body."

The further saying lacks all further comment.

XXV:X

1. A. He would say, "It is easier to rule the whole world than to sit and repeat Mishnah-traditions before people clothed in linen."

The rather odd final saying is not explained. My guess is that he is saying rich people cannot humble themselves to study the Torah.

The Fathers According to Rabbi Nathan

Chapter Twenty-Six

This chapter simply lays out sayings, with little or no secondary development over all.

R. Aqiba says, "Laughter and lightheadedness turn lewdness into a habit. Tradition is a fence for the Torah. Tithes are a fence for wealth. Vows are a fence for abstinence. A fence for wisdom is silence."

R. Eleazar the Modite says, "He who treats Holy Things as secular, and he who despises the appointed times, he who humiliates his fellow in public, he who removes the signs of the covenant of Abraham, our father, (may he rest in peace), and he who exposes aspects of the Torah not in accord with the law, even though he has in hand learning in the Torah and good deeds, will have no share in the world to come."

XXVI:I

XXVI:I.1 Sayings of Aqiba cited.

XXVI:II

XXVI:II.1 More sayings of Aqiba. Proof-text tacked on.

XXVI:III-V Further sayings of Aqiba.

XXVI:VI

XXVI:VI.1 Simeon b. Eliezer provides a restatement of Aqiba's view.

XXVI:VII

XXVI:VII.1 Eliezer the Modite's sayings.

XXVI:VIII-IX Further sayings of Aqiba.

XXVI:X-XI Sayings of Judah b. Ilai, Eliezer Haqqappar.

XXVI:I

1. A. R. Aqiba says, "A fence for honor is not acting in a silly way, **a fence for wisdom is silence, a fence for vows is abstaining [from vowing]**, a fence for sanctity is cleanness, a fence for humility is fear of sin."

The collection of sayings attributed to Aqiba follows the laconic form dominant in the document. Why the interest in the secondary precautions for primary concerns now recurs I cannot say. None of this was invoked in our amplification of those who made a fence around their words.

XXVI:II

1. A. He would say, "Do not come among gentiles, lest you learn from what they do. Do not eat bread with a priest who does not observe the rules of cultic cleanness properly, lest you commit sacrilege against Holy Things [given to the priest to eat, which the priest may not consume in accord with the law].

   B. "Do not break out in vows, lest you commit sacrilege [even] against oaths. Do not become accustomed to eating at banquets, lest you end up eating what is [Goldin] forbidden to you. Do not get involved in what is doubt[fully forbidden], lest you end up involved in what is certainly forbidden. And do not go outside of the Land [of Israel], lest you worship idols.

   C. "For lo, David is the one who says, *For they have driven me out this day that I should not cleave to the inheritance of the Lord, saying, Go serve other gods* (1 Sam. 26:19).

   D. "Now can you imagine that King David would ever have served idols? But this is what David said, 'Whoever abandons the Land of Israel and goes outside of the Land is regarded by Scripture as though he were an idolater.'"

The more usual presentation, an apophthegm followed by a biblical proof, either exemplary or textual, is now followed.

XXVI:III

1. A. He would say, "Whoever is buried in other lands is as though he were buried in Babylonia. Whoever is buried in Babylonia is as if he were buried in the Land of Israel. Whoever is buried in the Land of Israel is as if he were buried under the altar.

   B. "For the whole of the Land of Israel is suitable as a location for the altar.

   C. "And whoever is buried under the altar is as if he were buried under the throne of glory.

   D. "As it is said, *You throne of glory, on high from the beginning, you place of our sanctuary* (Jer. 17:12)."

The apophthegm is of course unitary, bearing its own proof-text, as in the former instance.

XXVI:IV

1. A. He would say, "A common person cannot be pious, nor can a shy person learn, nor can an impatient person teach."

XXVI:V

1. A. He would say, "Why do disciples of sages die young? Not because they commit adultery nor because they steal, but because they leave off the study of words of the Torah and take up idle conversation, and, furthermore, because they do not take up at the place at which they left off."

The repertoire of Aqiba's apophthegms unfolds with little secondary development.

XXVI:VI

1. A. R. Simeon b. Eliezer says, "Israelites who live outside of the Land worship idols [Goldin:] in all innocence.
   B. "How so? A gentile who makes a banquet for his son sends and invites all the Jews in his town. Even though they bring and eat their own food and drink their own wine and take along their own servant who stands over them and pours for them, Scripture regards them as though they had eaten from sacrifices of corpses, as it is said, *And they will invite you and you will eat of their sacrifice* (Ex. 34:15)."

Simeon expands on Aqiba's statement, which is why the passage is tacked on. This is a mark that we now turn to a new piece of material.

XXVI:VII

1. A. R. Eliezer the Modite says, "He who violates the Sabbath and treats the appointed times with contempt, **he who removes the signs of the covenant of circumcision, and he who exposes aspects of the Torah, even though he has in hand learning in the Torah and good deeds, will have no share in the world to come."**

Our version differs in some minor details from that in Avot.

XXVI:VIII

1. A. R. Aqiba says, "Whoever marries a woman inappropriate to his station in life violates no fewer than five negative commandments: *not taking vengeance* (Lev. 19:19), *not bearing a grudge* (Lev. 19:19), *not hating your brother in your heart* (Lev. 19:17), *loving your neighbor as yourself* (Lev. 19:18), *that your brother may live with you* (Lev. 25:36).

B. "Since he hates her, moreover, he wants her to die, and will therefore turn out to neglect the religious duty of procreation."

The point now is that the husband will not treat with esteem the wife who is unfit for him, and so he will violate the rules that prohibit a person from the deeds listed above. The saying itself is not provided with proof-texts, since the catalogue of verses of Scripture are integral.

XXVI:IX

1. A. He would say, "He who eats food which [Goldin:] does not agree with him violates three negative commandments, for he has treated himself with contempt, treated food with disrespect, and said a blessing [for the food] which is inappropriate [since the food has brought no blessing]."

XXVI:X

1. A. R. Judah b. Ilai says, "He who dies and left a son who has not learned the Torah from his father, and [after the father's death] goes and studies the Torah from other people – lo this one seeks compliments."

XXVI:XI

1. A. R. Eliezer Haqqappar says, "Do not be like the highest lintel, which people cannot reach up and touch, nor like the lintel on high, which... [what follows makes no sense], nor like the middle lintel, which bruises peoples' feet, but be like the lowest one, on which everyone tramples, for in the end, even though the entire building is demolished, that lintel still remains in its place."

The several sayings are simply laid forth without comment.

The Fathers According to Rabbi Nathan

Chapter Twenty-Seven

The chapter presents comments and expansions of a number of discrete sayings.

R. Yose says, "Whoever honors the Torah himself is honored by people. And whoever disgraces the Torah himself is disgraced by people."

R. Ishmael, his son, says, "He who learns so as to teach – they give him a chance to learn and to teach. He who learns so as to carry out his teachings – they give him a chance to learn, to teach, to keep, and to do."

He [Tarfon] would say: "It's not your job to finish the work, but you are not free to walk away from it. If you have learned much Torah, they will give you a good reward. And your employer· can be depended upon to pay your wages for what you do. And know what sort of reward is going to be given to the righteous in the coming time."

R. Eleazar Hisma says, "The laws of bird-offerings and of the beginning of the menstrual period – they are indeed the essentials of the Torah. Calculation of the equinoxes and reckoning the numerical value of letters are the savories of wisdom."

Rabbi Tarfon says: "The day is short, the work formidable, the workers lazy, the wages high, the employer impatient."

R. Eleazar b. Shammua says, "The honor owing to your disciple should be as precious to you as yours. And the honor owing to your fellow should be like the reverence owing to your master. And the reverence owing to your master should be like the awe owing to Heaven."

XXVII:I

XXVII:I.1 Yose cited and glossed with 1 Sam. 2:30.

XXVII:II

   XXVII:II.1 Further interpretation of 1 Sam. 2:30. Proof-text: Song 1:9.

   XXVII:II.2 Further interpretation of Song 1:9.

   XXVII:II.3 Reversion to **XXVII:II.1**.

   XXVII:II.4 As above.

XXVII:III

   XXVII:III.1 Ishmael cited.

XXVII:IV

   XXVII:IV.1 Tarfon cited.

XXVII:V

   XXVII:V.1 Eleazar Hisma cited.

XXVII:VI

   XXVII:VI.1 Foregoing complemented by Yohanan b. Nuri.

XXVII:VII

   XXVII:VII.1 More in name of Yohanan b. Nuri.

XXVII:VIII

   XXVII:VIII.1 Saying of Yohanan b. Danabai.

XXVII:IX

   XXVII:IX.1 Tarfon cited.

XXVII:X

   XXVII:X.1 Tarfon further cited, with parable.

XXVII:XI

   XXVII:XI.1 Eleazar b. Shammua cited and glossed.

XXVII:XII

   XXVII:XII.1 Saying included for no clear reason.

Apart from the final item, the plan and program of the chapter follow a clear plan.

XXVII:I

1. A. R. Yose says, "Whoever honors the Torah himself is honored by people. And whoever disgraces the Torah himself is disgraced by people."

B.   For it is said, *For those that honor me shall I honor, and those that abuse me will be treated as null* (1 Sam. 2:30).

A proof-text is tacked on to the cited saying.

XXVII:II

1. A.   Another interpretation of *For those that honor me shall I honor, and those that abuse me will be treated as null* (1 Sam. 2:30):

    B.   This refers to Pharaoh, king of Egypt, who treated with respect Him who spoke and by his word brought the world into being. For he came forth at the head of his retinue. His staff said to him, "The custom of the world is that all kings go forth only after their retinue, but you have gone forth at the head of your retinue."

    C.   "He said to them, "Am I going to greet a mortal king? Am I not going to greet the King of kings of kings, the Holy One, blessed be he?"

    D.   Therefore the Holy One, blessed be he, treated him with respect and exacted punishment only through his own personal intervention [not by angels],

    E.   as it is said, *I have compared you, O my love, to my own horse, which charged against Pharaoh's chariots* (Song 1:9).

2. A.   R. Pappias says, "[In the cited verse of Song of Songs,] the congregation of Israel was praising [Goldin: what God did against] the cavalry and chariotry of Pharaoh.

    B.   "For it is said, *You have trodden the sea with your horses* (Hab. 3:15)."

3. A.   R. Joshua b. Qorha says, "When Pharaoh came to the sea, he rode a stallion, and the Holy One, blessed be he, appeared to him on a mare,

    B.   "as it is said, *To my mare among Pharaoh's chariots* (Song 1:9)."

    C.   But is it not the case that he rode only on a cherub, as it is said, *And he rode upon a cherub and did fly, yes, he swooped down on the wings of the wind* (Ps. 18:11)?

    D.   The cherub appeared to Pharaoh's stallions as a mare and all of them [in heat] pursued it into the sea.

4. A.   *[For those that honor me shall I honor,] and those that abuse me will be treated as null* (1 Sam. 2:30):

    B.   This latter clause refers to Sennacherib, King of Assyria, as it is said, *By your servants have you taunted the Lord and have said, With the mass of my chariots I have come up to the heights of the mountains, to the innermost parts of Lebanon, and I have cut down the tall cedars of Lebanon, and the choice cypress trees thereof, and I have entered into his farthest height, the forest of his fruitful field* (Is. 37:24).

    C.   Accordingly, the Holy One, blessed be he, treated him with utter contempt, and exacted a penalty from him only through an angel,

    D.   as it is said, *And the angel of the Lord went forth and smote in the camp of the Assyrians a hundred and four score and five thousand, and when men rose up early in the morning, behold, they were all corpses* (Is. 37:36).

The proof-text cited above at No. 1 is given its own sizable amplification. Then, at No. 2, the proof-text of No. 1 is given a secondary treatment as well.

No. 3 contributes the same to the proof-text of No. 1. No. 4 then reverts to the primary proof-text of No. 1. So we introduce first Pharaoh, then Sennacherib, contrasting the honorable treatment of the one, who had treated God with respect, as against the contemptuous treatment accorded to the other.

XXVII:III

1. A. R. Ishmael says, He who learns so as to teach – they give him a chance to learn and to teach. He who learns so as to carry out his teachings – they give him a chance to learn, to teach, to keep, and to do.

XXVII:IV

1. A. He [Avot: Tarfon] would say: It's not your job to finish the study of the entire Torah, but you are not free to walk away from it. But to whoever puts in great effort and masters more [of the Torah] do they add a great reward.

XXVII:V

1. A. R. Eleazar b. Hisma says, The laws of bird-offerings and of the beginning of the menstrual period – they are indeed the essentials of the laws. Calculation of the equinoxes and reckoning the numerical value of letters are the savories of wisdom.

XXVII:VI

1. A. R. Yohanan b. Nuri says, "The laws, the rules of cultic cleanness, and the regulations on the menstrual period and on bird-offerings – lo, they are the essentials of the Torah."

XXVII:VII

1. A. He would say, "Laying out a sizable spread, building courts of justice and maintaining them bring good to the world."

After the citation of further sayings, **XXVII:III-V**, we have a minor development at **XXVII:VI-VIII** with some secondary additions.

XXVII:VIII

1. A. R. Yohanan b. Dahabai says, "He who says, 'This law does not make sense to me' has no share in the world to come."

XXVII:IX

1. A. Rabbi Tarfon says: The day is short, the work formidable, the workers lazy, the wages high, the employer impatient. And know that the reward that is coming to the righteous in the time to come is great.

XXVII:X

1. A. He would say, "Do not keep your distance from a good trait without limit and from labor without end.
   B. "There is a parable. To what may the matter be compared? To someone who was [hired for the purpose of] drawing water from the sea and pouring it out on the land. The one loses nothing, the other is not filled up.
   C. "He got impatient. People said to him, 'Fool, why get impatient? For the entire day of work, get your salary – which is a gold *denar*!'"

We have a further set of sayings. One bears a parable, as well it should. For its point is otherwise not explicit. One should indulge without limit in a good quality and study the Torah without stinting, even though he or she will never learn it all.

XXVII:XI

1. A. R. Eleazar b. Shammua says, The honor owing to your disciple should be as precious to you as yours. And the honor owing to your fellow should be like the reverence owing to your master. And the reverence owing to your master should be like the awe owing to Heaven.
   B. How do we know that the honor owing to one's disciple should be as precious to one as his own?
   C. Let everyone learn from the case of our lord, Moses, who said to Joshua, *Choose men for us* (Ex. 17:9).
   D. He did not say to him, "Choose men for *me*," but for *us*, teaching that he treated him like himself [as an equal], even though he was his master and Joshua was his disciple.
   E. How do we know that the honor owing to one's fellow should be like the reverence owing to his master?
   F. As it is said, *And Aaron said to Moses, Please, my lord* (Num. 12:11).
   G. Now was Moses not younger than he? But he treated him as his master.
   H. And how do we know that the reverence owing to one's master should be like the awe owing to Heaven?
   I. As it is said, *And Joshua b. Nun, servant of Moses from his youth, answered and said, My lord, Moses, destroy them* (Num. 11:28), so treating Moses as though he were equal [in power] to the Presence of God.

The cited saying is systematically spelled out with proof-texts.

XXVII:XII

1. A. Since to begin with people said, "There is grain in Judea, straw in Galilee, and chaff in Transjordan," they reverted and said, "There is no grain in Judah but straw, no straw in Galilee but chaff, and in Transjordan, neither this nor that."

I have no idea what this saying is meant to convey or why it is presented here.

The Fathers According to Rabbi Nathan

Chapter Twenty-Eight

While most of the sayings before us are not in Avot, the chapter treats the following saying:

> Hillel says: Do not walk out on the community. And do not have confidence in yourself until the day you die. And do not judge your companion until you are in his place. And do not say anything which cannot be heard, for in the end it will be heard. And do not say: When I have time, I shall study, for you may never have time.
>
> He would say: Lots of meat, lots of worms; lots of property, lots of worries; lots of women, lots of witchcraft; lots of slave girls, lots of lust; lots of slave boys, lots of robbery.   Lots of the Torah, lots of life; lots of discipleship, lots of wisdom; lots of counsel, lots of understanding; lots of righteousness, lots of peace. [If] one has gotten a good name, he has gotten it for himself.   [If] he has gotten teachings of the Torah, he has gotten himself life eternal.

The chapter follows a simple outline, citing and lightly glossing the materials its authorship has chosen as its base-sayings.

XXVIII:I

XXVIII:I.1   Saying of Nathan on the outstanding traits of various parties, e.g., the Torah, Land of Israel, Jerusalem, Rome, Persia, the Arabs, etc.

XXVIII:II

XXVIII:II.1   Further saying on the superiority of the Torah-study of Land of Israel.

XXVIII:III

XXVIII:III.1   Simeon b. Gamaliel-saying.

XXVIII:IV-V Gamaliel-sayings.

XXVIII:VI-VIII Judah the Patriarch-sayings.

XVIII:IX-X Hillel-sayings.

XXVIII:XI

   XXVIII:XI.1 Eleazar b. Shammua's sayings.

XXVIII:XII

XXVIII:XII.1 Judah b. Ilai's sayings.

Perhaps the group around the house of the patriarch, **XXVIII:III-X**, was assembled to join the names of those particular figures, but what is given fore and aft has no relationship. The overall themes of the several sayings do not seem to me cogent.

XXVIII:I

1. A. R. Nathan says, "You have no love like the love for the Torah, wisdom like the wisdom of the Land of Israel, beauty like the beauty of Jerusalem, wealth like the wealth of Rome, power like the power of Persia, lewdness like the lewdness of the Arabs, arrogance like the arrogance of Elam, hypocrisy like the hypocrisy of Babylonia —
   B. "as it is said, *And he said to me, to build her a house in the land of Shinar* [Zech. 5:11]) —
   C. "or witchcraft like the witchcraft of Egypt."

Apart from the proof-text at B, the saying is unadorned and not later on developed.

XXVIII:II

1. A. R. Simeon b. Eleazar says, "A sage who has dwelled in the Land of Israel and then left for overseas becomes flawed. One who remains in the Land is more praiseworthy than he.
   B. "And even though the former is flawed, he is nonetheless more praiseworthy than all those who live in other lands [never having lived in the Land].
   C. "The matter yields a parable. To what may it be likened? To Indian iron that comes from overseas. Even though it is less than it was, it is still better than the best iron made in all other lands."

Simeon expands on Nathan's statement that there is no wisdom like the wisdom of the sages of the Land of Israel. We may take for granted that our document originates in the Land of Israel.

XXVIII:III

1. A. R. Simeon b. Gamaliel says, "Whoever brings peace to his own household is credited by Scripture as though he brought peace in Israel, for every individual.

   B. "And whoever brings envy and contention into his household is as if he brought envy and contention in Israel.

   C. "For everyone is the monarch in his own household.

   D. "As it is said, *That every man should rule in his own household* (Est. 1:22)."

The apophthegm bears only a minor proof-text.

XXVIII:IV

1. A. R. Gamaliel says, "In four ways the empire [of Rome] supports itself: tolls, baths, theaters, and crop-levies."

XXVIII:V

1. A. He would say, "The words of Torah are as hard to acquire as garments made of fine wool and easy to destroy as linen garments.

   B. "Silly words and vulgarity are as easy to acquire and as hard to destroy as sack-cloth.

   C. "On occasion someone may buy a sack in the market place for a *sela* and use it for four or five years."

The apophthegm is clearly worked out and given a minor parable at C.

XXVIII:VI

1. A. R. Judah the Patriarch says, "From whoever is glad to get the pleasures of this world are held back the pleasures of the world to come.

   B. "And to whoever is not glad to get the pleasures of this world are given the pleasures of the world to come."

XXVIII:VII

1. A. He would say, "As to the righteous who have it bad in this world, to what are they compared? To a cook who fixes a meal for himself. Even though he has to trouble himself, he is preparing not for others but for himself.

   B. "But as to the wicked who have it bad in this world, to what are they compared? To a cook who fixes a meal for others. He has to trouble himself, and he is preparing not for himself but for others."

XXVIII:VIII

1. A. He would say, "Let your actions in secret in your own view be as though they were in public.

   B. "And something which it would be inappropriate [for a third party] to hear do not repeat to your fellow."

The several sayings are given in a plain way, without extensive development.

XXVIII:IX

1. A. Hillel says: Do not walk out on the community. And do not have confidence in yourself until the day you die. And do not judge your companion until you are in his place. And do not say anything which cannot be heard, for in the end it will be heard. And do not say: When I have time, I shall study, for you may never have time.

XXVIII:X

1. A. He would say: Lots of eating, lots of shitting. Lots of meat, lots of worms and maggots.
   B. Whoever does many good deeds brings peace for himself.

I assume that Hillel's statement about not saying anything which cannot be heard, linked in conception to XXVIII:VIII.1.B, explains why the entire passage has been inserted.

XXVIII:XI

1. A. R. Eleazar b. Shammua says, "There are three traits that may characterize disciples of sages: they may be like either hewn stone, a corner stone, or a polished stone.
   B. "A hewn stone: how so? This is a disciple who has studied exegesis. When a disciple of a sage comes to him and asks him an exegesis, he can report it to him. This then characterizes the hewn stone, who has only one surface [Goldin: for only one of its sides is exposed] [and in the case of the disciple, knows what he knows, that alone].
   C. "A corner stone: how so? This is a disciple who studies exegesis and laws. When a disciple of a sage comes and asks him something concerning exegesis, he can report it to him. If he should ask concerning laws, he can report it to him. This is the foundation stone, which has only two exposed surfaces.
   D. "A polished stone: how so? This refers to a disciple who has studied exegesis, laws, narratives, supplements. When a disciple of a sage comes and asks him something concerning exegesis, he can report it to him. If he should ask concerning laws, he can answer, concerning supplements, he can answer, concerning narratives, he can answer. This is a polished stone, which has four exposed surfaces, in all four directions."

Eleazar's saying is fully developed and applied to the life of sages. I see no connection with anything in its larger setting.

XXVIII:XII

1. A. R. Judah b. Ilai says, "Whoever treats the words of the Torah as the main thing and earning a living as trivial is treated as the main thing in the world to come.

   B. "...earning a living as the main thing and the words of the Torah as second is treated as trivial in the world to come.

   C. "There is the following parable: to what may the matter be compared?

   D. "To a path that goes between two roads, one of fire, the other of snow. If one walks toward the fire, lo, he is burned by the fire, and if he walks toward the snow, low, he is frozen by the cold.

   E. "What should he do? He should go between the two and take care not to be burned by the fire or frozen by the cold."

The saying is supplied with a parable, indicating that one should hold in the balance studying the Torah and earning a living. But the parable then contradicts Judah's statement, which says that one should stress only the former and treat the latter as secondary and trivial.

The Fathers According to Rabbi Nathan

Chapter Twenty-Nine

The chapter rather austerely presents sayings of sages, with slight amplification of any kind. That makes all the more puzzling the rather rich selection of sayings with no counterpart in Avot, such as we have reviewed in the current sequence of chapters.

> R. Simeon b. Eleazar says, Do not try to make amends with your fellow when he is angry, or comfort him when the corpse of his beloved is lying before him, or seek to find absolution for him at the moment at which he takes a vow, or attempt to see him when he is humiliated.
>
> R. Matya b. Harash says, Greet everybody first, and be a tail to lions. But do not be a head of foxes.

All I see is a sequence of cited sayings, most of them lacking all development.

XXIX:I-IV Simeon b. Eleazar cited.

XXIX:V

    XXIX:V.1 Abba Saul b. Nannos: Four traits in a disciple.

XXIX:VI

    XXIX:VI.1 Hanania b. Jacob's sayings.

XXIX:VII

    XXIX:VII.1-3 Eliezer Haqqappar's sayings.

XXIX:VIII

    XXIX:VIII.1 Mattia consults Eleazar Haqqappar [sic] on a teaching of Ishmael.

XXIX:IX

    XXIX:IX.1 Issi b. Judah's saying.

XXIX:X-XII Isaac b. Phineas's sayings.

XXIX:I

1. A. R. Simeon b. Eleazar says in the name of R. Meir, **Do not try to make amends with your fellow when he is angry, or comfort him when the corpse of his beloved is lying before him, or seek to find absolution for him at the moment at which he takes a vow,** or come to his house on a day on which he has suffered a reverse, **or attempt to see him when he is humiliated.**

XXIX:II

1. A. He would say, "If you have friends, some of him give you criticism and some of whom give you praise, love the ones who give you criticism and hate the ones who give you praise.

   B. "For the ones who give you criticism will bring you to the life of the world to come, while the ones who give you praise will remove you from the world."

XXIX:III

1. A. He would say, "Wherever a person goes, his heart follows. If he stops, his heart stops. If he sits, things settle down for him [Goldin: wheresoever he sits, things are clarified for him]."

XXIX:IV

1. A. He would say, "To whoever pays careful attention to teachings of the Torah they give those who will keep watch over him.

   B. "And to whoever pays slight attention to the words of the Torah they give [Goldin:] [forces] that will make him idle,

   C. "for instance, a lion, wolf, panther, leopard, snake.

   D. "bandits or muggers will come and surround him and exact a penalty from him,

   E. "as it is said, *God has his chastisers on the earth* (Ps. 58:12)."

The sequence of sayings bears slight amplification, except at the end. There are variations in wording, as indicated, and the further sayings are not in Avot.

XXIX:V

1. A. Abba Saul b. Nannos says, "There are four traits in a disciple of a sage:

   B. "There is one who studies for himself but does not teach others, there is one who teaches others but does not teach himself, there is one who teaches himself and others, and one who does not teach himself or others.

   C. "There is one who studies for himself but does not teach others: how so? If someone repeats one or two or even three divisions [of the Mishnah] but does not repeat them to others, occupying himself with them and not forgetting them, this is someone who studies for himself but does not teach others.

D. "There is one who teaches others but does not teach himself: how so? If someone studied a division or two or three and repeated them for others, but did not occupy himself with them and ultimately forgot them, this is someone who teaches others but does not teach himself.

E. "There is one who teaches himself and others: how so? If someone repeated a division, two or three, and repeated them for others and occupied himself with them and did not forget them, held on to them and the others do too, that is one who teaches himself and others.

F. "And one who does not teach himself or others: how so? If someone repeated a division two or three times but did not repeat them for others and did not occupy himself with them and ultimately forgot them, this is one who does not teach himself or others."

The saying is fully spelled out as given.

XXIX:VI

1. A. R. Hanania b. Jacob says, "He who wakes up in the middle of the night on account of words of the Torah has a good omen for himself. If it is on account of the words of an idle conversation he may have had, it is a bad omen for him."

B. R. Jacob b. Hanania says, "He who wakes up in the middle of the night and does not open his mouth with words of the Torah, it would have been befitting for him and better for him had the afterbirth of his mother been turned over on his face [to suffocate him as an infant] so that he should not go forth into the air of the world or see the world."

B's rather ferocious saying simply repeats the sentiment of A.

XXIX:VII

1. A. R. Eliezer Haqqappar says, "Whoever honors his fellow for the sake of money in the end will take his leave from him in disgrace, but whoever treats his fellow lightly on account of [a prior obligation to perform] a religious duty in the end will take his leave from him in dignity."

B. "And how do we know that whoever honors his fellow for the sake of money in the end will take his leave from him in disgrace?

C. "For so we find in the case of the wicked Balaam, who paid honor to Balak for monetary considerations, as it is said, *And Balaam answered and said to the servants of Balak, if Balak would give me his house full of silver and gold* (Num. 22:19).

D. "And how do we know that in the end he took his leave from him in disgrace? As it is said, *Therefore now flee you to your own place...but lo, the Lord has kept you back from honor* (Num. 24:11).

E. "And how do we know that whoever treats his fellow lightly on account of a religious duty in the end will take his leave from him in dignity?

F. "For so we find in the case of our lord, Moses, who treated Pharaoh lightly on account of performing a religious duty, as it is said, *And all these servants of yours will come down to me and bow down to me, saying* (Ex. 11:8)."

2. A. And was Pharaoh standing on the room and Moses standing down on the ground?

   B. But this is what Moses said to Pharaoh, "Even if all your servants who are standing and prostrating themselves before you at your dais were to stand and beg me, I shall not listen to them."

3. A. "And how do we know that in the end he took his leave from him in dignity?

   B. "As it is said, *And he called for Moses and Aaron by night and said, Rise up, go forth from among my people* (Ex. 12:31).

   C. "They said to him, 'Are we thieves that we should go out by night? But wait for us until the Holy One, blessed be he, brings for us seven clouds of glory and we shall leave following them with rejoicing and [Goldin:] in broad daylight,

   D. "'as it is said, *On the morrow after the Passover the children of Israel went forth with a high hand* (Num. 33:3).'"

The exposition of Eleazar's saying is full and complete, bearing its own internal gloss as well.

XXIX:VIII

1. A. In order to investigate four types of atonement R. Mattia b. Harash went to R. Eleazar Haqqappar in Laodicea to visit him. He said to him, "Have you heard about the four types of atonement that R. Ishmael expounded?"

   B. He said to him, "I heard indeed, but they are three, but with each of them repentance is required.

   C. "One verse of Scripture says, *Return, you backsliding children, says the Lord, I will heal your backsliding* (Jer. 3:22). A second says, *For on this day shall atonement be made for you to cleanse you* (Lev. 16:30). And a third says, *Then I will visit their transgression with the rod and their iniquity with strokes* (Ps. 89:33), and a fourth: *Surely this iniquity shall not be expiated by you until you die* (Is. 22:14).

   D. "How so? If someone has violated a religious duty involving an act of commission but has repented, he does not move from that spot before he is forgiven forthwith. In this regard it is said, *Return, you backsliding children, says the Lord, I will heal your backsliding* (Jer. 3:22).

   E. "If someone has transgressed a negative commandment but has repented, repentance suspends the punishment and the Day of Atonement atones. In this regard it is said, *For on this day shall atonement be made for you to cleanse you* (Lev. 16:30).

   F. "If someone has transgressed a rule, the penalty of which is extirpation or judicially inflicted capital punishment, but has repented, repentance and the Day of Atonement suspend the matter, and suffering on the other days of the year effect atonement, and in this regard it is said, *Then I will visit their transgression with the rod and their iniquity with strokes* (Ps. 89:33).

   G. "But one who has profaned the name of heaven – repentance has not got the power to effect suspension of the punishment, nor suffering to wipe it out, nor the Day of Atonement to atone, but repentance and suffering suspend the punishment, and death will wipe out the sin with them, and in this regard it is said, *Surely this iniquity shall not be expiated by you until you die* (Is. 22:14)."

The story once more fully spells out the teaching, leaving no need for any further gloss or exposition.

XXIX:IX

1. A. Issi b. Judah says, "On what account do disciples of sages die before their time?
    B. "It is not because they commit adultery or steal but because they treat themselves lightly [Goldin: they despise themselves]."

This matter is not spelled out, and I see no point in the prior materials to which it is relevant.

XXIX:X

1. A. R. Isaac b. Phineas says, "Whoever has mastered exegesis but not laws has never tasted the flavor of wisdom.
    B. "Whoever has mastered laws but not exegesis has never tasted the flavor of fear of sin."

XXIX:XI

1. A. He would say, "Whoever has mastered exegesis but has not mastered laws is a mighty man who is not armed.
    B. "Whoever has mastered laws but not exegesis is armed but a weakling.
    C. "If one has mastered both, he is a well-armed mighty man."

XXIX:XII

1. A. He would say, "**Be careful to greet other people first,** and to not get involved in contention, and do not try to be [following Goldin:] seen in session with disciples of sages,
    B. "and **be a tail to lions but do not be head of foxes.**"

The sayings bear no amplification of any kind.

The Fathers According to Rabbi Nathan

Chapter Thirty

The chapter presents the exposition of several sayings, some fully, some perfunctorily.

> R. Jonathan says, "Whoever keeps the Torah when poor will in the end keep it in wealth. And whoever treats the Torah as nothing when he is wealthy in the end will treat it as nothing in poverty."

XXX:I.1-XXX:II.1 Citation of Nathan b. Joseph's sayings.

XXX:III-IV Further sayings that make the same point, that merely thinking is tantamount to doing.

XXX:V

XXX:V.1 Secondary amplification of a minor detail of **XXX:IV.2**.

XXX:VI.1-XXX:VII.1 Sayings of Ahai b. Josiah on a separate point entirely.

XXX:I

1. A. R. Nathan b. Joseph says, Whoever neglects the words of the Torah when he is wealthy in the end will neglect the Torah when he is poor, and whoever carries out the words of the Torah when he is poor in the end will carry out the Torah when he is wealthy.

XXX:II

1. A. He would say, "Bringing words of consolation to mourners, visiting the sick, and carrying out acts of loving-kindness bring good to the world."

Apart from the slightly different order of the words and the changed attribution, the version of what we have in Avot is the same, and the second saying is a banality.

XXX:III

1. A. R. Meir says, "Whoever as a matter of doubt thinks that he has committed a transgression [of sacrilege, e.g., unknowingly eating food that is in the status of Holy Things] is regarded by Scripture as though he had assuredly done it [so that he pays the penalty that would accrue had he actually committed sacrilege, as we shall now see].

   B. "How so? If someone has inadvertently committed a sin and his sin is made known to him, he brings a sin-offering worth a *sela* and a tenth of an *ephah* of fine flour, worth a *pondion*.

   C. "If he is in doubt whether or not he has sinned, he brings an offering for sacrilege and [makes up the full value of the sacrilege plus a penalty of] a fifth more of the value of the sacrilege, he brings a guilt-offering worth two *selas*. [This is a considerably more substantial penalty than the other.]

   D. "Now which of the divine traits is the greater, the trait of bestowing good or the trait of inflicting punishment? One must say it is the trait of doing good.

   E. "Then that yields an argument *a fortiori*: if the trait of inflicting punishment, which is the lesser, yields the rule that whoever as a matter of doubt thinks that he has committed a transgression [of sacrilege, e.g., unknowingly eating food that is in the status of Holy Things] is regarded by Scripture as though he had assuredly done it [and penalized heavily on that account, as we have seen], all the more so will be the rule governing the trait of doing good, which is the greater. [Then if someone thinks he has done an act of goodness, Scripture credits it to him as if he had actually done it.]"

2. A. R. Nathan b. Joseph says, "Whoever inadvertently commits a transgression is regarded by Scripture as though he had done it deliberately.

   B. "How so? If one inadvertently has killed someone and gone into exile to a city of refuge, and the redeemer of the blood of the deceased found him [outside of the refuge], and killed him, he is exempt. If, however, he had killed someone deliberately and the redeemer of the blood found the killer and killed him, lo, this redeemer of the blood is put to death on that account.

   C. "Now which of the divine traits is the greater, the trait of bestowing good or the trait of inflicting punishment? One must say it is the trait of doing good. Then that yields an argument *a fortiori*:

   D. "if the trait of inflicting punishment, which is the lesser, yields the rule that whoever inadvertently commits a transgression is regarded by Scripture as though he had done it deliberately, all the more so will be the rule governing the trait of doing good, which is the greater. [Then if someone deliberately has done an act of goodness, all the more so does Scripture credits it to him for a reward.]"

The set-piece composition is inserted because Nathan b. Joseph is one of the two authorities. There is no tie to the foregoing, which means that the thematic principle that governed the formation of **XXX:III.1-2** has been set aside by the principle of conglomeration of materials in the name of a single authority that governs in Avot.

XXX:IV

1. A. R. Aqiba says, "Whoever associates with transgressors, even though he does not do the things they do, lo, this one receives a punishment like theirs. And whoever associates with those who do religious deeds, even though he does not do the things they do, lo, this one receives a reward like theirs.

   B. "How so? If two witnesses give testimony against someone, saying, 'This man has killed someone,' and the two are found to be a conspiracy for the purpose of perjury, and the verdict governing them, for the death penalty, is completed, and when they are being brought to the place of stoning, someone ran and came after them, saying, 'I have testimony to give in this case,' so they say to the person, 'Come and testify.' [That testimony is found to be null, with the result that] this one too is found to be part of the conspiracy for perjury, and he too is sentenced to death.

   C. "Now when they are taking him to the place of stoning, he says, 'Woe is me, for if I had not come, then I would not have been sentenced to be put to death. Now that I have come along with them, I too am sentenced to be put to death.'

   D. "They say to him, 'Empty-head! Even if a hundred men had come after them and been found conspiratorial perjurers, all of them would have been put to death.

   E. "Now which of the divine traits is the greater, the trait of bestowing good or the trait of inflicting punishment? One must say it is the trait of doing good. Then that yields an argument *a fortiori*:

   F. "if the trait of inflicting punishment, which is the lesser, yields the rule that whoever associates with transgressors, even though he does not do the things they do, lo, this one receives a punishment like theirs, all the more so as to the trait of bestowing good, which is the greater [so that if someone associates with those who do good, even if he does not do the same, he will be rewarded]."

Aqiba's saying, No. 1, continues the line of thought begun at **XXX:III**. What one intends and what one does are weighed, and the former takes precedence. If someone does not do evil deeds but associates with those who do, he is penalized. Obviously Aqiba's materials are inserted for thematic reasons, and, it follows, the composition beginning in **XXX:III** continues here.

XXX:V

1. A. R. Simeon says, "The punishment of a liar is that even when he is telling the truth, people do not believe him.

   B. "For so we find in the case of the sons of Jacob. When they first deceived their father, he believed them, as it is said, *And they took the cloak of Joseph and slaughtered a young goat...and he recognized it and said, It is the cloak of my son* (Gen. 37:31, 33).

   C. "But in the end, even though they told the truth before him, he did not believe them, as it is said, *And they told him, saying, Joseph is still alive, and his heart melted, for he did not believe them, but when he saw the wagons* (Gen. 45:26, 27)."

D.   And some say, "It was the Holy Spirit that had departed from our father, Jacob, that rested on him at that moment, for it is said, *And the spirit of Jacob, their father, revived* (Gen. 45:26)."

The prior theme, conspiratorial perjury, accounts for the inclusion of this thematically intersecting composition. But the principle established at **XXX:III-IV** is not in play at all. So, as we see, a further redactional principle takes over: association of a thematic character, with stress on secondary and tangential themes now made central.

XXX:VI

1.   A.   R. Ahai b. Josiah says, "One who has to buy grain in the market place – to what is he compared? To an infant whose mother died, and whom people pass from door to door among wetnurses, but who is not satisfied.
     B.   "He who has to buy baked bread from the market place – to what is he compared? It is as if he is dead and buried.
     C.   "He who eats bread of his own household's baking is like an infant who is raised on his mother's breasts."

XXX:VII

1.   A.   He would say, "When someone eats of his own [produce], his mind is serene.
     B.   "But if someone eats food even of his father, his mother, his children, his mind is not serene,
     C.   "and it is not necessary to say, if he eats food of someone else."

We have an independent saying, undeveloped. First we have a metaphor, then an apodictic version of the same saying.

The Fathers According to Rabbi Nathan

Chapter Thirty-One

The chapter works its way through the basic theme, the creation of the world, but makes its own point on that theme, which is that the human being is equivalent to the whole of creation. This point emerges in the exposition, item after item.

> By ten acts of speech was the world made. And what does Scripture mean [by having God say *say* ten times]? But it is to exact punishment from the wicked, who destroy a world which was created through ten acts of speech, and to secure a good reward for the righteous, who sustain a world which was created through ten acts of speech.

XXXI:I

XXXI:I.1 Whoever carries out one religious duty is as if he sustained the whole world. This point leads to the one of importance: a human being is equivalent to the whole of creation.

XXXI:I.2 The point repeated, now for Cain.

XXXI:I.3 The point repeated in general terms.

XXXI:I.4 Secondary appendix added because of thematic association.

XXXI:II

XXXI:II.1 Ten acts of speech linked to the Torah, thus reversion to original assertion.

XXXI:III

XXXI:III.1 Man is equivalent to created world.

We see that the exposition of the phrase and theme of Avot is systematic and subtle.

XXXI:I

1. A. **By ten acts of speech was the world made:**
   B. Now why do people need to be told that? It is to teach you that whoever carries out a single religious duty, whoever observes a single Sabbath,

whoever saves a single life [Goldin, p. 204, n. 4 does not read *of Israel*] is credited by Scripture as though he had sustained the entire world that was created by ten words.

C. And whoever commits a single transgression, whoever violates a single Sabbath, whoever destroys a single life, is credited by Scripture as though he had destroyed the entire world that was created by ten words.

2. A. So we find in the case of Cain, who killed Abel his brother, as it is said, *The voice of the bloods of your brother cry out to me* (Gen. 4:10).

B. He spilled the blood of a single human being, but Scripture speaks of bloods in the plural.

C. This teaches that the blood of his children, grandchildren, and all the coming heirs to the end of all generations that were destined to come forth from him, all of them were standing and crying out before the Holy One, blessed be he.

D. So you learn that one person is equivalent to all the works of creation.

3. A. R. Nehemiah says, "How do we know that a single person is equivalent to all the words of creation?

B. "As it is said, *This is the book of the generations of man, in the day that God created man, in the likeness of God he made him* (Gen. 5:1), and, elsewhere, *These are the generations of heaven and earth when they were created* (Gen. 12:4).

C. "Just as in that latter passage we speak of creating and making, so in the former were creating and making.

D. "This teaches that the Holy One, blessed be he, showed him all the generations that were destined to come forth from him, as though they were standing and [Goldin:] rejoicing before him."

E. Some say that he showed him only the righteous alone, as it is written, *All those who were written unto life in Jerusalem* (Is. 4:3).

4. A. R. Joshua b. Qorha says, "Lo, it is written, *Your eyes did see my unformed substance and in your book they were all written* (Ps. 139:16).

B. "This teaches that the Holy One, blessed be he, showed to Adam each generation and its teachers, each generation and its responsible authorities, each generation and its leaders, each generation and its prophets, each generation and its heroes, each generation and its sinners, each generation and its exemplars of piety,

C. "[saying,] 'In such and such a generation, king so-and-so will arise,' 'in such and such a generation, the sage so-and-so will flourish.'"

Once the point is made that a single person is equivalent to all of creation, we move on to a concrete example of that view, Nos. 1, 2. No. 3 then provides a proof-text for the same proposition. The relevance of No. 4 is not equivalently obvious. My guess is that the associative principle has taken over, and, once the theme of creation is introduced, together with the theme of showing someone the future (Cain, the future generations of Abel that he had destroyed), we move along that same line to a tangential point, which is that God showed Adam the future leadership of the world. That is relevant only by the principle of thematic association.

XXXI:II

1. A. R. Eliezer, son of R. Yose the Galilean, says, "Nine hundred seventy-four generations before the world was created, the Torah was written down and resting in the bosom of the Holy One, blessed be he, reciting song with the ministering angels.

   B. "For it is said, *Then I was with him as a nursling, and I was daily all delight, playing before him* (Prov. 8:30), and it says, *Playing in his habitable earth, and my delights are with the sons of men* (Prov. 8:31)."

I take it the point of relevance is the notion, attached elsewhere to the cited verse, that God looked into the Torah and created the world. Then the amplification of the ten acts of speech by which the world was created is fully exposed: the speech took place in the giving of the Torah.

XXXI:III

1. A. R. Yose the Galilean says, "Whatever the Holy One, blessed be he, created on earth, he created also in man. To what may the matter be compared? To someone who took a piece of wood and wanted to make many forms on it but had no room to make them, so he was distressed. But someone who draws forms on the earth can go on drawing and can spread them out as far as he likes.

   B. "But the Holy One, blessed be he, may his great name be blessed for ever and ever, in his wisdom and understanding created the whole of the world, created the heaven and the earth, above and below, and created in man whatever he created .in his world.

   C. "In the world he created forests, and in man he created forests: the hairs on his head.

   D. "In the world he created wild beasts and in man he created wild beasts: lice.

   E. "In the world he created channels and in man he created channels: his ears.

   F. "In the world he created wind and in man he created wind: his [Goldin:] breath.

   G. "In the world he created the sun and in man he created the sun: his forehead.

   H. "Stagnant waters in the world, stagnant waters in man: his nose, [namely, rheum].

   I. "Salt water in the world, salt water in man: his urine.

   J. "Streams in the world, streams in man: man's tears.

   K. "Walls in the world, walls in man: his lips.

   L. "Doors in the world, doors in man: his teeth.

   M. "Firmaments in the world, firmaments in man, his tongue.

   N. "Fresh water in the world, fresh water in man: his spit.

   O. "Stars in the world, stars in the man: his cheeks.

   P. "Towers in the world, towers in man: his neck.

   Q. "[Goldin:] masts in the world, masts in man: his arms.

   R. "Pins in the world, pins in man: his fingers.

   S. "A King in the world, a king in man: his head [Goldin: heart].

T. "Grapeclusters in the world, grapeclusters in man: his breasts.

U. "Counsellors in the world, counsellors in man: his kidneys.

V. "Millstones in the world, millstones in man: his intestines [which grind up food].

W. "[Goldin:] mashing mills in the world, and mashing mills in man: the spleen.

X. "Pits in the world, a pit in man: the belly button.

Y. "Flowing streams in the world and a flowing stream in man: his blood.

Z. "Trees in the world and trees in man: his bones.

AA. "Hills in the world and hills in man: his buttocks.

BB. "[Goldin:] pestle and mortar in the world and pestle and mortar in man: the joints.

CC. "Horses in the world and horses in man: the legs.

DD. "The angel of death in the world and the angel of death in man: his heels.

EE. "Mountains and valleys in the world and mountains and valleys in man: when he is standing, he is like a mountain, when he is lying down, he is like a valley.

FF. "Thus you have learned that whatever the Holy One, blessed be he, created on earth, he created also in man."

The general theme of creation accounts for the inclusion of this catalogue, which also underlines the opening point: a human being is equivalent to the entire world. Accordingly, the associative principle of redaction blends exquisitely with the expository one, since the theme and the point the redactor wished to make from the start to the finish now join together, the mark of a stunning piece of redaction.

The Fathers According to Rabbi Nathan

Chapter Thirty-Two

The chapter works out the theme at hand – the generation of Noah. The stress is on the long-suffering character of God.

> There are ten generations from Adam to Noah, to show you how long-suffering is [God]. For all those generations went along spiting him until he brought the water of the flood upon them. There are ten generations from Noah to Abraham, to show you how long-suffering is [God]. For all those generations went along spiting him, until Abraham came along and took the reward which had been meant for all of them.

XXXII:I

XXXII:I.1 Why is it necessary to count the generations? To show how long-suffering God is. He waited for Methuselah to die.

XXXII:I.2 God waited for them to repent but they did not.

XXXII:I.3 God gave them signals that something was wrong, but they did not listen.

XXXII:I.4 God showed them what they would lose.

XXXII:II

XXXII:II.1 Exegesis of Gen. 6:3: God gave them their reward in this world.

XXXII:II.2 Good impulse/evil impulse.

XXXII:II.3 Same as above.

XXXII:II.4 Exegesis of Gen., 6:3: God paid reward coming to the righteous.

XXX:II.5 They were arrogant.

XXXII:II.6 They did not believe there was judgment.

XXXII:II.7 They did not set up courts.

XXXII:I

1. A. **There are ten generations from Adam to Noah:**
   B. Now why was it necessary to tell people this? It is to teach you that all those generations people continued to anger [God], but he did not bring the flood on them on account of the righteous and pious people among them.
   C. And some say that all the time that Methuselah was alive, the flood did not come down on the world, but when Methuselah died, the flood was held back for seven days after his death.
   D. For it is said, *And it came to pass after the seven days that the waters of the flood were upon the earth* (Gen. 7:10).
   E. What were these seven days? They were the days of mourning for that righteous man, Methuselah, who prevented the punishment from coming onto the world.
   F. That is why it is said, *And it came to pass after the seven days.*

2. A. Another explanation of the verse, *And it came to pass after the seven days* :
   B. This teaches that the Holy One, blessed be he, set a time for them after one hundred twenty years, that they might repent, but they did not do so.
   C. Therefore it is said *And it came to pass after the seven days* .

3. A. Another matter: it teaches that the Holy One, blessed be he, changed the order of the world on their account, so that the sun came up in the west and set in the east,
   B. so that they might understand and fear and repent, but they did not do so.
   C. Therefore it is said *And it came to pass after the seven days* .

4. A. Another matter: The Holy One, blessed be he, laid out his table for them and showed them some of that goodness that would come in the world to come, so that they would take heed of themselves and say, "Woe to us for the goodness that we have lost."
   B. It is because they had corrupted their way on earth,
   C. for it is said, *And God saw the earth and behold it was corrupt, for all flesh had corrupted their way upon the earth* (Gen. 6:12).

The pattern is identical to that at Chapter Thirty-One. Once the explanation of our base-clause is introduced, No. 1, the interpretation of the proof-text takes over. The proof-text's explanations do not draw us back to the main point, which is that God spared the world because of the righteous. Now he spared the world as long as he did so that people might repent, which they failed to do. So the movement from the proof-text outward, Nos. 2-4, changes the point made at No. 1.

XXXII:II

1. A. R. Eleazar b. Parta says, "Lo, Scripture says, *My spirit shall not judge man in this world* (Gen 6:3).
   B. "Said the Holy One, blessed be he, I shall not judge them until I double the reward that is coming to them [Goldin: until I have given them their reward in full], as it is said, *They spend their days in prosperity, but then they go down to Sheol* (Job 21:13)."

2. A. R. Yose the Galilean says, Lo, Scripture says, *My spirit shall not judge man in this world* (Gen 6:3).

   B. "Said the Holy One, blessed be he, 'I shall not treat as equivalent the impulse to do evil and the impulse to do good.'

   C. "When is that the case? Before the decree has been sealed, but once the decree has been sealed, both of them are equal as to transgression."

3. A. R. Yose the Galilean used to say, "From the righteous the evil impulse is taken away and the good impulse is given in its place,

   B. "as it is said, *My heart is wounded within me* (Ps. 109:22).

   C. "But from the wicked the good impulse is taken away and the evil impulse is given in its stead, as it is said [Goldin's translation, verbatim:], *Says transgression to the wicked in the midst of his heart. There is no fear of God before his eyes* (Ps. 36:2).

   D. "As to the people in the middle, both this and that are given to them. The one who comes to the evil impulse is judged by that, the one who comes to the good impulse is judged by that,

   E. "as it is said, *Because he stands at the right hand of the needy, to save him from them that judge his soul* (Ps. 109:34)."

4. A. R. Simeon b. Eleazar says, "Lo, Scripture says, *My spirit shall not punish man in this world* (Gen 6:3).

   B. "Said the Holy One, blessed be he, 'I shall not judge them until I have paid the reward that is coming to the righteous.'

   C. "When is this the case? In this world.

   D. "But as to the world to come, His breath goes forth, he returns to the dust in that very day (Ps. 146:4)."

5. A. R. Aqiba says, "Lo, Scripture says, *My spirit shall not judge man in this world* (Gen 6:3).

   B. "Said the Holy One, blessed be he, 'They did not come to a correct judgment of themselves, that they are mortal, but they behaved arrogantly toward the heights,

   C. "as it is said, *Yet they said to God, Depart from us, we do not want the knowledge of your ways* (Job 21:14)."

6. A. R. Meir says, "Lo, Scripture says, *My spirit shall not judge man in this world* (Gen 6:3).

   B. "Said the Holy One, blessed be he, 'That generation has said, "The Lord will not judge, there is no judge in the world, God has abandoned the world."'"

7. A. Rabbi says, "Lo, it says, *My spirit shall not judge man in this world* (Gen 6:3).

   B. "Said the Holy One, blessed be he, 'They did not call sanhedrins into session on earth, lo, I shall call into session a sanhedrin in heaven.'"

The several expositions of Gen. 6:3 amplify the common theme of God's patience and ultimate judgment. Nos. 1, 4-7 clearly are relevant to the larger context. What Nos. 2, 3 contribute is more difficult to say.

The Fathers According to Rabbi Nathan

Chapter Thirty-Three

Once we have a brief amplification, through glosses, of the base-statements, the appendices take over.

There are ten generations from Noah to Abraham, to show you how long-suffering is [God]. For all those generations went along spiting him, until Abraham came along and took the reward which had been meant for all of them.

Ten trials were inflicted upon Abraham, our father, may he rest in peace, and he withstood all of them, to show you how great is His love for Abraham, our father, may he rest in peace.

XXXIII:I

XXXIII:I.1 Base-statement cited and glossed.

XXXIII:I.2-3 Appendix on Abraham.

XXXIII:II

XXXIII:II.1 Base-statement cited and glossed.

XXXIII:III

XXXIII:III.1 In response to the ten trials, Holy One performed ten miracles in Egypt, ten plagues on the Egyptians in Egypt, ten miracles for Israelites at the sea, ten plagues on Egyptians at the sea.

XXXIII:IV

XXXIII:IV.1 Foregoing statement given a thematic appendix, in which what the Egyptians did to Israel has as its counterpart what the Holy One did to the Egyptians.

XXXIII:V

XXXIII:V.1 Miracles done at the sea for the Israelites. No reference to foregoing.

The opening is the same as at **XXXI:I.1** and **XXXII:I.1**, and the point is the same as well. We see that at **XXXIII:I, II**, the base-statement is given some attention, but then the appendices go their own way.

XXXIII:I

1. A. **There are ten generations from Noah to Abraham:**
   B. And what need was there for people to be told this?
   C. It is to teach you that **all those generations went along spiting him,**
   D. and there was none of them that would go in the ways of the Holy One, blessed be he,
   E. **until Abraham** our father **came along** and went in the ways of the Holy One, blessed be he.
2. A. Thus it is said, *Because Abraham obeyed me and kept my charge, my commandments, and my statutes and my laws* (Gen. 26:5) – one Torah is not written here but many Torahs.
   B. How did he know them?
   C. It teaches that the Holy One, blessed be he, designated for Abraham, our father, two reins, like two sages, who gave him understanding and advised him and taught him wisdom all night long.
   D. So it is said, *I will bless the Lord, who has given me counsel, yes in the night seasons my reins instruct me* (Ps. 16:7).
3. A. Not only so, but Abraham, our father, would first carry out acts of philanthropy and only then acts of justice.
   B. So it is said, *For I have known him to the end that he may command his children and his household after him that they may keep the way of the Lord to do charity and justice* (Gen. 18:19).
   C. When two litigants would come before our father Abraham with a case, and one said concerning his fellow, "This one owes me a *mina*," Abraham, our father, would produce a *mina* of his own and give it to him and say to him, "Lay out your case before me."
   D. They laid out their case before him. When a decision had been reached that one of them owed the other a *mina*, he would say to the one who held the *mina*, "Give the *mina* to your fellow." Or, if not, he would say to them, "Divide the *mina* between yourselves and go in peace."
   E. But King David did not do it that way, but first he did justice, then philanthropy, as it is said, *And David did philanthropy and justice for all his people* (2 Sam. 8:15).
   F. When litigants came for justice before King David, he would say to them, "Lay out your case." When one of them turned out to owe his fellow a *mina*, he would then take out a *mina* of his own and give it to him, and if not, he would say to them, "Divide what is incumbent on you and go in peace."

No. 1 lightly glosses the base-statement of Avot. What follows is assembled as a thematic complement, but the thesis of No. 1 is never taken up again. On the contrary, No. 2 has no bearing on the original statement. It makes its own point, in exegesis of the cited verse. No. 3 is certainly independent of the present contrast, since all it does is contrast the procedure of Abraham and David, and the contrast is not invidious.

XXXIII:II

1. A. **Ten trials were inflicted upon Abraham,** our father, before the Holy One, blessed be he, and in all of them he came out whole.

   B. These are they: two in the passage, "Go forth" [Goldin: twice, when ordered to move on]; two in connection with his two sons; two in connection with his two wives; one with the kings; one in the covenant between the pieces; one in the furnace of the Chaldeans; one in connection with circumcision.

   C. And why all of these trials?

   D. So that when Abraham our father would come to receive his reward, when the nations of the world would complain, "More than all of us, more than everyone, Abraham is worthy of receiving his reward."

   E. And in connection with him, Scripture says, *Go your way, eat your bread with joy and drink your wine with a merry heart, for God has already accepted your works* (Qoh. 9:7).

The amplification of the base-statement is necessary and to the point.

XXXIII:III

1. A. In response to the ten trials inflicted upon Abraham, our father, from all of which he emerged whole, the Holy One, blessed be he, performed ten miracles for his children in Egypt.

   B. And corresponding to them also, the Holy One, blessed be he, brought ten plagues on the Egyptians in Egypt.

   C. And corresponding to them also, ten miracles were done for the Israelites at the sea.

   D. And corresponding to them also, he brought ten plagues on the Egyptians at the sea.

The exposition of the base-statement continues, entirely to the point.

XXXIII:IV

1. A. The Egyptians [Goldin:] thundered at Israel with their voices, so the Holy One, blessed be he, raised his voice against them, as it is said, *The Lord thundered from heaven, and the Most High gave forth his voice* (2 Sam. 22:14).

   B. The Egyptians attacked them with bow and arrow, so the Holy One, blessed be he, attacked them with bow and arrow, as it is said, *Your bow is made quite bare* (Hab. 3:9), and it further says, *And he sent out his arrows and scattered them* (Ps. 18:15).

   C. The Egyptians attacked them with swords, so the Holy One, blessed be he, attacked them with swords and spears, as it is said, *And he sent out his arrows and scattered them, and he shot forth lightnings and discomfited them* (Hab. 3:9). The word for lightning bears the meaning of sword, as it is said, *A sword, a sword is sharpened and also polished, it is sharpened to make a heavy slaughter, it is polished so as to glitter* (Ez. 21:14).

D The Egyptians took pride in their shield and buckler, so the Holy One, blessed be he, did the same, as it is said, *Take hold of shield and buckler and rise up to my help* (Ps. 35:2).

E. The Egyptians attacked them with spears, so the Holy One, blessed be he, attacked them with spears, as it is said, *At the shining of your glittering spear* (Hab. 3:11).

F. The Egyptians attacked them with stones and slingshots, so the Holy One, blessed be he, exalted himself over them with hailstones, as it is said, *At the brightness before him, there passed through his thick clouds hailstones and coals of fire* (Ps. 18:13).

The passage is autonomous of the present context, since it hardly carries forward the allegations of the preceding one. It now alleges that God responded to what the Egyptians did to the Israelites, rather than what Abraham did as acts of faith.

XXXIII:V

1. A. When our fathers stood at the sea, Moses said to them, "Get up and pass through."

B. They said to him, "We are not going to pass through until the sea is turned into passages." Moses took his staff and hit the sea, and the sea was turned into passages, as it is said, *You have hit through with rods, the head of his rulers* (Hab. 3:14).

C. Moses said to them, "Get up and pass through."

D. They said to him, "We are not going to pass through until the sea is turned a valley before us." Moses took his staff and hit the sea, and the sea was turned into a valley before them, as it is said, *He made a valley of the sea and caused them to pass through* (Ps. 78:13), and it is said, *As the cattle that go down into the valley, so did you lead your people* (Is. 63:14).

E. Moses said to them, "Get up and pass through."

F. They said to him, "We are not going to pass through until the sea is cut into two parts before us." Moses took his staff and hit the sea, and the sea was cut into two parts before them, as it is said, *To him who divided the Red Sea into two parts* (Ps. 136:13).

G. Moses said to them, "Get up and pass through."

H. They said to him, "We are not going to pass through until the sea is turned clay for us." Moses took his staff and hit the sea, and the sea was turned into clay, as it is said, *You have trodden on the sea with your horses, through the clay of mighty waters* (Hab. 3:15).

I. Moses said to them, "Get up and pass through."

J. They said to him, "We are not going to pass through until the sea is turned into a wilderness before us." Moses took his staff and hit the sea, and the sea was turned into a wilderness, as it is said, *And he led them through the deep as through a wilderness* (Ps. 106:9).

K. Moses said to them, "Get up and pass through."

L. They said to him, "We are not going to pass through until the sea is turned into pieces before us." Moses took his staff and hit the sea, and the sea was turned into pieces, as it is said, *You broke the sea in pieces by your strength* (Ps. 74:13).

M. Moses said to them, "Get up and pass through."

N. They said to him, "We are not going to pass through until the sea is turned rocks before us." Moses took his staff and hit the sea, and the sea was turned into rocks, as it is said, *You shattered the heads of the sea monsters* (Ps. 74:13). And where does one smash the heads of the sea monsters? One must conclude that they are shattered only on rocks.

O. Moses said to them, "Get up and pass through."

P. They said to him, "We are not going to pass through until the sea is turned into dry land before us." Moses took his staff and hit the sea, and the sea was turned into dry land, as it is said, *He turned the sea into dry land* (Ps. 66:6), and further, *But the children of Israel walked on dry land in the midst of the sea* (Ex. 14:29). '

Q. Moses said to them, "Get up and pass through."

R. They said to him, "We are not going to pass through until the sea is turned into walls before us." Moses took his staff and hit the sea, and the sea was turned into walls, as it is said, *And the waters were a wall for them on their right hand and on their left* (Ex. 14:29).

S. Moses said to them, "Get up and pass through."

T. They said to him, "We are not going to pass through until the sea [stands up and is] turned into the shape of a bottle before us." Moses took his staff and hit the sea, and the sea was turned into the shape of a bottle, as it is said, *The water stood upright like a bottle containing liquid* (Ex. 15:8).

U. Fire came down and licked up the water between the parts, as it is said, *When fire caused that which melts to disappear, and the fire lapped up the water, to make your name known to your adversaries* (Is. 64:1).

V. And the bottles let out oil and honey into the mouths of infants, and they sucked from them, as it is said, *And he made them suck honey out of the rock* (Deut. 32:13).

W. And some say, "They produced fresh water from the sea and they drank it in the paths,

X. "(for sea water is salty),

Y. "[continuing W] as it is said, *Flowing streams* (Deut. 32:13), and *flowing streams* refers only to sweet water, as it is said, *A well of living water and flowing streams from Lebanon* (Song 4:15)."

Z. And clouds of glory were above them, so that the sun should not smite them, and the Israelites passed through in such a way that they were not distressed.

AA. R. Eliezer says, "The great deep covered them over from above, and the Israelites passed through, so that they were not distressed."

BB. R. Eliezer and R. Simeon say, "The upper water and the lower water tossed the Egyptians up and down, as it is said, *And the Lord tossed the Egyptians up and down in the midst of the sea* (Ex. 14:27)."

We have yet another thematic appendix, with no relationship to the proposition that introduced this collection.

The Fathers According to Rabbi Nathan

Chapter Thirty-Four

This rather disappointing chapter enriches the base-statement simply by giving numerous illustrations of it, specifically, lists of ten things (one of eleven!) to run parallel to the list of ten things with which we begin. It is surprising that, after so many rich and thoughtful reworkings of themes as well as ideas, the framers could do no better than they have done here. But that the plan is part of a larger program is made obvious by the chapters to come, many of which consist simply of lists of ten, seven, four or three items, no list having any bearing on any other in its classification.

> Ten trials did our fathers inflict upon the Omnipresent, blessed be he, in the Wilderness, as it is said, *Yet they have tempted me these ten times and have not listened to my voice* (Num. 14:22).

XXXIV:I

XXXIV:I.1 Ten trials plus systematic amplification and proof-texts.

XXXIV:II

XXXIV:II.1 Ten terms of praise apply to God.

XXXIV:III

XXXIV:III.1 Ten terms of denigration apply to idolatry.

XXXIV:IV

XXXIV:IV.1 Two signifying markers occur in a single passage.

XXXIV:V

XXXIV:V.1 More of same.

XXXIV:VI

XXXIV:VI.1 Ten passages in the Torah are dotted.

XXXIV:VII

XXXIV:VII.1 Eleven passages in which the word for *she* is written with a Y.

XXXIV:VIII

XXXIV:VIII.1 Ten descents of God's presence into the world.

XXXIV:IX

XXXIV:IX.1 Ten ascents out of the world.

XXXIV:X

XXXIV:X.1 Prophet called by ten names.

XXXIV:XI

XXXIV:XI.1 Holy spirit called by ten names.

XXXIV:XII

XXXIV:XII. Joy called by ten names.

XXXIV:XIII

XXXIV:XIII.1 Ten are called living.

After the excellent beginning, **XXXIV:I.1**, I see nothing but a sequence of catalogues, some of them matched, many of them lacking all point of contact with our passage.

XXXIV:I

1. A. Ten trials did our fathers inflict upon the Omnipresent, blessed be he, in the Wilderness,
   B. And these are they: *In the wilderness, at Arabah, over against Suph, in the neighborhood of Paran and Tophel, and Laban, and Hazeroth, and Dizahab* (Deut. 1:1).
   C. *In the wilderness*, where they made the golden calf: *And they made the calf in Horeb* (Ps. 106:19).
   D. *...at Arabah*, at the bitter water, as it is said, *And the people thirsted there for water* (Ex. 17:3). And some say that this refers to the idol of Micah.
   E. *...over against Suph*, for they rebelled at the Red Sea.
   F. R. Judah says, "They rebelled at the sea and they were rebellious in the sea: *But they were rebellious at the sea, even in the Red Sea* (Ps. 106:7)."
   G. *...in the neighborhood of Paran*: this refers to the matter of the spies: *And Moses sent them from the wilderness of Paran* (Num. 13:3).
   H. *...and Tophel:* this refers to the foolish words that they said about the manna.

I. ...*and Laban:* this refers to dispute with Korach.

J. ...*and Hazeroth:* this refers to the quail.

K. Lo, there are seven. And further: *And at Taberah, at Massah, and at Dibroth-hattavah you made the Lord angry* (Deut. 9:22).

L. *and Dizahab*: Said to them Aaron, "The sin that you committed in bringing the gold for the calf is enough [DY] for you."

M. R. Eliezer b. Jacob says, "This sin is sufficient to bring punishment for Israel until the dead will live."

The exegesis of the base-sentence by the provision of a biblical verse which supplies the required facts is completely successful.

XXXIV:II

1. A. Ten terms of praise are applied to the Holy One, blessed be he, and these are they:

    B. Lord, Yahweh, God, Deity, Your God, Your [pl.] God, Mighty, I am, Almighty, and Hosts.

    C. Said R. Yose, "I differ as to Hosts, as it is said, *Captains of hosts shall be appointed at the head of the people* (Deut. 20:9)."

The appendices for the base-sentence provide more lists of ten items, having no point of intersection with the original one.

XXXIV:III

1. A. Ten terms of denigration are applied to idolatry, and these are they:

    B. abominations, idols, molten idols, graven images, non-gods, Asherim, sun-gods, shapes, evil, and teraphim.

This set matches the foregoing.

XXXIV:IV

1. A. There are two signifying markers stated in the Torah in one brief passage, and which one is it? It is the one that begins: *And it came to pass when the ark set forward, that Moses said...And when it rested, he said...* (Num. 10:35f.).

    B. Rabban Simeon b. Gamaliel says, "That passage is destined to be uprooted from its present location and moved to another location in the Torah."

I have no idea why this passage has been introduced here.

XXXIV:V

1. A. Along these same lines: *And Jonathan, the son of Gershom, the son of Manasseh* (Jud. 18:30):

    B. Was he the son of Manasseh and not the son of Moses?

C. But since his deeds were not like those of Moses, his father, he is assigned to Manasseh.

D. Along these same lines: *These are the two anointed ones that stand by the Lord of the whole earth* (Zech. 4:14):

E. This refers to Aaron and the Messiah, but I do not know which of the two is more beloved.

F. When it is said, *The Lord has sworn and will not repent, you are a priest forever after the manner of Melchizedek* (Ps. 110:4), one must conclude that the king-messiah is more beloved than the righteous priest.

2. A. Lo, Scripture says, *The boar out of the wood ravages it* (Ps. 80:14).

B. But what is written is, *The boar out of* the river *ravages it.*

C. *The boar out of the* wood *ravages it* refers to the Roman government. For when the Israelites do not carry out the will of the Omnipresent, the nations of the world appear to them like a boar out of the *forest*.

D. Just as a boar out of the forest kills people and injures them and hurts them, so too upon Israel, so long as they do not carry out the will of the Omnipresent, the nations of the world inflict death, injury, and hurt.

E But so long as the Israelites do carry out the will of the Omnipresent, the nations of the world cannot rule over them,

F. like the boar out of the river.

G. That is why it is written, *The boar out of* the river *ravages it.*

As it stands, the passage scarcely intersects with anything that we have yet seen.

XXXIV:VI

1. A. There are ten passages in the Torah that are dotted: *May the Lord judge between me and you* (Gen. 16:4).

B. The presence of dots in the wording here, *the Lord judge between me and you*, indicates that Sarah's statement to Abraham concerned Hagar alone, and some say it concerns those who bring strife between him and her.

C. Along these same lines: *They said to him, 'Where is Sarah, your wife'* (Gen. 19:33).

D. The presence of dots in the wording here, *Where*, indicates that they knew where she was but raised the question anyhow.

E. Along these same lines: *And he did not know when she lay down or when she rose up* (Gen. 19:33).

F. The presence of dots over the word *when she lay down* indicates that he did not know when she lay down, but he did know when she got up.

G. Along these same lines: *And he kissed him* (Gen. 33:4).

H. The presence of dots over the word, *and he kissed him*, indicates that he did not do so sincerely.

I. R. Simeon b. Eleazar says, "As a matter of fact, it is perfectly clear that that particular kiss he gave him with all his heart, but all the others were insincere."

J. Along these same lines: *His brothers went to pasture the flock of their father in Shechem* (Gen. 37:12).

K. The presence of dots indicates that they went there only to eat, drink, and make merry [and not in their father's interest].

L.   Along these same lines: *All that were numbered of the Levites, whom Moses and Aaron numbered* (Num. 3:39). This addition of dots over *Aaron* teaches that Aaron was not included in the count.

M.   *...afar off on a journey:*

N.   There are dots over the letter H, indicating that even if someone is merely in the area beyond the threshold of the Temple court on a nearby trip but is unclean, he would not carry out the passover offering with them].

O.   Along these same lines: *While the fire spreads onward to Medeba* (Num. 21:30).

P.   The presence of dots indicates that they destroyed the nations but not the towns.

Q.   Along these same lines: *A tenth ephah, a tenth ephah* (Num. 29:15).

R.   The presence of dots indicates that only a single tenth *ephah* was involved.

S.   Along these same lines: *The things that are hidden belong to the Lord, our God, and the revealed things to us and to our children forever"* (Deut. 29:28).

T.   There are dots over *to us* and *to our children* [following Sifré Num. 69:] to indicate, "Just as you have made things public, so I shall tell you secret things.]"

U.   For this is what Ezra said, "If Elijah comes and says to me, 'On what account did you write this,' I shall say to him, I have placed dots over them, and if he says to me, You wrote them properly, I shall remove the dots from them.

All I see is another catalogue of ten items.

XXXIV:VII

1.   A.   There are eleven passages in which the word for *she* [or it] is written in the Torah with a Y.

B.   The first: *And the king of Bela – it is Zoar* (Gen. 14:2).

C.   *Did he himself not say to me, She is my sister? And she, even she herself said, He is my brother* (Gen. 20:5)

D.   *When she was brought forth, she sent to her father in law, saying* (Gen. 38:25).

E.   *And if any beast of, which you may eat, die* (Lev. 11:39).

F.   *And it have turned the hair white* (Lev. 13:10).

G.   *But if the priest look on it...but it be dimmed* (Lev. 13:21).

H.   *And she see his nakedness* (Lev. 20:17).

I.   *She profanes her father* (Lev. 21:9).

J.   And in the chapter on the accused wife [Num. 5]:

K.   *She being defiled secretly...neither she be taken in the act* (Num. 5:13).

L.   *Or if the spirit of jealousy come upon him and he be jealous of his wife, and she be not defiled* (Num. 5:14).

Another list of items is before us, making no more interesting a point than any other. Why a list of eleven belongs I cannot say. But given the character of the chapter, who can say why any item belongs or does not belong?

XXXIV:VIII

1. A. There were ten descents that the Presence of God made into the world.
   B. One into the Garden of Eden, as it says, *And they heard the sound of God walking in the garden* (Gen. 3:5).
   C. One in the generation of the tower of Babylon, as it is said, *And the Lord came down to see the city and the tower* (Gen. 11:5).
   D. One in Sodom: *I shall now go down and see whether it is in accord with the cry that has come to me* (Gen. 18:21).
   E. One in Egypt: *I shall go down and save them from the hand of the Egyptians* (Ex. 3:8).
   F. One at the sea: *He bowed the heavens also and came down* (2 Sam. 22:10).
   G. One at Sinai: *And the Lord came down onto Mount Sinai* (Ex. 19:20).
   H. One in the pillar of cloud: *And the Lord came down in a pillar* (Num. 11:25).
   I. One in the Temple: *This gate will be closed and will not be open for the Lord, God of Israel, has come in through it* (Ez. 44:2).
   J. And one is destined to take place in the time of Gog and Magog: *And his feet shall stand that day on the mount of Olives* (Zech. 14:4).

Yet another list of ten items is worked out.

XXXIV:IX

1. A. In ten upward stages the Presence of God departed, from one place to the next: from the ark cover to the cherub, from the cherub to the threshold of the temple-building; from the threshold of the temple to the two cherubim; from the two cherubim to the roof of the sanctuary; from the roof of the sanctuary to the wall of the temple court; from the wall of the temple court to the altar; from the altar to the city; from the city to the Temple mount; from the temple mount to the wilderness.
   B. from the ark cover to the cherub: *And he rode upon a cherub and flew* (2 Sam. 22:11).
   C. from the cherub to the threshold of the temple-building: *And the glory of the Lord mounted up from the cherub to the threshold of the house* (Ez. 10:45).
   D. from the threshold of the temple to the two cherubim: *And the glory of the Lord went forth from off the threshold of the house and stood over the cherubim* (Ez. 10:18).
   E. from the two cherubim to the roof of the sanctuary: *It is better to dwell in a corner of the housetop* (Prov. 21:9).
   F. from the roof of the sanctuary to the wall of the temple court: *And behold the Lord stood beside a wall made by a plumbline* (Amos 7:7).
   G. from the wall of the temple court to the altar: *I saw the Lord standing beside the altar* (Amos 9:1).

H. from the altar to the city: *Hark, the Lord cries to the city* (Mic. 6:9).
I. from the city to the Temple mount: *And the glory of the Lord went up from the midst of the city and stood upon the mountain* (Ez. 11:23).
J. from the temple mount to the wilderness: *It is better to dwell in a desert land* (Prov. 21:19).
K. And then to on high: *I will go and return to my place* (Hos. 5:15).

The simple form, first the list, then the proof-texts, is once more followed.

XXXIV:X
1. A. A prophet may be called by ten names, and these are they:
   B. agent, faithful, servant, messenger, seer, visionary, one who sees, dreamer, prophet, man of God.

XXXIV:XI
1. A. The Holy Spirit may be called by ten names, and these are they:
   B. [Goldin:] parable, metaphor, riddle, word, speech, beauty, command, burden, prophecy, vision.

XXXIV:XII
1. A. Joy may be called by ten names, and these are they:
   B. rejoicing, joy, gladness, sounding forth, singing, dancing, jubilation, delight, cheerfulness, exultation.

XXXIV:XIII
1. A. Ten are called the living, and these are they:
   B. [God is called living:] *But the Lord God is the true God, he is the living God* (Jer. 10:10)
   C. The Torah is called living: *She is a tree of life to those that lay hold of her* (Prov. 3:18).
   D. Israel is called living: *But you that cleave to the Lord your God are alive every one of you this day* (Deut. 4:4).
   E. The righteous man is called living: *The fruit of the righteous is a tree of life* (Prov. 11:30).
   F. The Garden of Eden is called living: *I shall walk before the Lord in the lands of the living* (Ps. 116:9).
   G. Trees are called living: *The tree of life also in the midst of the garden* (Gen. 2:9).
   H. The Land of Israel is called living: *And I will place glory in the land of the living* (Ez. 26:20).
   I. Acts of loving-kindness is called living: *For your loving-kindness is better than life, my lips shall praise you* (Ps. 63:4).
   J. Sages are called living: *The teaching of the sage is a fountain of life* (Prov. 13:14).
   K. Water is called living: *In that day ...living water shall go out of Jerusalem* (Zech. 14:8).

Apart from the arrangement that permits an eschatological finish, I find nothing of interest here.

The Fathers According to Rabbi Nathan

Chapter Thirty-Five

Another sizable saying is given a full and systematic exegesis.

Ten wonders were done for our fathers in the Temple: (1) A woman never miscarried on account of the stench of the meat of Holy Things. (2) And the meat of the Holy Things never turned rotten. (3) A fly never made an appearance in the slaughter house. (4) A high priest never suffered a nocturnal emission on the eve of the Day of Atonement. (5) The rain never quenched the fire on the altar. (6) No wind ever blew away the pillar of smoke. (7) An invalidating factor never affected the 'omer, the Two Loaves, or the show bread. (8) When the people are standing, they are jammed together. When they go down and prostrate themselves, they have plenty of room. (9) A snake and a scorpion never bit anybody in Jerusalem. (10) And no one ever said to his fellow, *"The place is too crowded for me* (Is. 49:20) to sleep over in Jerusalem."

XXXV:I

XXXV:I.1 Ten wonders saying amplified.

XXXV:II

XXXV:II.1 Ten rulings in connection with Jerusalem.

XXXV:III

XXXV:III.1-3 Appendix on Jerusalem.

XXXV:IV

XXXV:IV.1 Ten wonders done for our fathers in the Temple.

XXXV:IV.2-3 Appendix on wonders in Temple.

XXXV:I

1. A. Ten wonders were done for our fathers in the Jerusalem: A woman never miscarried on account of the stench of the meat of Holy Things.
   B. No one was ever attacked in Jerusalem.

C. No one ever stumbled in Jerusalem.

D. A conflagration never broke out in Jerusalem.

E. No building ever collapsed in Jerusalem.

F. No one ever said to his fellow, "I have not found in Jerusalem an oven in which to roast Passover-offerings."

G. No one ever said to his fellow, "I have not found in Jerusalem a bed in which to sleep."

H. **And no one ever said to his fellow,** *"The place is too crowded for me* (Is. 49:20) to sleep over in Jerusalem."

The citation of the base-saying is followed by a fine and systematic amplification of its main point, now in terms of Jerusalem, rather than the Temple.

XXXV:II

1. A. Ten rulings were made in connection with Jerusalem:

B. Jerusalem is not susceptible to uncleanness by reason of plagues [such as are described in Lev. 14].

C. It is not subject to trial on the count of an apostate city.

D. On account of the consideration of transmitting corpse-uncleanness by means of overshadowing, people may not build over the public way projections on their houses, such as beams, balconies, or sockets.

E. A corpse may not be kept there overnight.

F. Human bones may not be transported in that city.

G. A place for a resident alien is not made there.

H. Graves are not kept there, except for the graves of the house of David and Huldah the prophetess, for they were located there from the days of the early prophets.

I. When they cleared out the graves, why did they not clean out those?

J. They said, "There was a passage-way which gave egress to the uncleanness into the Kidron brook.

K. People may not plant plantings there.

L. People may not plant gardens and orchards there, except for rose gardens, which were located there from the time of the early prophets.

M. People may not raise in Jerusalem geese or chickens, and one need hardly say pigs.

N. People may not keep rubbish heaps there, because of the possibility of uncleanness.

O. "An incorrigible and rebellious child's trial may not be held there," the words of R. Nathan.

P. For it is said, *Then his father and mother shall lay hold on him and bring him out to the elders of his city, to the gate of his place* (Deut. 21:19) – and this is not *his* city or *his* place.

Q. When people sell houses there, they sell only what is located from the ground up [on a leasehold, not on a freehold of the real property].

R. A house is not sold in perpetuity there after the passage of twelve months [from the issuance of a loan secured by the house, which is to be repaid in a year's time. If the loan is not repaid, the house may then be permanently alienated. But that rule does not apply in Jerusalem.]

S. People do not accept payment for use of a bed there.

T. R. Judah says, "Or even for the use of bed coverings."

U. People did not purchase there the hides of Holy Things.

V. What did they do with them?

W. Rabban Simeon b. Gamaliel says, "They hand them over to innkeepers. The guests would stay inside, and the innkeepers outside. The innkeepers practice deception and purchase [Goldin:] painted sheep, whose hides were worth four or five selas, and the men of Jerusalem would receive their fees from them."

This list of ten items is thematically cogent, but it does not emphasize the miraculous character of Jerusalem, as the first list does. So it has been included solely for thematic reasons. On the rather odd item at W, see Goldin, p. 210, n. 27, but that picture seems to me farfetched. The next item is tacked on as an appendix to O-P above.

XXXV:III

1. A. One verse of Scripture says, *The place which the Lord shall choose in one of your tribes* (Deut. 12:14), and the other says, *Out of all your tribes* (Deut. 12:5).

   B. *The place which the Lord shall choose in one of your tribes* refers to Judah and Benjamin.

   C. And *Out of all your tribes* refers to Jerusalem, for all Israelites are partners in that city.

   D. What part fell into the territory of Judah? The Temple mount, the treasuries, and the courts.

   E. What part fell into the territory of Benjamin? The sanctuary, porch, and house of the Holy of Holies.

   F. A triangular strip of land protruded, entering and leaving [Benjamin's portion, but connected to Judah's], and on that strip of land the altar was built.

   G. [Because] Benjamin enjoyed sufficient merit, he was made into the landlord of the All-mighty, as it is said, *And he dwells between his shoulders* (Deut. 33:12).

2. A. At that time said Joshua, "I know that the chosen house is destined to be established between the border of Judah and of Benjamin. I shall go and prepare a pasture in Jericho."

   B. Who ate the produce of that pasture all those years [prior to the building of the Temple]?

   C. The sons of the Kenites, Moses' father-in-law, as it is said, *And the children of the Kenite, Moses' father-in-law, went up out of the city of palm trees* (Jud. 1:16).

   D. They said, "When the Holy One, blessed be he, reveals his Presence, he is destined to pay a good reward to Jethro and his sons."

   E. And whence did the sons of Jethro get their living? From pottery: *And the families of scribes that lived at Jabez...these are the Kenites who came from Hammath, the father of the house of Rehab* (1 Chr. 2:55), and *These are the potters and those that dwelled among plantations* (1 Chr. 4:23).

F. They had been important people, householders and landlords and vintners. In the service of the King of kings of kings, the Holy One blessed be he, they left it all and went their way.

G. Where did they go?

H. To Jabez, to study the Torah.

I. They became a people of the Omnipresent.

3. A. At that time Jabez was a good man, solid, a man of truth, pious, who went into session and expounded the Torah,

B. for it is said, *And Jabez called on the God of Israel, saying, Oh that you would bless me indeed...And God granted him what he asked* (1 Chr. 4:10).

The little composition is inserted solely because of its relevance to the theme of Jerusalem as the property of the nation as a whole, pertinent to the statement of Nathan. The connection is attenuated. Nos. 2 and 3 are tacked on for a further thematic reason.

XXXV:IV

1. A. **Ten wonders were done for our fathers in the Temple:**

B. **A fly never made an appearance in the slaughter house:**

C. **A high priest never suffered a nocturnal emission on the eve of the Day of Atonement.**

D. There is the exception in the case of R. Ishmael b. Qimhit. He went out to converse with a local authority, and spit of that man splattered and fall on his garments [rendering him unclean, as the spit of a gentile will do], so his brother took his place and served as the high priest in his stead, and their mother saw the two of them on the same day as high priests.

E. Sages witnessed the matter and said to her, "What sort of merit was to your credit [for such an unusual honor to come to you]?"

F. She said, "The beams of my house have never seen the hair on my head."

G. No one was ever attacked in Jerusalem. No one ever stumbled in Jerusalem.

H. **A woman never miscarried on account of the stench of the meat of Holy Things:**

I. The priests never spoiled Holy Things by forming the intention of eating them outside of their proper time or place.

J. When they ate a great deal of meat of Holy Things, they would drink the words of Siloam and the meat would be digested in their bellies as food is ordinarily digested.

K. **An invalidating factor never affected the *'omer*, the Two Loaves, or the show bread.**

L. If a clay pot broke, the sherds were swallowed up on the spot.

M. **No wind ever blew away the pillar of smoke.**

N. When the pillar of smoke arose from the altar, it would rise straight up like a staff, until it reached the sky.

O. And when the pillar of incense came up from the golden altar, it would enter on its way into the house of the Holy of Holies.

P. When the people are standing, they are jammed together. When they go down and prostrate themselves, they have plenty of room.

Q. When the Israelites go up to prostrate themselves to their Father in heaven, when they are seated [in the prayer], they are seated crowded together, so that no one can squeeze a finger between them, but when they prostrate themselves, they prostrate themselves in plenty of space.

R. But the greatest among all [the miracles] is that even if a hundred people bowed down at one time, the leader of the congregation did not announce, saying, "Make room for your brothers."

2. A. Miracles were done in the courtyard, for even if all Israel were to enter the courtyard, the courtyard would hold them all.

B. A still greater miracle: when the Israelites stand up in reciting the Prayer, they are crowded together, so that no one can squeeze a finger between them, but when they prostrate themselves, there was enough space between each of of them for the full height of a person.

3. A. Rabban Simeon b. Gamaliel says, "Jerusalem is destined to have all the nations and kingdoms gathered together in its midst.

B. "For it is said, *And all the nations shall be gathered into it, to the name of the Lord, to Jerusalem* (Jer. 3:17).

C. "And further: *Let the waters under the heaven be gathered together to one place* (Gen. 1:9).

D. "Just as the gathering stated in that passage refers to a gathering of all the waters of creation to one place, so the gathering referred to here means the gathering of all the nations and kingdoms into it, as it is said, *And all the nations shall be gathered into it.*"

The original list is exquisitely glossed and amplified, with some new, but entirely appropriate items. It seems to me that all the materials are cogent to the single purpose at hand, which is why I see no natural dividing line among the diverse entries of No. 1. But No. 2 clearly starts off on its own rubric, the courtyard in particular. It is well-connected to the immediately preceding entry. No. 3 is independent but inserted for a valid reason of connection to the foregoing. So No. 2, which goes over the materials of No. 1, and No. 3, together serve as a valid appendix. We again notice a tendency to conclude the amplifications with an eschatological finish.

The Fathers According to Rabbi Nathan

Chapter Thirty-Six

The present chapter corresponds to the chapter in which Avot addresses the lists of sevens, fours, and threes. Since one of the items before us speaks of those seven who have no share in the world to come, the vast composition, which certainly is autonomous of Avot and has no clear bearing on anything in the corresponding chapter of Avot, has found its place here.

XXXVI:I

XXXVI:I.1 Men of Sodom and world to come (Eliezer vs. Joshua).

XXXVI:II

XXXVI:II.1 Minor children of wicked and world to come, last judgment (Eliezer vs. Joshua).

XXXVI:III

XXXVI:III.1 Korach and his party (Eliezer vs. Joshua).

XXXVI:IV

XXXVI:IV.1 Generation of wilderness (Eliezer vs. Joshua).

XXXVI:V

XXXVI:V.1 Ten tribes.

XXXVI:VI

XXXVI:VI.1 Seven who have no share in the world to come.

XXXVI:VII

XXXVI:VII.1 Continuation of foregoing.

XXXVI:VII.2 Others who have no share in the world to come.

XXXVI:I

1. A. "The men of Sodom will not live [in the world to come] or be brought to judgment, for it is said, *Now the men of Sodom were wicked and sinners against the Lord exceedingly* (Gen. 13:13).

B.   *"Now the men of Sodom were wicked* toward one another.

C.   *"and sinners* in sexual misconduct.

D.   *"against the Lord –* this refers to blasphemy.

E.   *"exceedingly* – for they sinned deliberately," the words of R. Eliezer.

F.   R. Joshua says, "They will come to judgment, for it is said, *Therefore the wicked shall not stand in the judgment, nor sinners in the congregation of the righteous* (Ps. 1:5).

G.   "In the congregation of the righteous they shall not stand, but they shall stand in the congregation of the wicked."

H.   R. Nehemiah says, "Even in the congregation of the wicked they will not stand, for it is said, *Let sinners cease out of the earth and let the wicked be no more* (Ps. 104:35)."

XXXVI:II

1.   A.   "Minor children of the wicked will not live [in the world to come] nor stand in judgment, as it is said, *For behold the day comes, it burns as a furnace, and all the proud, and all who do wickedness, shall be stubble, and the day is coming that will set them afire, says the Lord of hosts, so that they shall leave neither root nor branch* (Mal. 3:19)," the words of R. Eliezer.

B.   R. Joshua says, "They will come [to judgment, like everyone else,] for it is said, *He cried aloud and said this: cut down the tree and cut off its branches, shake off its leaves and scatter its fruit* (Dan. 4:11). And it further says, *Nevertheless leave the stump of its roots in the earth, even in a band of iron and brass* (Dan. 4:12). The word root occurs in both passages. Just as the word root appearing in the one means the tree itself [that is cut down], so when the word occurs in the other passage, it means the man himself.

C.   "If so, how shall I explain the statement, *so that they shall leave neither root nor branch* ?

D.   "It means that they will not find merit for them on which to reply [such as the children of the righteous have. The children of the wicked have only that merit that they themselves accomplish.]"

E.   Others say, "They will come [to judgment], for concerning them Scripture says, *One shall say, I am the Lord's, and another shall call himself by the name of Jacob, and another shall subscribe with his hand to the Lord, and another will take as his surname the name of Israel* (Is. 44:5).

F.   *"One shall say, I am the Lord's:* this refers to the people who are wholly righteous.

G.   *"and another shall call himself by the name of Jacob:* this refers to the minor children of the wicked.

H.   *"and another shall subscribe with his hand to the Lord:* this refers to the wicked who separated from their ways and took a different way and carried out repentence.

I.   *and another will take as his surname the name of Israel:* this refers to sincere proselytes."

XXXVI:III

1.   A.   "Korach and his party will not live or be judged, as it is said, *And the earth closed on them and they perished from among the assembly* (Num. 16:33)," the words of R. Eliezer.

B. R. Joshua says, "They will come to judgment, for concerning them it is said, *The Lord kills and brings alive, he brings down to the grave and brings up again* (1 Sam. 2:6).

C. "In the passage concerning Korach the word grave occurs: *So they and all that pertained to them went down alive into the grave* (Num. 16:33), and in the passage cited from the book of Samuel, the word grave also occurs.

D. "Just as in the latter, the word *grave* occurs, with the meaning, *he brings down to the grave and brings up again* , so here, where the same word appears, the sense is that they went down but are destined to come up again."

E. Said to him R. Eliezer, "How then do you explain the statement, *And the earth closed on them and they perished from among the assembly?*

F. He said to him, "From the congregation they perished, from the world to come they did not perish."

XXXVI:IV

1. A. "The generation of the wilderness will not live or be judged, as it is said, *In the wilderness they shall be consumed, and there they shall die* (Num. 14:35), and, further, *Wherefore I swore in my anger that they shall not enter into my rest* (Ps. 95:11)," the words of R. Eliezer.

B. R. Joshua says, "They shall indeed enter into judgment, and concerning them it is written, *Gather my saints together to me, those that have made a covenant with me by sacrifice* (Ps. 50:15)."

C. Said to him R. Eliezer, "How do you interpret the verse, *Wherefore I swore in my anger that they shall not enter into my rest?*"

D. He said to him, "This refers to the spies and all the wicked of that generation."

E. Said R. Joshua to him, "How do you interpret the verse *Gather my saints together to me, those that have made a covenant with me by sacrifice?*

F. He said to him, "This refers to Moses and Aaron and all the pious people of the generation of the tribe of Levi."

G. [Following Goldin's reordering of the text of Schechter, cf. Goldin, p. 150 and n. 21:] R. Yose the Galilean says, "They will not enter judgment, for it is said, *In this wilderness they shall be consumed and there they shall die* (Num. 21:4), and further, *And they shall break the heifer's neck there in the valley* (Deut. 21:4).

H. "Just as the word *there* in the one passage concerning the heifer the neck of which is broken means that the beast dies there and does not move from the spot, so the word *there* stated here means that they shall die and not move from their place."

I. They answered him, "Concerning the wicked, the word *there* is used, but concerning the righteous, is not the word *there* used too? [It certainly is used of the righteous as well, so the proof is not possible, as in the following instances;] *There they buried Abraham and Sarah his wife* (Gen. 49:312). *In my grave which I dug for myself in the land of Canaan, there you will bury me* (Gen. 50:5). *And Miriam died there and was buried there* (Num. 20:1). *And Aaron the priest went up...and died there* (Num. 33:38). *So Moses the servant of the Lord died there in the land of Moab, according to the word of the Lord* (Deut. 34:5)."

J. Others say, They shall indeed come to judgment, and concerning him Scripture states, *Go and cry in the ears of Jerusalem, saying...I remember to your credit the loyalty of your youth* (Jer. 2:2)."

XXXVI:V

1. A. The ten tribes will not live nor come to judgment, for it is said, *And the Lord rooted them out of their land...and cast them into another land as at this day* (Deut. 29:27).

   B. R. Simeon b. Judah says, "Just as the day goes and does not come back, so they will not come back."

   C. R. Aqiba says, "Just as a day grows dark and then becomes light, so the darkness that is theirs is destined to become bright."

2. A. Rabban Gamaliel says, "Lo, Scripture says, *That your days may be many and the days of your children* (Deut. 11:21), but it also says, *The fathers shall not die on account of the children* (Deut. 24:16).

   B. "So long as the father lives a long life, so the son will live a long life If the father does not live a long life, the son will not live a long life."

   C. R. Yose the Galilean supports the position of R. Eliezer, and Rabban Gamaliel supports the position of R. Joshua.

The opening composition is a set-piece dispute, neatly worked out in its own terms and following a tight pattern. Its relevance will become clear only later.

XXXVI:VI

1. A. There are seven who have no share in the world to come, and these are they: a scribe, a teacher of beginning students, the best among all physicians, one who serves as judge in his own town, a diviner, a head [of a congregation], and a butcher.

   B. Three kings and four ordinary folk have no share in the world to come.

   C. The three kings are Jeroboam, Ahab, and Manasseh.

   D. The four ordinary folk are Balaam, Doeg, Ahitophel, and Gahazi.

   E. R. Judah says, "Take Manasseh off the list, for he repented: *And he prayed to him and he was entreated of him and heard his supplication and brought him back to Jerusalem to his kingdom* (2 Chr. 33:13)."

   F. They said to him, "Had it been written, 'They brought him back *to Jerusalem*,' and then said nothing more, we should have concurred with you. But when Scripture specifies, *to his kingdom*, the meaning is, to his kingdom [here and now] they brought him back, but they did not bring him back to the life of the world to come."

   G. R. Meir says, "Absalom has no portion in the world to come."

   H. R. Simeon b. Eleazar says, "Jeroboam, Ahab, Manasseh, Basha, Ahaziah, and all the kings of Israel who were wicked will have no portion in the world to come."

   I. R. Yohanan b. Nuri says, "Also one who pronounces the divine name with all of its letters spelled out has no portion in the world to come."

XXXVI: VII

1. A. He would say, "One who warbles the Song of Songs, who whispers over a wound, who spits on a wound and says, *I will put none of the diseases on you that I have put upon the Egyptians, for I am the Lord who heals you* (Ex. 15:26) has no portion in the world to come."

    B. And sages say, "Any disciple of a sage who first repeated [traditions] and then left the fold has no portion in the world to come, for it is said, *Because he has despised the word of the Lord...that soul shall be utterly cut off* (Num. 15:31), and further, *What unrighteousness have your fathers found in me that they are gone far from me* (Jer. 2:5)."

2. A. R. Meir says, "Whoever has a study-house in his town but does not go there has no portion in the world to come."

    B. R. Aqiba says, "Also one who does not serve as a disciple to disciples of sages has no portion in the world to come."

My best guess is that the base-number, seven, important in the chapter of Avot to which the present series of chapters corresponds, accounts for the inclusion of the whole, from the beginning to the end. The interest in *the seven who have no share in the world to come* – a statement that formally can find a comfortable position in the counterpart chapter in Avot – explains the inclusion of the entire sequence of compositions, which, of course, is happily situated in Sanhedrin Chapter Ten, from the Mishnah through the Bavli, in diverse versions of the same theme.

The Fathers According to Rabbi Nathan

Chapter Thirty-Seven

The interest in listing seven items bearing a trait in common accounts for the presentation of a set of lists of sevens, sixes, and the like. The one pertinent passage of Avot is as follows:

> There are seven traits that characterize an unformed clod, and seven to a sage. (1) A sage does not speak before someone greater than he in wisdom. (2) And he does not interrupt his fellow. (3) And he does not answer hastily. (4) He asks a relevant question and answers properly. (5) And he addresses each matter in its proper sequence, first, then second. (6) And concerning something he has not heard, he says, "I have not heard the answer." (7) And he concedes the truth [when the other party demonstrates it]. And the opposite of these traits apply to a clod.

XXXVII:I

XXXVII:I.1 Seven categories of created beings.

XXXVII:II

XXXVII:II.1 Continuation of foregoing: Six traits have been stated with respect to humanity, three like traits of a beast, three like traits of ministering angels.

XXXVII:III

XXXVII:III.1 Continuation of foregoing: Six traits have been stated with respect to demons.

XXXVII:IV

XXXVII:IV.1 Seven types of Pharisee.

XXXVII:V

XXXVII:V.1 Seven things which in large volume are bad and in small volume are good.

XXXVII:VI

    XXXVII:VI.1 With seven things did the Holy One, blessed be he, create his world.

XXXVII:VII

    XXXVII:VII.1 Seven attributes serve before the throne of glory.

XXXVII:VIII

    XXXVII:VIII.1 Seven stages [to the universe].

XXXVII:IX

    XXXVII:IX.1 Seven points of distinction between one righteous person and another.

XXXVII:X

    XXXVII:X.1 There are seven exegetical principles by which Hillel the Elder interpreted [Scripture] before the sons of Batera.

XXXVII:XI

    XXXVII:XI.1 There are seven traits that characterize an unformed clod, and seven a sage.

XXXVII:XII

    XXXVII:XII.1 Clarification of foregoing.

XXXVII:XIII

    XXXVII:XIII.1 As above.

XXXVII:XIV

    XXXVII:XIV.1 As above.

XXXVII:XV

    XXXVII:XV.1 As above.

XXXVII:XVI

    XXXVII:XVI.1 As above.

XXXVII:XVII

    XXXVII:XVII.1   As above.

Once we reach our base-passage, the framer systematically expounds its statements. But up that point all we find is a sequence of unrelated catalogues, most of them involving seven items. There is no rhyme or reason for the inclusion of the catalogues we have.

XXXVII:I

1. A. There are seven categories of created beings, one above the next [in importance].
   B. On high he created the firmament.
   C. More important than the firmament, he created stars that give light to the world.
   D. More important than the stars, he created trees, [which are superior,] for trees produce fruit, while stars do not produce fruit.
   E. More important than trees he created strong winds, [which are superior,] for strong winds go here and there, while trees do not move from their place.
   F. Above the strong winds he created cattle, [which are superior,] for cattle work and eat, while strong winds do not work and do not eat.
   G. More important than cattle he created humanity, [which is superior,] for humanity has intelligence, and in beasts is no intelligence.
   H. Above humanity he created the ministering angels, [which are superior,] for the ministering angels go from one end of the world to the other, while humanity does not do so.

The composition has been inserted only because it catalogues seven items. I see no cogent message that would link to any other in this chapter. But the interesting point of the catalogue, starting on high, then working down to earth via the stars, should not be missed, since the hierarchical scheme is odd and striking. The following carries forward the same point.

XXXVII:II

1. A. Six traits have been stated with respect to humanity, three like traits of a beast, three like traits of ministering angels.
   B. Three in which humanity is like the beast: people eat and drink like a beast, procreate like a beast, and shit like a beast.
   C. Three in which humanity is like ministering angels: people have understanding like ministering angels, they walk standing up, like ministering angels, and they make use of the Holy Language, like ministering angels.

The catalogue is autonomous but has been added as a complement to the foregoing.

XXXVII:III

1. A. Six traits have been stated with respect to demons, three like human beings, three like ministering angels.
   B. Three like human beings: they eat and drink like human beings, they procreate like human beings, and they die like human beings.

C.   Three like ministering angels: they have wings, like ministering angels; they know what is going to happen, like ministering angels; they go from one end of the world to the other, like ministering angels.

D.   And some say, "They also [Goldin:] change their appearance to any likeness they please."

E.   And they can see but not be seen.

This list surely matches the foregoing and was made up to go along with it.

XXXVII:IV

1.   A.   There are seven types of Pharisee:

B.   the shoulder-Pharisee [ostentatiously carrying his good deeds on his shoulder, for show], the "excuse-me-I-have-to-do-a-religious-duty"-Pharisee, the ...-Pharisee, the Pharisee who had a trade, the "what-is-my-duty-that-I-may-do-it"-Pharisee; the Pharisee who separates from his evil impulse; the Pharisee out of fear.

Our text has an inferior version of the materials at hand. I have followed my translation of B. Sotah 22b. The text here is defective. Compare Goldin, p. 153, and p. 213, ns. 5-13.

XXXVII:V

1.   A.   There are seven things which in large volume are bad and in small volume are good:

B.   wine, work, sleep, wealth, business, hot water, and blood-letting.

XXXVII:VI

1.   A.   With seven things did the Holy One, blessed be he, create his world.

B.   And these are they: with knowledge, understanding, might, loving-kindness, mercy, justice, and [Goldin:] decree.

C.   And in the same way in which the Holy One, blessed be he, created his world, so he created the three patriarchs and four matriarchs.

D.   The three patriarchs: Abraham, Isaac, and Jacob.

E.   The four matriarchs: Sarah, Rebecca, Rachel, and Leah.

XXXVII:VII

1.   A.   Seven attributes serve before the throne of glory.

B.   And these are they: wisdom, righteousness, loving-kindness, mercy, truth, peace,

C.   as it is said, *And I will betroth you to me for ever, yes, I will betroth you to me in righteousness, justice, loving-kindness, compassion. And I will betroth you to me in faithfulness and you shall know the Lord* (Hos. 2:21-22).

D.   R. Meir says, "Why does Scripture state, *and you shall know the Lord* ? It is to teach you that any person in whom are these traits knows the mind of the Omnipresent."

XXXVII:VIII

1. A. There are seven stages [to the universe]:
   B. the upper stage, the lower stage, the airspace of the world, and the four [Goldin:] upper spheres.
   C. R. Meir says, "There are seven firmaments:
   D. "[Goldin:] the Velum, the Firmament, the Skies, the Habitation, the Dwelling Place, the Foundation, the Clouds.
   E. "And matching them he assigned to the earthly regions seven names: earth, ground, land, dry ground, dry land, world, abode.
   F. "[Goldin:] Why is it called World? Because it is rich in everything."
   G. Another matter: because it ordinarily takes in but does not ordinarily give out.

XXXVII:IX

1. A. There are seven points of distinction between one righteous person and another:
   B. one's wife is prettier than the other's; one's children are pretty than the other's.
   C. Two eat in a single bowl, this one tasting the food in accord with his deeds, the other in accord with his.
   D. Both dye wool in a single kettle. For this one the wool comes up lovely, for that one it comes up ugly.
   E. [Further points of distinction are in] wisdom, knowledge, stature, as it is said, *One righteous man excels his friend, but the way of the wicked leads them astray* (Prov. 12:16).

This item seems to have been poorly articulated, with only three items at B, then another three at E, with something not entirely clear at C, D. But the overall point, such as it is, is clear.

XXXVII:X

1. A. There are seven exegetical principles by which Hillel the Elder interpreted [Scripture] before the sons of Batera, and these are they:
   B. the argument *a fortiori*, the argument by analogy, the argument by deduction from one verse of Scripture; the argument by deduction from two; the argument that moves from the general to the particularization of the general; the argument that moves from the particular to the generalization of the particular; the argument by reference to similar usage elsewhere; the argument by deduction from context.
   C. These are the seven exegetical principles by which Hillel the Elder expounded Scripture before the sons of Betera.

It seems to me all we have is a sequence of compositions joined for one reason only, as is given.

XXXVII:XI

1. A. There are seven traits that characterize an unformed clod, and seven a sage. (1) A sage does not speak before someone greater than he in wisdom. (2) And he does not interrupt his fellow. (3) And he is not at a loss for an answer. (4) He asks a relevant question and answers properly. (5) And he addresses each matter in its proper sequence, first, then second. (6) And concerning something he has not heard, he says, "I have not heard the answer." (7) And he concedes the truth [when the other party demonstrates it]. And the opposite of these traits apply to a clod.

XXXVII:XII

1. A. A sage does not speak before someone greater than he in wisdom.
   B. This refers to Moses, for it is said, *And Aaron spoke all the words which the Lord has spoken to Moses and did the signs in the sight of the people* (Ex. 4:30).
   C. Now who was the more worthy to speak, Moses or Aaron?
   D. One has to say it was Moses.
   E. For Moses had heard the message from the mouth of the Almighty, while Aaron heard it from Moses.
   F. But this is what Moses said: "Is it possible for me to speak in a situation in which my elder brother is standing?"
   G. Therefore he said to Aaron, "Speak."
   H. Thus it is said, *And Aaron spoke all the words which the Lord had spoken to Moses* (Ex. 4:30).

We find ourselves in a quite different world. The purpose is to provide suitable examples for the statement cited from Avot.

XXXVII:XIII

1. A. And he does not interrupt his fellow.
   B. This refers to Aaron.
   C. For it is said, *Then Aaron spoke...Behold, this day have they offered their sin-offering and their burnt-offering...and such things as these have happened to me* (Lev. 10:19).
   D. He kept silence until Moses had finished speaking and did not say to him, "Cut it short."
   E. But afterward he said to Moses, *Then Aaron spoke...Behold, this day have they offered their sin-offering and their burnt-offering...and such things as these have happened to me*.
   F. "And we are in mourning."
   G. Some say that Aaron drew Moses apart from the group and said to him, "My brother, if of tithes, which are of lesser sanctity, it is forbidden for one who has yet to bury his deceased to eat, a sin-offering, of greater sanctity, all the more so should be forbidden as a meal to a person who has yet to bury his deceased."

H. Moses immediately agreed with him, as it is said, *And when Moses heard it, it was well-pleasing in his sight* (Lev. 10:20),

I. and in the view of the Almighty as well.

2. A. Along these same lines: *And Moses was angry with Eleazar and with Ithamar, the sons of Aaron* (Lev. 10:16):

B. On the basis of this passage they have said, When someone makes a banquet for his disciples, he should face only the greatest among them, but when he expresses anger, he expresses anger only against the least,

C. as it is said, *And Moses was angry with Eleazar and with Ithamar,* [and the statement, *the sons of Aaron*] teaches that [in point of fact] he was enraged also with Aaron.

3. A. Aaron was greater than Moses, and the Holy One, blessed be he, was greater than Aaron.

B. Why did he not speak with Aaron?

C. It was because he had no sons who would stand in the breach, for if his sons, Eleazar and Ithamar, had stood in the breach, no sin would have affected Nadab and Abihu.

4. A. Along these same lines [we find] in the case of our father, Abraham, when he was praying for the men of Sodom, the Holy One, blessed be he said to him, *If I find in Sodom fifty righteous, then I will forgive all the place for their sake* (Gen. 18:26).

B. But it was perfectly clear before him who spoke and brought the world into being that were there only three or five righteous men in the town, transgression would not have affected the town, but the Holy One, blessed be he, waited on Abraham until he completed his plea, and afterward he replied to him,

C. as it is said, *And the Lord went his way when he had completed speaking to Abraham* (Gen. 18:33).

D. It is as if he said to him, "Lo, I am taking my leave,"

E. as it is said, *And Abraham returned to his place* (Gen. 18:33).

Not only is the material discursive and interesting, it also matches the foregoing in form and purpose and surely comes from a single authorship. The exposition is diverse and rich.

XXXVII:XIV

1. A. **He does not answer hastily.**

B. This is exemplified by Elihu ben Barachel the Buzite.

C. For it is said, *I am young and you are very old, which is why I held back and did not tell you my opinion. I said, Days should speak, and the multitude of years should teach wisdom* (Job 32:6).

D. This teaches that they remained seated in silence before Job. When he stood up, they stood up. When he sat down, they sat down. When he ate, they ate. When he drank, they drank. Then he took permission from them and cursed his day:

E. *After this Job opened his mouth and cursed his day and said, Let the day perish when I was born, and the night in which it was said, A man-child is brought forth* (Job 3:1).

F.   *Let the day perish* on which my father came to my mother and she said to him, "I am pregnant."

G.   And how do we know that they answered not out of turn? *Then Job answered and said* (Job 3:2). *Then answered Eliphaz the Temanite and said* (Job 4:1). *Then answered Bildad the Shuhite and said* (Job 8:1). *Then answered Zophar the Naamathite and said* (Job 11:10. *Then Elihu the son of Barachel the Buzite answered and said* (Job 32:1).

H.   Scripture arranged them one by one so as to let everyone in the world know that **a sage does not speak before someone greater than he in wisdom. And he does not interrupt his fellow. And he does not answer hastily.**

XXXVII:XV

1.   A.   **He asks a relevant question and answers properly:**

B.   This is exemplified by Judah, who said, *I will be surety for him* (Gen. 43:9).

C.   Not asking a relevant question is exemplified by Reuben, as it is said, *And Reuben said to his father, You shall slay my two sons* (Gen. 42:37).

XXXVII:XVI

1.   A.   **And he addresses each matter in its proper sequence, first, [then second]:**

B.   This is exemplified by Jacob.

C   And some say, this is exemplified by Sarah.

D.   **then second:**

E.   This is exemplified by the men of Haran.

XXXVII:XVII

1.   A.   **And he concedes the truth:**

B.   This is exemplified by Moses: *And the Lord said to me, They have said well that which they have spoken* (Deut. 18:17).

C.   It is further exemplified by the Holy One, blessed be he: *The Lord spoke to Moses, saying, The daughters of Zelophehad speak right* (Num. 27:6).

The systematic and orderly exposition of the base-statement continues with further biblical examples of the recommended traits.

The Fathers According to Rabbi Nathan

Chapter Thirty-Eight

We have a systematic and orderly exposition of the statements of Avot, with proof-texts and cases illustrative of the theme, if not the proposition, at hand. In a few cases we have a different wording for matters.

There are seven forms of punishment which come upon the world for seven kinds of transgression. (1) [If] some people give tithes and some people do not give tithes, there is a famine from drought. So some people are hungry and some have enough. (2) [If] everyone decided not to tithe, there is famine of unrest and drought. (3) [If all decided] not to remove dough-offering, there is a famine of annihilation. (4) Pestilence comes to the world on account of the death-penalties which are listed in the Torah but which are not in the hands of the court [to inflict]; and because of the produce of the Seventh Year [which people buy and sell]; (5) A sword comes into the world because of the delaying of justice and perversion of justice, and because of those who teach the Torah not in accord with the law. (6) A plague of wild animals comes into the world because of vain oaths and desecration of the Divine Name. (7) Exile comes into the world because of those who worship idols, because of fornication, and because of bloodshed, and because of the neglect of the release of the Land [in the year of release].

XXXVIII:I
XXXVIII:I.1 Amplification of causes of famine.

XXXVIII:II
XXXVIII:II.1 Josiah on causes of famine.

XXXVIII:III
XXXVIII:III.1 Neglect of the gifts to the poor.

XXXVIII:IV
XXXVIII:IV.1 Case illustrative of the foregoing.

XXXVIII:V

XXXVIII:V.1 Base-saying cited.

XXXVIII:V.2 Base-saying illustrated.

XXXVIII:V.3 Secondary expansion of foregoing.

XXXVIII:VI

XXXVIII:VI.1 Base-sayings supplied with proof-texts.

There is an orderly exposition of the base-sayings, with a pattern of secondary expansion through stories.

XXXVIII:1

1. A. There are seven forms of punishment which come upon the world for seven kinds of transgression. (1) [If] some people give tithes and some people do not give tithes, there is a famine from drought.
   B. If some people do, and some people do not, set aside the portion for the priestly ration, a famine because of tumult comes upon the world.
   C. If some people do, and some do not set aside dough-offering, there is a famine of annihilation that comes upon the world.
   D. (2) [If] everyone decided not to tithe, the heavens will be closed up so as not to yield dew and rain, and people will labor but not suffice.

I see only a slightly different wording of the base-sayings as we have them in Avot.

XXXVIII:II

1. A. R. Josiah says, "On account of the sin of neglecting the dough offering, a blessing does not come upon the produce, so that people labor but do not suffice.
   B. "On account of the sin of neglecting the separation of a portion of the crop for the priestly ration and the separation of tithes, the heavens will be closed up so as not to yield dew and rain, and people will be handed over to the government [to be sold into slavery for non-payment of their taxes in kind]."

Josiah has a somewhat different view of matters, exchanging some of the wording. But the presentation of the base-saying remains the centerpiece.

XXXVIII:III

1. A. Pestilence comes to the world on account of neglect of the requirement to leave in the fields the defective grape, the forgotten sheaf,

and the corner of the field, as well as to separate tithe for the poor person.

There is yet another version of the matter, now emphasizing the gifts to the poor. The next item provides a precedent for the same matter.

XXXVIII:IV

1. A. There is the case of a woman who lived in the neighborhood of a landlord, and her two sons went out to gather [the crops that are to be left for the poor], but did not find any produce in the field.
   B. Their mother said, "When my sons come from the field, perhaps I'll find something in their hands to eat."
   C. For their part, they were saying, "When we get home, perhaps we'll find something in mother's hands to eat."
   D. She found nothing with them, nor they with her, to eat. They put their heads on their mother's lap, and all three of them died on one day.
   E. The Holy One, blessed be he, said to them, "You people have exacted from them their lives! By your lives! I shall exact from you your lives."
   F. And so Scripture says, *Do not rob from the weak, because he is weak, nor crush the poor in the gate, for the Lord will plead their cause and take the life of those who despoil them* (Prov. 22:22-23).

The case is not made up to illustrate the matter of pestilence in particular, but serves nonetheless as an appendix to the foregoing.

XXXVIII:V

1. A. A sword comes into the world because of the delaying of justice and perversion of justice, and because of those who teach the Torah not in accord with the law.
2. A. When they seized Rabban Simeon b. Gamaliel and R. Ishmael on the count of death, Rabban Simeon b. Gamaliel was in session and was perplexed, saying, "Woe is us! For we are put to death like those who profane the Sabbath and worship idols and practice fornication and commit murder."
   B. Said to him R. Ishmael b. Elisha, "Would it please you if I said something before you?"
   C. He said to him, "Go ahead."
   D. He said to him, "Is it possible that when you were sitting at a banquet, poor folk came and stood at your door, and you did not let them come in and eat?"
   E. He said to him, "By heaven [may I be cursed] if I ever did such a thing! Rather, I set up guards at the gate. When poor folk came along, they would bring them in to me and eat and drink with me and say a blessing for the sake of Heaven."
   F. He said to him, "Is it possible that when you were in session and expounding [the Torah] on the Temple mount and the vast populations of Israelites were in session before you, you took pride in yourself?"

G. He said to him, "Ishmael, my brother, one has to be ready to accept his failing. [That is why I am being put to death, the pride that I felt on such an occasion.]"

H. They went on appealing to the executioner for grace. This one [Ishmael] said to him, "I am a priest, son of a high priest, kill me first, so that I do not have to witness the death of my companion."

I. And the other [Simeon] said, "I am the patriarch, son of the patriarch, kill me first, so that I do not have to witness the death of my companion."

J. He said to him, "Cast lots." They cast lots, and the lot fell on Rabban Simeon b. Gamaliel.

K. The executioner took the sword and cut off his head.

L. R. Ishmael b. Elisha took it and held it in his breast and wept and cried out: "Oh holy mouth, Oh faithful mouth, Oh mouth that brought forth beautiful gems, precious stones and pearls! Who has laid you in the dust, who has filled your mouth with dirt and dust!

M. "Concerning you Scripture says, *Awake, O sword, against my shepherd and against the man who is near to me* (Zech. 13:7)."

N. He had not finished speaking before the executioner took the sword and cut off his head.

O. Concerning them Scripture says, *My wrath shall wax hot, and I will kill you with the sword, and your wives shall be widows, and your children fatherless* (Ex. 22:23).

3. A. Since it is said *I will kill you with the sword*, do I not know that *your wives shall be widows*?

B. They will be widows but not really widows, for they will not find witnesses [that you have died, so as] to permit them to remarry.

C. The example is Betar, from which not a single one escaped so as to give testimony that someone has died and his wife may remarry.

D Since it is said, *your wives shall be widows*, do I not know that *your children will be fatherless*?

E. But they will be fatherless and not fatherless [for the same reason as before], so that the property they are to inherit will remain in the domain of their father, with the result that they will not be permitted to inherit and to transact business with that property [being unable to settle the estate].

The story about the execution by the sword of the two great rabbis surely cannot illustrate the notion that they were responsible for a delay of justice or the perversion of justice or taught the Torah not in accord with the law. It is simply tacked on as a story about how people died by the sword – unless some remarkably perverted redactor had in mind to condemn the high priesthood and the patriarchate. But the power and nobility of the story testify against that unlikely possibility. So it is simply another case of assembling thematically relevant, but substantively autonomous, materials around a tangential topic: death by the sword, in this case. The secondary expansion of the exegesis of the proof-text points to that same conclusion.

XXXVIII:VI

1. A. Exile comes into the world because of those who worship idols, because of fornication, and because of bloodshed, and because of the neglect of the release of the Land [in the year of release].

   B. On account of idolatry, as it is said: *And I will destroy your high places...and I will scatter you among the nations* (Lev. 26:30, 33).

   C. Said the Holy One, blessed be he, to Israel, "Since you lust after idolatry, so I shall send you into exile to a place in which there is idolatry."

   D. Therefore it is said, *And I will destroy your high places...and I will scatter you among the nations*.

   E. [Following Goldin's ordering of the text:] **Because of fornication:** Said R. Ishmael b. R. Yose, "So long as the Israelites are lawless in fornication, the Presence of God takes its leave of them,"

   F. as it is said, *That he not see an unseemly thing in you and turn away from you* (Deut. 23:15).

   G. [Following Goldin:] **Because of bloodshed:** *So you shall not pollute the land in which you are located, for blood pollutes the land* (Num. 35:33).

   H. **Because of neglect of the release of the Land in the year of release:** how do we know that that is the case?

   I. Then shall the land be paid her Sabbaths (Lev. 26:34).

   J. Said the Holy One, blessed be he, to Israel, "Since you do not propose to give the land its rest, it will give you a rest. For the number of months that you did not give the land rest, it will take a rest on its own."

   K. That is why it is said, *Even then shall the land rest and repay her Sabbaths, As long as it lies desolate it shall have rest, even the rest that it did not have on your sabbaths, when you lived on it* (Lev. 26:35).

The systematic exposition of the base-statement follows a disciplined program.

The Fathers According to Rabbi Nathan

Chapter Thirty-Nine

This chapter is composed of a sequence of sayings that can as well have appeared in Avot. I see slight effort to amplify or otherwise gloss and expound what is before us.

> He [Aqiba] would say, "Precious is the human being, who was created in the image [of God]. It was an act of still greater love that it was made known to him that he was created in the image [of God]. as it is said, *For in the image of God he made man* (Gen. 9:6).

> "Precious are Israelites, who are called children to the Omnipresent. It was an act of still greater love that it was made known to them that they were called children to the Omnipresent, as it is said, *You are the children of the Lord your God* (Deut. 14:1).

> "Precious are Israelites, to whom was given the precious thing. It was an act of still greater love that it was made known to them that to them was given that precious thing with which the world was made, as it is said, *For I give you a good doctrine. Do not forsake my Torah* (Prov. 4:2)."

> "Everything is foreseen, and free choice is given. In goodness the world is judged. And all is in accord with the abundance of deed[s]."

> He would say, "(1) All is handed over as a pledge, (2) And a net is cast over all the living. (3) The store is open, (4) the storekeeper gives credit, (5) the account-book is open, and (6) the hand is writing.

> "(1) Whoever wants to borrow may come and borrow. (2) The charity-collectors go around every day and collect from man whether he knows it or not. (3) And they have grounds for what they do. (4) And the judgment is a true judgment. (5) And everything is ready for the meal."

XXXIX:I

XXXIX:I.1 Further sayings.

XXXIX:II

XXXIX:II.1 Further sayings.

XXXIX:III

XXXIX:III.1 Aqiba cited, with some glosses.

XXXIX:IV

XXXIX:IV.1 As above.

XXXIX:V

XXXIX:V.1 Further sayings.

XXXIX:VI

XXXIX:VI.1 Further sayings.

XXXIX:VII

XXXIX:VII.1 Further sayings.

XXXIX:VIII

XXXIX:VIII.1 Further sayings.

XXXIX:IX

XXXIX:IX.1 Further sayings.

XXXIX:X

XXXIX:X.1 Parable *possibly* illustrative of **XXIX:VII.1.**

XXXIX:XI

XXXIX:XI.1 Further sayings: list of six items.

XXXIX:XII

XXXIX:XII.1 As above.

XXXIX:XIII

XXXIX:XIII.1 As above.

XXXIX:I

1. A. Five sorts are beyond forgiveness:
   B. one who repents a lot, one who sins a lot, one who sins in a generation of righteous people, one who sins intending to repent, and whoever [Goldin:] has on his hands [the sin of] profaning the Name.

XXXIX:II

1. A. On account of his sin, it is not accorded to humanity to know [Goldin:] what likeness is above.
    B. And were it not for that same reason, the keys would have been handed over to humanity to know out of what heaven and earth were made.

XXXIX:III

1. A. **Everything is foreseen,** and all is revealed, and all accords with human intention.

XXXIX:IV

1. A. He would say, "(1) All is handed over as a pledge, (2) And a net is cast over all the living. (3) The store is open, (4) the storekeeper gives credit, (5) the account-book is open,
    B. "the judge is in session,
    C. "the charity-collectors go around every day and collect from man whether he knows it or not. (3) And they have grounds for what they do,
    D. "with or without one's consent."

XXXIX:V

1. A. The repentance of genuinely wicked people suspends [their punishment], but the decree against them has been sealed.
    B. The prosperity of the wicked in the end will go sour.
    C. Dominion buries those that hold it.
    D. Repentance suspends [punishment] and the Day of Atonement achieves atonement.
    E. Repentance suspends [punishment] until the day of death, and the day of death atones, along with repentance.

XXXIX:VII

1. A. They [immediately, in this world] pay off the reward owing to the wicked [for such good as they may do], while they credit to the righteous [the reward that is coming to them, but do not pay it off, rather paying them off in the world to come].
    B. They pay off the reward owing to the wicked [in this world] as though they were people who had carried out the Torah ungrudgingly, in whom no fault had ever been found.
    C. They credit to the righteous [the reward that is coming to them, but do not pay it off, rather paying them off in the world to come], as though they were people lacking all good traits.
    D. They thus give a little bit to each party, with the bulk of the remainder laid up for them.

XXXIX:VIII

1. A. He would say, "Everyone goes along out of this world naked,
    B. "and would that people left the way they came in."

We have a long sequence of unadorned sayings.

XXXIX:IX

1. A. R. Meir says, "Precious is the human being, who was created in the image [of God]. [Lacking here: It was an act of still greater love that it was made known to him that he was created in the image [of God],] as it is said, For in the image of God he made man (Gen. 9:6).

   B. "Precious are Israelites, who are called children to the Omnipresent. [Lacking here: It was an act of still greater love that it was made known to them that they were called children to the Omnipresent,] as it is said, You are the children of the Lord your God (Deut. 14:1).

   C. "Precious are Israelites, to whom was given the precious thing. [Lacking here: It was an act of still greater love that it was made known to them that to them was given that precious thing with which the world was made,] as it is said, For I give you a good doctrine. Do not forsake my Torah (Prov. 4:2)."

We have a slightly defective version of the materials in Avot.

XXXIX:X

1. A. R. Eliezer bar Sadoq says, "To what are the righteous compared in this world?

   B. "To a tree that is standing in a clean place, with its foliage extending from it to an unclean place.

   C. "What do people say? 'Cut off the foliage from the tree so that the whole of it may be clean, as is its character.'

   D. "To what are the wicked compared in this world?

   E. "To a tree that is standing in an unclean place, with its foliage extending from it to a clean place.

   F. "What do people say? 'Cut off the foliage from the tree, so that the whole of it may be unclean, as is its character.'"

If this item were located after **XXXIX:VII**, I should have taken it to be a parable expressing the main point of the saying of that unit. As it stands, I see no necessary context in which to read the parable.

XXXIX:XI

1. A. [Following Goldin verbatim:] By six names is the lion called: *ari, kefir, labi, layish, shahal, shahas.*

XXXIX:XII

1. A. [Following Goldin verbatim:] By six names is the serpent called: *nahash, sharaf, tannin, tsifoni, efeh, akshub.*

XXXIX:XIII

1. A. [Following Goldin verbatim:] By six names is Solomon called: *[Solomon,] Jedidiah, Kohelet, Ben Jakeh, Agur, Lemuel.*

I see only lists of six items, making no particular point.

The Fathers According to Rabbi Nathan

Chapter Forty

The lists of four cover a great deal of ground, but a single theme, four types of disciple, unifies only a few of them. The chapter in general glosses the materials of Avot and presents a variety of lists made up of four items.

He who brings merit to the community never causes sin. And he who causes the community to sin – they never give him a sufficient chance to attain penitence. Moses attained merit and bestowed merit on the community. So the merit of the community is assigned to his [credit], as it is said, *He executed the justice of the Lord and his judgments with Israel* (Deut. 33:21). Jeroboam sinned and caused the community of the Israelites to sin. So the sin of the community is assigned to his [debit], as it is said, *For the sins of Jeroboam which he committed and wherewith he made Israel to sin* (I Kings 15:30).

There are four sorts of people. (1) He who says, "What's mine is mine and what's yours is yours" – this is the average sort. (And some say, "This is the sort of Sodom.") (2) "What's mine is yours and what's yours is mine" – this is a boor. (3) "What's mine is yours and what's yours is yours" – this is a truly pious man. (4) "What's mine is mine and what's yours is mine" – this is a truly wicked man.

There are four sorts of personality: (1) easily angered, easily calmed – he loses what he gains; (2) hard to anger, hard to calm – what he loses he gains; (3) hard to anger and easy to calm – a truly pious man; (4) easy to anger and hard to calm – a truly wicked man.

There are four types of disciples: (1) quick to grasp, quick to forget – he loses what he gains; (2) slow to grasp, slow to forget – what he loses he gains; (3) quick to grasp, slow to forget – a sage; (4) slow to grasp, quick to forget – a bad lot indeed.

There are four traits among those who sit before the sages: a sponge, a funnel, a strainer, and a sifter. (1) A sponge – because he sponges everything up; (2) a funnel – because he takes in on one side and lets out on the other; (3) a strainer – for he lets out the wine and keeps in the

lees; (4) and a sifter — for he lets out the flour and keeps
in the finest flour.

[In] any loving relationship which depends upon
something, [when] that thing is gone, the love is gone.
But any which does not depend upon something will never
come to an end.   What is a loving relationship which
depends upon something?   That is the love of Amnon and
Tamar [II Sam. 13:15].   And one which does not depend
upon something: That is the love of David and Jonathan.

Any dispute which is for the sake of Heaven will in the
end yield results, and any which is not for the sake of
Heaven will in the end not yield results.   What is a
dispute for the sake of Heaven?   This is the sort of
dispute between Hillel and Shammai.   And what is one
which is not for the sake of Heaven?   It is the dispute of
Korach and all his party.

XL:I

XL:I.1 List of four items.

XL:II

XL:II.1 List of four items.

XL:III

XL:III.1 Secondary expansion of foregoing.

XL:IV

XL:IV.1 Matched sayings on the penalties of causing public sin and the
rewards of bringing about public merit.

XL:V

XL:V.1 Continuation of foregoing.

XL:VI

XL:VI.1 Four types of persons.

XL:VII

XL:VII.1 More of the same, in the model of the foregoing.

XL:VIII

XL:VIII.1 Four types of disciples.

XL:IX

XL:IX.1 Four types of disciples.

XL:X

XL:X.1 Four types of disciples.

XL:XI

XL:XI.1 Four sorts [of sources] of bad things.

XL:XII

XL:XII.1 Four sorts of sages whom one might see in a dream.

XL:XIII

XL:XIII.1 Three sorts of sages whom one might see in a dream.

XL:XIV

XL:XIV.1 Three sorts of prophets whom one might see in a dream.

XL:XV

XL:XV.1 Three sorts of writings one might see in a dream.

XL:XVI

XL:XVI.1 Death, sleep, quiet.

XL:XVII

XL:XVII.1 Four rules for the privy.

XL:XVIII

XL:XVIII.1 Verbatim transcription of saying in Avot.

XL:XIX

XL:XIX.1 As above.

XL:XX

XL:XX.1 Further example of the same.

XL:I

1. A. There are four things that a person does, the fruit of which one enjoys in this world, while the [Goldin:] stock endures for his advantage in the world to come.

    B. These are they: honoring father and mother, acts of loving-kindness, bringing peace between people, and study of Torah outweighs all the rest.

XL:II

1. A. There are four things which a person does, and on account of which he suffers a penalty in this world and also in the world to come.

B. These are they: idolatry, fornication, murder, and gossip outweighs the rest.

XL:III

1. A. As to merit, it has [Goldin:] stock and also fruit, as it is said, *Say of the righteous that it will be well with him, for they shall eat the fruit of their deeds* (Is. 3:10).

   B. As to transgression, it has stock but no fruit, as it is said, *Woe for the wicked person, it shall be ill with him, for the work of his hands shall be done to him* (Is. 3:11).

   C. Some say, "Transgressions have fruit, as it is said, *Therefore they shall eat of the fruit of their own way and be filled with their own devices* (Prov. 1:31)."

The lists of four are unrelated, but the final item carries forward the theme of principal and dividend, or, in Goldin's good rendering, stock and fruits.

XL:IV

1. A. Whoever increases the store of merit accruing to the community at large will never bring about transgression resulting in his disciples' inheriting the world to come while he goes down to Sheol,

   B. for it is said, *You will not abandon my soul to the netherworld* (Ps. 16:10).

   C. And whoever brings about sin on the part of the community at large will never suffice to accomplish repentance resulting in his disciples' going down to Sheol while he inherits the world to come,

   D. as it is said, *A man that is laden with the blood of any person shall hasten his steps to the pit* (Prov. 28:17).

My view is that this passage glosses the cited materials of Avot. This is a more fully worked out saying than we have seen, one in which we have proof-texts along with the base-saying.

XL:V

1. A. He who says, "I shall sin and repent" will never suffice to carry out repentance.

   B. "I will sin and the Day of Atonement will accomplish atonement" – the Day of Atonement will not accomplish atonement.

   C. "I shall sin and the day of death will wipe away the sin" – the day of death will not wipe away the sin.

   D. R. Eliezer b. R. Yose says, "He who sins and repents and then proceeds in an unblemished life does not move from his place before he is forgiven.

   E. "He who says, 'I shall sin and repent' is forgiven three times but no more."

This seems to me to carry forward the theme of the foregoing, if only in a general way.

XL:VI

1. A. There are four sorts of people. (1) He who says, "What's mine is mine and what's yours is yours" – this is the average sort. (And some say, "This is the sort of Sodom.") (2) "What's mine is yours and what's yours is mine" – this is a boor. (3) "What's mine is yours and what's yours is yours" – this is a truly pious man. (4) "What's mine is mine and what's yours is mine" – this is a truly wicked man.

The base-saying is simply cited. We shall now have some more lists of four types of persons.

XL:VII

1. A. There are four sorts of disciples:
   B. One who wishes to learn and to see others learn is generous.
   C. One who wishes to learn but not to see others learn is grudging.
   D. One who wishes for others to learn but not to learn himself is average.
   E. And some say, "This is the sort of Sodom."
   F. One who wishes not to learn and for others not to learn: this is a completely wicked person.

This seems to me to conform to the model of the foregoing and to have been generated to amplify it. I find it difficult to imagine the problem addressed here, that is, someone not wanting third parties to study.

XL:VIII

1. A. There are four types of persons who go to the school house:
   B. One who takes a place near [the master] and sits down enjoys a reward.
   C. One who takes a place near and sits down enjoys no reward.
   D. One who takes a place distant and sits down enjoys a reward.
   E. One who takes a place distant and sits down has no reward.
   F. One who asks questions and gives answers has a reward.
   G. One who asks questions and gives answers has no reward.
   H. One who sits silently has a reward.
   I. One who sits silently has no reward.
   J. One who takes a place near [the master] and sits down in order to listen and learn enjoys a reward.
   K. One who takes a place near and sits down so that people will say, "Mr. So-and-so takes a place near the sage and sits down" enjoys no reward,
   L. One who takes a place distant and sits down so as to pay respect to someone greater than himself enjoys a reward.

M. One who takes a place distant and sits down so that people will say, "Mr. So-and-so has no need to listen to a sage" has no reward.

N. One who asks questions and gives answers so as to listen and learn has a reward.

O. One who asks questions and gives answers so that people will say, "Mr. So-and-so asks questions and gives answers before a sage" has no reward.

P. One who sits silently to listen and to learn has a reward:

Q. One who sits silently so that people will say, "Mr. So-and-so sits silently before sages" has no reward.

This beautifully articulated unitary composition makes its point many times over, which is that people should not make a show out of learning. It is included not because of any point of intersection with the earlier lists, but because it does pursue the same theme: four types of disciple. That theme continues.

XL:IX

1. A. **There are four traits among those who sit before sages: a sponge, a funnel, a strainer, and a sifter [ARNA: sponge, sifter, funnel, strainer]. (1) A sponge, because he sponges everything up; (2) a funnel, because he takes in on one side and lets out on the other; (3) a strainer, for he lets out the wine and keeps in the lees; (4) and a sifter, for he lets out the flour and keeps in the finest flour.**

   B. Like a sponge: how so? This is an experienced disciple, who sits before sages and studies Scripture, Mishnah, exegesis, laws and narratives, just like a sponge that sops up everything. So that student sops up everything.

   C. Like a sifter: how so? This is a smart disciple, who sits before disciples of sages and listens to Scripture, Mishnah, exegesis, laws and narratives. Just as a sifter lets out the coarse flour and keeps the fine, so this disciple lets out the bad and keeps in the good.

   D. Like a funnel: how so? This is a foolish disciple, who sits before disciples of sages. He hears Scripture, Mishnah, exegesis, laws and narratives. Just as with a funnel, one pours in on one side and it lets out on the other, so whatever is put into the disciple's ears goes in one side and comes out the other. What he hears first he forgets first and goes his way.

   E. Like a strainer: how so? This is a wicked disciple, who sits before a sage and hears Scripture, Mishnah, exegesis, laws and narratives. Just as a strainer lets out the wine and holds back the lees, so this one lets out the worthwhile and keeps the bad.

2. A. R. Eliezer b. Jacob calls him, "A perforated horn, one lacking a head [a stump].

   B. "How so? There is a child to whom they give pearls, then a piece of bread. He throws out the pearls and takes the bread. If they go and give him a piece of pottery, he throws away the bread and keeps the pottery. So in the end he is left only with a sherd."

The passage of Avot is given an elaborate and handsomely composed amplification, followed by a simile. I cannot imagine a more amply spelled out idea. The next catalogue continues the same theme. The parallel at [1] and [2] to Tarfon and Aqiba is not drawn, because the interest here is in hierarchization and classification, not in precedent and narrative.

XL:X

1. A. In the matter of disciples Rabban Gamaliel the Elder gave an exegesis covering four classifications: an unclean fish, a clean fish, a fish from the Jordan, a fish from the Great Sea:
   B. "An unclean fish: how so? This is the son of a poor family who has studied Scripture, Mishnah, laws, and lore, but has no intelligence.
   C. "A clean fish: how so? This is the son of a rich family who has studied Scripture, Mishnah, laws, and lore, and has intelligence.
   D. "A fish from the Jordan, how so? This is a disciple of a sage who has studied Scripture, Mishnah, exegesis, laws and lore, but has no intelligence to compose an answer.
   E. "A fish from the Great Sea, how so? This is a disciple of a sage who has studied Scripture, Mishnah, laws, and lore, and has intelligence to compose an answer."

We go over the same matter in another way. There is a clear effort at hierarchization here.

XL:XI

1. A. There are four sorts [of sources of bad things]: [those that are] seeing and seen, seen but not seeing, seeing but not seen, not seeing and not seen.
   B. Seeing and seen: for instance, the wolf, lion, panther, bear, leopard, snake, bandit, robber. They see and are seen.
   C. Seen but not seeing: for instance, the sword, bow, spear, knife, stick, staff. These are seen but unseeing.
   D. Seeing but not seen: for example, the blow of an evil spirit.
   E. Not seeing and not seen: for example, a belly ache.

XL:XII

1. A. There are four sorts of sages [who, in a dream, present omens of what is to come]:
   B. One who sees R. Yohanan b. Nuri in a dream may expect to attain fear of sin.
   C. [One who sees] R. Eleazar b. Azariah may expect worldly greatness and wealth.
   D. [One who sees] R. Ishmael may expect wisdom.
   E. [One who sees] R. Aqiba should fear punishment.

The lists of fours are not so arranged that all those involving sages are grouped together. This suggests that the redactor had no interest in theme, but simply strung out whatever he had in hand.

XL:XIII

1. A. Three sorts of sages [one might see as omens in a dream]:
   B. One who sees Ben Azzai in a dream may look forward to piety.
   C. [One who sees] Ben Zoma may look forward to wisdom.
   D. [One who sees] Elisha b. Abuyah should worry about coming punishment.

XL:XIV:I

1. A. There are three sorts of prophets [one might see in a dream as an omen]:
   B. One who sees the books of Kings in a dream may look forward to greatness and wealth.
   C. One who sees Isaiah may look forward to consolation.
   D. One who sees Jeremiah should watch out for punishment.

XL:XV:I

1. A. Three sorts of writings one might see in a dream [and interpret as omens of what is to come]:
   B. One who in a dream sees the book of Psalms may look forward to humility.
   C. One who in a dream sees the book of Proverbs may look forward to wisdom.
   D. One who in a dream sees the book of Job should watch out for punishment.

XL:XVI

1. A. Death for the wicked is fitting for them and fitting for the world. For the righteous it is bad for them and bad for the world.
   B. Sleep for the wicked is fitting for them and fitting for the world. For the righteous it is bad for them and bad for the world.
   C. Quiet for the wicked is bad for them and bad for the world. For the righteous it is good for them and good for the world.

The lists of threes run on, following a fairly stable form to the end.

XL:XVII

1. A. One should not stand naked facing the house of the Holy of Holies.
   B. One who enters a privy should not turn his face either east or west but to the sides.
   C. And one should uncover himself not standing but sitting.
   D. And one should wipe himself not with the right hand but with the left.
   E. On what account did they rule that one should wipe himself not with the right hand but with the left?
   F. R. Eliezer says, "Because with the right one points to the words of the Torah."
   G. R. Joshua says, "Because one eats and drinks with the right hand."

My guess is that this composition is included because it contains four rules. I see no other point of contact, fore or aft.

XL:XVIII

1. A. [In] any loving relationship which depends upon something, [when] that thing is gone, the love is gone. But any which does not depend upon something will never come to an end.

    B. What is a loving relationship which depends upon something? That is the love of Amnon and Tamar [II Sam. 13:15]. And one which does not depend upon something: That is the love of David and Jonathan.

XL:XIX

1. A. Any dispute which is for the sake of Heaven will in the end yield results, and any which is not for the sake of Heaven will in the end not yield results.

    B. What is a dispute for the sake of Heaven? This is the sort of dispute between Hillel and Shammai. And what is one which is not for the sake of Heaven? It is the dispute of Korach and all his party.

XL:XX

1. A. Any assembly which is for the sake of heaven in the end will yield results, and one that is not for the sake of heaven in the end will not yield results.

    B. What is an assembly that is for the sake of heaven? It is for instance the congregation of Israel before Mount Sinai.

    C. And one that is not for the sake of heaven?

    D. It is for instance the assembly of the generation of the dispersion.

The final entry cites one passage of Avot and composes a parallel.

The Fathers According to Rabbi Nathan

Chapter Forty-One

We proceed to the end of Avot, so far as the authorship of ARNA wishes to comment on the concluding materials.

> R. Simeon says, There are three crowns: the crown of the Torah, the crown of priesthood, and the crown of sovereignty. But the crown of a good name is best of them all.
>
> Judah b. Tema says, Be strong as a leopard, fast as an eagle, fleet as a gazelle, and grave as a lion, to carry out the will of your Father who is in heaven.
>
> He would say, The shameless go to Gehenna, and the diffident to the garden of Eden.
>
> *"May it be found pleasing before you, O Lord our God, that you rebuild your city quickly in our day and set our portion in your Torah."*

XLI:I

XLI:I.1 Exposition of three-crowns saying of Avot.

XLI:II

XLI:II.1 Amplification of Torah-theme, with story about a rabbi and blasphemy.

XLI:III

XLI:III.1 Story about a rabbi, relevant to blasphemy.

XLI:IV

XLI:IV.1 Further lists of threes.

XLI:V

XLI:V.1 As above.

XLI:VI

XLI:VI.1 As above.

XLI:VII

XLI:VII.1 A set of six, complementing the foregoing.

XLI:VIII

XLI:VIII.1 Set of three.

XLI:IX

XLI:IX.1 Set of three.

XLI:X

XLI:X.1 Set of four.

XLI:XI

XLI:XI.1 Another set of four.

XLI:XII

XLI:XII.1 Set of three.

XLI:XIII

XLI:XIII.1 Judah b. Tema's saying.

XLI:XIV

XLI:XIV.1 Further sayings of Judah b. Tema.

XLI:XV

XLI:XV.1 As above.

XLI:XVI

XLI:XVI.1 As above.

XLI:XVII

XLI:XVII.1 Five things that were made and hidden away.

XLI:XVIII

XLI:XVIII.1 [Conjectural: Five things done for a bride.]

XLI:XIX

XLI:XIX.1 Five who have no portion in the world to come.

XLI:XX

XLI:XX.1 World to come-appendix.

XLI:XXI.1-XLI:XXII.1 Liturgical conclusion.

XLI:I

1. A. R. Simeon says, "There are three crowns: and these are they: the crown of the Torah, the crown of priesthood, and the crown of sovereignty. But the crown of a good name is best of them all."

    B. The crown of the priesthood: how so? Even if one should give all the silver and gold in the world, people still cannot bestow on him the crown of the priesthood, for it is said, *And he and his descendants after him shall have the covenant of an everlasting priesthood* (Num. 25:13).

    C. The crown of sovereignty: Even if one should give all the silver and gold in the world, people still cannot bestow on him the crown of sovereignty, as it is said, *And my servant David shall be their prince for ever* (Ez. 37:25).

    D. But the crown of the Torah is not that way. As to the labor of the Torah, whoever wants to undertake it may come and undertake it, as it is said, *Let all who thirst come for water* (Is. 51:1).

The systematic and orderly exposition of the list of the crowns produces a fresh and important point.

XLI:II

1. A. Labor in words of the Torah and do not occupy yourself with words of no worth.

    B. There is the case of R. Simeon b. Yohai, who would visit the sick. He came across a person who was bloated and suffering with a belly ache, and [in pain] blaspheming before the Holy One, blessed be he.

    C. He said to him, "Empty head! You should have sought mercy for yourself instead of blaspheming."

    D. He said to him, "May the Holy One, blessed be he, arise from me and alight on you."

    E. He said to him, "The Holy One, blessed be he, did to you what is coming to you, for you have neglected words of the Torah and occupied yourself with words of no worth."

The theme of the third saying is carried forward, now with a precedent to complement the proof-text already cited.

XLI:III

1. A. There is the case of R. Simeon b. Eleazar, who was coming from the house of his master in Migdal Eder, riding on an ass and making his way along the sea shore. He saw an unusually ugly man. He said to him, "Empty head! what a beast you are! Is it possible that everyone in your town is as ugly as you are?"

    B. He said to him, "And what can I do about it? Go to the craftsman who made me and tell him, 'How ugly is that utensil that you have made!'"

C. When R. Simeon b. Eleazar realized that he had sinned, he got off his ass and prostrated himself before the man, saying to him, "I beg you to forgive me."

D. He said to him, "I shall not forgive you until you go to the craftsman who made me and tell him, 'How ugly is that utensil that you have made!'"

E. He ran after the man for three miles. The people of the town came out to meet him. They said toward him, "Peace be to you, my lord."

F. He said to them, "Whom do you call, 'my lord'?"

G. They said to him, "To the one who is going along after you."

H. He said to them, "If this is a 'my lord,' may there not be many more like him in Israel."

I. They said to him, "God forbid! and what has he done to you?"

J. He said to them, "Thus and so did he do to me."

K. They said to him, "Nonetheless, forgive him."

L. He said to them, "Lo, I forgive him, on the condition that he not make a habit of acting in that way."

M. On that same day R. Simeon entered the great study-house that was his and gave an exposition: "'One should always be as soft as a reed and not as tough as a cedar.'

N. "In the case of a reed, all the winds in the world can go on blowing against it but it sways with them, so that when the winds grow silent, it reverts and stands in its place. And what is the destiny of a reed? In the end a pen is cut from it with which to write a scroll of the Torah.

O. "But in the case of a cedar it will not stand in place, but when the south wind blows against it, it uproots the cedar and turns it over. And what is the destiny of a cedar? Foresters come and cut it down and use it to roof houses, and the rest they toss into the fire.

P. "On the basis of this fact they have said, 'One should always be as soft as a reed and not as tough as a cedar.'"

The only reason I can see for including this story is that Simeon blasphemed in his address to the man. Otherwise I find no point of contact with the present exercise. Nor do I see the connection between M-P and the prior story. What made the rabbi's conduct "as tough as a cedar" I cannot say.

XLI:IV

1. A. Three qualities [in regard to philanthropic policy] apply to people:
    B. one who gives charity – may a blessing come upon him.
    C. One who lends [at no interest] is better than he.
    D. One who gives [to the poor] a half-share in his capital and in his profit is the best of them all.

XLI:V

1. A. Three qualities in regard to disciples of sages: one who asks a question and gives an answer is a sage.
    B. One who asks but does not give an answer is less than he.
    C. One who does not ask and does not give an answer is least of them all.

XLI:VI

1. A. There are three kinds of sweat that are good for the body: the sweat of the sick person, the sweat of the steam bath, the sweat of hard work.
    B. The sweat of the sick person heals.
    C. The sweat of the steam bath – there is nothing like it.

XLI:VII

1. A. There are six kinds of tears, three that are good, three bad.
    B. Tears of weeping, smoke, and the privy are bad.
    C. Tears of medicine, laughter, and herbs are good.

XLI:VIII

1. A. There are three traits stated with regard to a clay utensil:
    B. it absorbs,
    C. but it does not excrete,
    D. and it does not make what is in it rot.

XLI:IX

1. A. There are three traits stated with regard to a glass utensil:
    B. It does not absorb what is in it,
    C. and it does not excrete what is in it,
    D. and it displays whatever is in it.
    E. In a hot place it is hot, in a cold place, cold.

The lists of three continue, each providing another instance of hierarchization. My guess is that the item on tears is included not only as a double set of threes but also as a complement to the theme of sweat. The list of traits of disciples, **XLI:V.1**, goes over the theme of the earlier exposition in Chapter Forty. **XLI:VI.1** is slightly flawed. The addition of a fourth item at **XLI:IX.1.C** marks the end of the pattern.

XLI:X

1. A. Four circumstances are hard for sexual relations:
    B. coming home from a trip,
    C. leaving a physician,
    D. recovering from a sickness,
    E. getting out of prison.

XLI:XI

1. A. Whoever accepts upon himself responsibility to carry out four matters is accepted as a fellow [in a commensal group]:
    B. Not to go to a cemetery, not to raise small cattle, not to hand over priestly rations and tithes to a priest who is a common person, not to prepare with a common person food requiring conditions of cultic cleanness,
    C. and eating unconsecrated food in a condition of cultic cleanness.

In the sets of four I see nothing cogent with what has preceded or what is to follow. The random character of the collection is seen at **XLI:XI.1**. That item gives five components and breaks all patterns.

XLI:XII

1. A. [Following Goldin, supply through B:] [Three returned to their place of origin: Israel, the silver of Egypt, and the heavenly writing:

   B. Israel dwelt beyond the river, as it is said, *Your father dwelt of old time beyond the river, even Terah, the father of Abraham* (Joshua 24:2). And how do we know that they returned to their place of origin? As it is said, *But because our fathers had provoked the God of heaven, he gave them into the hand of Nebuchadnezzar...who...carried the people away into Babylon* (Ezra 5:12).]

   C. The silver of Egypt returned to its place, as it is said, *And they robbed Egypt* (Ez. 12:36). And it says, *And Joseph collected all the silver* (Gen. 47:14). But then it says, *In the fifth year of King Rehoboam Shishak, king of Egypt came up...and he took the treasuries of the house of the Lord* (2 Chr. 12:2, 9).

   D. The heavenly writing returned to its place, as it is said, *Will you set your eyes upon it? It is gone, for it surely makes wings for itself, like an eagle that flies toward heaven* (Prov. 23:5).

To complete the composition, we have to follow Goldin's reconstruction, based on parallels. Only C is fully spelled out, with an account of how the silver got into Israelite hands and then reverted to Egyptian ones. This completes the sets of threes.

XLI:XIII

1. A. **Judah b. Tema says, "Be strong as a leopard, fast as an eagle, fleet as a gazelle, and grave as a lion, to carry out the will of your Father who is in heaven."**

XLI:XIV

1. A. He would say, "One should love Heaven, fear Heaven, and tremble and rejoice in all religious duties.

   B. "If you have done a minor act of meanness to your fellow, treat it as a major one. But if you have done a major favor for your fellow, treat it as nothing.

   C. "If your fellow has done you a minor favor, treat it as a big deal. If he has done you a major act of meanness, treat it as nothing."

XLI:XV

1. A. "A sponge and a utensil covered with pitch – these are what scholars are like.

   B. "A funnel and a tube – these are what wicked are like.

XLI:XVI

1. A. "Be like a skin that has no opening to let in air.

B. "Be educated to accept pain.

C. "Be forgiving of what insults you."

We have a sequence of unadorned sayings to add to Judah b. Tema's item in the catalogue of Avot.

XLI:XVII

1. A. Five things were made but then hidden away, and these are they:

B. The tent of meeting and the utensils that were in it, the ark and the sherds of the tablets, the jar of manna, the cruse of anointing oil, the staff [of Moses], that of Aaron, its almond blossoms and flowers, the priestly garments, the garments of the anointed priest.

C. But the mortar of the house of Abtinas, the table, candlestick, curtain of the ark, and plate are still kept in Rome [and not reverently hidden away].

I am not sure why this list of five items has been entered.

XLI:XVIII

1. A. [Following Goldin, p. 220, n. 45, add: Five things to be done for a bride: Wash her, anoint her, dress her up, dance before her, and take her to her husband's house:]

B. There was a case involving R. Tarfon, who was in session and repeating traditions for his disciples, when a bride passed before him.

C. [Interrupting the class], he gave orders concerning her and they brought her into his house.

D. He said to his mother and his wife, "Wash her, anoint her, dress her up, dance before her, until she goes to the house of her husband."

Goldin's note explains why this item is included. Topically of course it is no more irrelevant than any other. The exposition – rule, then case – follows one familiar pattern.

XLI:XIX

1. A. These are the ones who, sages have stipulated, have no share in the world to come: five kings;

B. and six who sought greatness: Cain, Korach, Balaam, Ahitophel, Doeg, and Gahazi.

XLI:XX

1. A. R. Yose says, "As to the wholly righteous, they are not purified [in purgatory], and as to the wholly wicked, they too are not purified. Who are purified? The mediocre.

B. "*I beg you, O Lord, deliver my soul* (Ps. 116:4) – from the judgment of Gehenna."

C. The House of Shammai say, "[The mediocre] go down and are purified there and [Goldin:] are singed and come up from there, as it is said, *And I will bring the third part through the fire and will refine them as silver is refined and will try them as gold is tried* (Zech. 13:9)."

D. The House of Hillel say, "[The mediocre] do not see [Gehenna] at all, as it is said, *For your loving kindness is good to them who are without life, my lips will praise you* (Ps. 63:4), and it says, *And spare them according to the greatness of your mercy* (Neh. 13:22),

E. "so that they may be saved from the judgment of Gehenna."

The reference to five accounts for the inclusion of **XLI:XIX.1**, and, therefore, the appendix on the theme of the world to come.

XLI:XXI

1. A. Whatever the Holy One, blessed be he, has created in his world he has created only for his glory,

   B. as it is said, *Everyone that is called by my name, him I have created for my glory, I have formed him, yes I have made him* (Is. 43:7).

   C. And it says, *The Lord shall reign forever and ever* (Ex. 15:18).

XLI:XXII

1. A. Said R. Hanania b. Aqashia, "The Holy One, blessed be he, wanted to bestow merit on Israel. Therefore he gave them in abundance both the Torah and religious duties,

   B. "as it is said, *The Lord was pleased for his righteousness' sake to make the Torah great and glorious* (Is. 42:21)."

The liturgical conclusion is tacked on.

Index